T0369092

GROWING UP IN MEXICO

GROWING UP IN MEXICO

Peggy Brown Balderrama

iUniverse, Inc.
New York   Bloomington

Growing up in Mexico

iUniverse books may be ordered through booksellers or by contacting:

iUniverse
1663 Liberty Drive
Bloomington, IN 47403
www.iuniverse.com
1-800-Authors (1-800-288-4677)

ISBN: 978-1-4401-6272-5 (sc)
ISBN: 978-1-4401-6270-1 (dj)
ISBN: 978-1-4401-6271-8 (ebook)

Library of Congress Control Number: 2009936713

Printed in the United States of America

iUniverse rev. date: 9/9/2009

To my two loves, Frank and Tony,
And to my precious grandchildren,
Anthony Francis, Sophia Raphaela,
And Allegra Isabella

When I was but thirteen or so
I went into a golden land,
Chimborazo, Cotopaxi
Took me by the hand.

I walked in a great golden dream
To and fro from school—
Shining Popocatepetl
The dusty streets did rule.

I walked home with a gold dark boy,
And never a word I'd say,
Chimborazo, Cotopaxi
Had taken my speech away;

I gazed entranced upon his face
Fairer than any flower—
O shining Popocatepetl
It was thy magic hour:

The houses, people, traffic seemed
Thin fading dreams by day.
Chimborazo, Cotopaxi
They had stolen my soul away!

Exerpt from "ROMANCE" by W. J. Turner

VERACRUZ

"Which one is my father?" I asked my mother in a high pitched voice as we hung over the railing of the ocean liner which had just docked in the port of Veracruz. Several passengers standing nearby chuckled and one kidded my mother fondly, "Go on, Louise, tell your little girl who her father is!" My mother laughed while scanning the crowd on the wharf below. "My goodness, I can't seem to find him. He has to be somewhere out there." And then, suddenly waving wildly. "Oh, there he is, there he is, see darling, all in white with the Panama hat!" and she pointed to a man standing a little back from the crowd who was shading his eyes and looking up at the ship's railing, trying to find us. Apparently he was unsuccessful as he did not wave back. He was too far away yet to recognize his wife and child whom he had not seen for over a year.

"Come on Louise, we're starting to disembark." said one of the fellow passengers urging my mother to start moving toward the gangway. I can remember, as we started toward the wharf , the sudden swarm of flies in my face and an unpleasant smell in the air.

"Mama, Mama, I don't like this, I want to go back to the ship!" and I clung to my mother's hand with both of my small ones. By the time we arrived at the bottom of the gangway, mercifully my father had spied us and was there with open arms to welcome us to Mexican soil. He kissed my mother full on the lips, looking at her fondly and then slowly turned down to me, still hanging on her skirts. "And here is my little 'Pegitus' he smiled, and reached down to tilt my face up to his. I turned away. I was upset that this only vaguely familiar stranger had dared kiss my mother so intimately, and I wanted no part of this reunion. Besides, I did not take fondly to the nickname he had given me of 'Pegitus' when my name was Peggy.

"I was beginning to think you'd never arrive!" he said. "What on earth took the ship so long? I've been waiting here in Veracruz for five days! What happened?"

The shipping company had wired the offices in Veracruz of the return to Antwerp, although not disclosing the reason. He took my mother's hand luggage and urged her forward. She said "I'll explain later, darling, but just a moment," and turned back to reach out for a tall older man who was coming alongside. "Tommy, please come, I want you to meet my husband, Fred Brown. Fred, this is Tommy Wilkinson who was a fellow passenger and helped us so much throughout the voyage."

"So pleased to meet you finally, Mr. Brown. Your wife has told us all so much about you. She really is such a charming shipmate. She kept us all enthralled with her lively conversation and her experiences. I'm sure you're very happy to finally have her with you." They shook hands, and then Mr. Wilkinson said, "Well, cheerio, most probably be seeing you again before leaving for Mexico City. I understand we'll be staying at the same hotel here, so good luck, and congratulations, Mr. Brown, that you have your family with you at last." He moved on.

The voyage from England had been a long one. After the train trip from London to Southampton in the middle of May 1939, we had boarded a Belgian ship to take us to Antwerp, where we changed over to a German ship of the Hamburg America Line, the "Orinoco", and set sail for America, final destination— Veracruz, Mexico. But after a few days at sea we docked at Lisbon and all the passengers were suddenly asked to hand in their passports to one of the officers. Terror gripped the faces of our fellow shipmates and I clearly remember my mother standing in one of the hallways with a group of people after handing in her British passport, discussing in low voices the reasons for this request, and hearing snippets of conversations and theories about the likelihood of war being declared between England and Germany, in which case we might all be taken as prisoners. Finally we set sail again, but to my mother's alarm she found out from one of the stewards that the ship was retracing its route to Hamburg, where it had started, because there were "illegal" passengers aboard who had to be returned to their original point of departure. By that time my mother had made friends with two lovely Jewish couples who sat with us at our luncheon table every day and who had disappeared from the scene ever since the passports had been collected. Whether they had preferred to remain in their cabins, or had been held prisoners on board I will never know. All I know is that when we docked at Hamburg, I was peeking over the side of the boat when German uniformed officers urged several passengers down the gangway--among them, the Jewish couples. Realizing the seriousness of the moment, even in my childlike mind, I ran to our cabin for my little Brownie camera, a gift from my sister for the voyage, and took a couple of pictures of this memorable event. Somewhere in one of our old scrapbooks the two tiny photographs still remain.

My mother and I were coming out to live with my father again. He had been working in Mexico for many years with the American Smelting Company, faithfully sending money to my mother, first to the U. S., where I was born, and where she and my siblings were living while they were attending school, and then to London so that the children, all older than I, could be educated " in the English manner". I was barely a year old at the time, so my first seven years were spent in London, with visits from my father every six or seven months, or whenever he could afford the long ocean voyage.

During those years my mother had become a completely independent self-sufficient mother of seven from necessity. When we finally left London to avoid the imminent war, my sister, Victoria, was twenty-four years old, and had recently married a fine British interior decorator; my brother, Fred, was twenty-two and had just joined the Grenadier Guards; my brother, Dick, had run away from home and joined the Merchant Marines; Ted and Bob were in the Royal Air Force, and Bill, the youngest boy had dropped out of school and been tempted by his older brother to follow him into the Merchant Marines. So my mother felt free to take her youngest child and flee to Mexico to escape the clearly oncoming war. Also, she was eager to celebrate her 25th silver wedding anniversary with my father. He, bless his heart, had thought it would be wonderful for his wife and child to enjoy the warm weather and seaside in Veracruz before leaving for Mexico City, so had reserved the hotel room for another week, to my mother's complete dismay. She, being accustomed now to living in a cosmopolitan city such as London, was eager to return to Mexico City and renew old acquaintances there to whom she had bid goodbye several years before.

As for me, that week in Veracruz holds very few good memories. It was hot and sticky weather; the flies were everywhere, and at night they were exchanged for a swarm of mosquitoes, so that we were forced to cover ourselves completely with mosquito netting before turning out the light. In the morning my father would order cereal for me, but the milk was boiled and tasted terrible. However I did go for the mound of pancakes and golden slices of fresh pineapple which I had never seen before, and I ate too much, so that on the third day I had a terrible case of dysentery and had to remain in bed taking an ill-tasting medicine. The one pastime I remember fondly was riding up and down several times a day in the golden cage elevator of the hotel. A young dark-skinned boy worked it, obviously enjoying my amusement and stopping at any floor I desired over and over again.

In the mornings, my mother, father and I would set out after a breakfast of sorts to see the city's sites, and to my delight sometimes boarded a rickety open-air street car which had no doors, only one step up to the wooden seat we chose. We visited San Juan de Ulúa, the dark dank jail and dungeons where prisoners used to be interned, and which originally served as a repository for the silver and gold the Spaniards shipped out to their mother country during the sixteenth century after the conquest of Mexico. I found out more about its importance when my husband and I returned to Veracruz many years later so that I could relive my first impressions of Mexico. My parents and I would then stop at some restaurant for lunch, and from there to the hotel to spend the hotter part of the day indoors for a long nap.

Luckily for me, I had started to read when I was five, and had brought along several of my children's books, one of which was the popular story, The Water Babies, by the Reverend Charles Kingsley, which my mother had already read to me, facilitating the re-reading for me, as it was rather advanced even for a precocious seven year old.

In the evenings we would stroll around the main plaza in front of our hotel and end up stopping for refreshments at the sidewalk café where we would be serenaded by music from nearby marimbas. I would invariably ask for a "limonada preparada", which was a cool lemonade made with bottled water, while my parents would usually ask for a good cold beer.

Somehow the week went by and we finally took the train to Mexico City where my father checked us into a lovely downtown hotel, The Guardiola, in front of the famous Sanborns Restaurant, known as The House of Tiles. My mother promptly set about calling all her old friends which she had not seen since she left Mexico in 1929.

I should clear up the fact that my mother and father and my siblings had already lived in Mexico. I was the only child born in the United States, and was whisked off to London shortly after.

My mother had originally come out to Mexico from England as a child, with her parents, when her father, John B. Hardy, had been offered the position of Superintendent of the Huasteca Oil Company, "El Águila". It was one of the first foreign companies which had been established when oil was discovered in the Gulf area in 1900. At that time prime jobs were being offered to foreigners under the government of President Porfirio Diaz, who had stabilized the nation after many years of bloodshed and who had opened up the country to foreign investment, which had poured millions into refineries, mining ventures, railroads, and work on the infrastructure.

As Lucy Louise grew, she was first sent to New Orleans to the Sacred Heart Academy, and later on, to a business school in Dallas, Texas. When my father, Frederick A. Brown, came out to Tampico from England to work as an accountant at the Huasteca, he and Lucy met. They were the only two Britishers about the same age at the time, and it did not take long for them to fall in love and marry in 1914, during the Mexican Revolution.

They only married by civil law, as Catholic priests were being persecuted by the rebels, so they traveled overnight to San Antonio, Texas, for their honeymoon, where they were married in the church, after being reprimanded by the priest for traveling together before their union was blessed. Later, they moved to the southern part of Mexico, and spent a little over a year on a sugar plantation on the Isthmus of Tehuantepec, in the state of Veracruz. That is where their first child was born, fair of face, dark-haired, and named Victoria, for the late Queen Victoria, of course, and Louise, one of my mother's names. A year later they moved to Mexico City where four of my brothers were born, first a boy, named Frederick Archibald, (poor boy) after my father, followed shortly by Richard, named for Richard the Lionhearted, Twelfth Century King of England, and then Edward Albert, for King Edward the VII and "Albert" for Queen Victoria's adored husband. When the next boy arrived two years later, my mother had run out of royal names, so she took the first two names of her favorite poet, Robert Louis Stevenson.

My father was offered a better job in Pachuca, in the state of Hidalgo, and with the family growing so quickly, and the need for higher wages, they moved to this small mining town, north of Mexico City. Here, the youngest of my five brothers, William Hardy, was born. "William", for William the Conqueror, and "Hardy", my mother's maiden name.

After a few years, my parents moved to Mexico City, where they decided that my mother should travel to the U. S. with the children for their education. My father remained in Mexico, where he held down a good position with another mining company, while making frequent trips back and forth to San Antonio, Texas, to see his large family. Then, after a few years, when my sister Victoria was seventeen years old and the youngest of my brothers was eight, my mother became pregnant with me, surprising the whole family. It turned out that she had planned the pregnancy, intentionally traveling to Mexico to visit my father during her fertile period because she had always wanted to have another little girl. But I have often wondered how my poor father took the news, for supporting a wife and six children must have become a burden, and I imagine the prospect of a seventh child did not meet with exultation on his part. I was the only child to be born in the United States, but before I could enjoy my good fortune, the whole family left for England, where they had decided to move again for the further education of the children, as well as a long-promised visit to my father's mother and family. So, brave adventurers that they were, the entire family took the boat and went to live in London. I was named Margaret Diana, the first name after her long departed mother, and the second after the Goddess of hunting and chastity. What a name to live up to. My maternal grandmother had been a delicate Welsh porcelain beauty, judging from the sepia-colored photograph my mother kept on her dressing table. One could tell from the pose the Honorable Margaret Rowena affected, her left hand held daintily up to her cheek, heavy lace and satin gown clinging to her full bosom, that she had been a "grande dame" back in Wales, only daughter of Lady Margaret Richards and Sir William Richards. As one can imagine, they were not happy about my grandfather's courtship of their daughter, he, being her second cousin, and penniless at the time. So the couple eloped and went to London, and it was there that my mother was born.

Dreamer that my mother was, I imagine she must have had visions of Eton and Cambridge for the boys, a finishing school for Victoria, and a home which looked out onto a lush back lawn surrounded by tulips and daffodils in the springtime while she sat in the drawing room sipping tea from lovely patterned Bone china with her new lady friends who would wear hats and pearls. She yearned to hear English "the way it should be spoken" with her mother and father's accent. She could imagine robins sitting on her windowsill in the mornings, and could recall her parents' description of long walks down country lanes in their youth. My father would work in The City and I'm sure she even saw him coming home from the office every evening and setting down his bowler hat on the hallstand before joining the family before a crackling fire in the drawing room. In reality it turned out to be heartbreakingly different.

My father, with the self-confidence of a man who had worked for years in Mexico in high-salaried positions, had assumed he could easily find work in England where he had started out. But he was wrong. That period in their lives would be a difficult one, and after having to take a succession of lower paying jobs, he decided to return to Mexico because he found doors in London closed to him. He had not worked in his native country for over twenty years, and found that all the letters of recommendation he carried were of no value whatsoever there. Disappointed, disillusioned and depressed, he sailed again for Mexico, where upon his return, he almost immediately landed another well-paying position enabling him to send money to his wife and family for their support. But returning to our arrival in London in the spring of 1932, it is a story I have heard recounted many times from various members of my family, each one slightly different from the other.

LONDON

My dad had advised his mother that he and his family would be arriving by train from Southampton, so she had rented a house within walking distance of her own home in Finsbury Park. She had signed signed a two year contract, clearly hoping to keep her dear son nearby after all those years when he had been living in "that heathen country". Also she had thoughtfully furnished the bedrooms with beds, sheets and blankets so we would not have to stay at a hotel that first night. She had put a few items in the larder and the pantry for our first meals, plus necessary china and cutlery. A cellarful of coal which would last us for at least a month had also been ordered. Looking back, I am amazed at her forethought and arrangements -- a marvellous feat for a woman who was almost seventy years old and not financially well-off to say the least. How she wangled it I'll never know, but I do know that my mother resented the fact that she had tied us to a monster of a house while she probably had visions of arriving at a fancy hotel, not taking into consideration the money my father would have had to pay for an indeterminate time while they house-hunted.

Anyway, this was to be the big family reunion. None of them knew what to expect, and the thought of having a daughter-in-law who was brought up in a foreign country, with seven children of all ages ranging from seventeen years to six months, descend upon my grandmother, must have been more than intimidating.

So, after a two week voyage from Galveston to Le Havre in France, and from there another ship to Southampton, we finally boarded the train to London, and were met at Victoria Station by Grandmother Brown and the whole family. In Dad's absence, his father, William, had passed away, and Mrs. Brown had remarried a charming old gentleman named Edward Beer. He too was at the station, and I'm afraid my father's reaction to the new addition to his family was not the most gracious. His brothers, Alfred and Frank, and Esther, Frank's wife were there, along with his sisters Elsie and Mabel and Frank's sons, Peter and Rodney. Quite an impressive welcome committee, but no less impressive than the arrival of our family as we stepped off the train.

I can just imagine my sedate little grandmother Brown's first impression of "the Mexican Browns" (as our London relatives came to call us). Of course, the first off the train was my father, straight into his mother's waiting open arms. He picked up the diminutive little gray figure and kissed her fondly, and I imagine he had tears running down his cheeks, for he was a most sentimental man. "My son, my dear son", was all she was able to say, according to my mother, years later, and even she, admitted it was a moving moment.

He hugged each of the other family members and was stiffly introduced to his step-father. Turning proudly toward the train, he helped my mother down, babe in arms (me), my sister Victoria, splendid in a red wrap-around overcoat with fur collar, red painted toenails showing from her open-toed high-heeled sandals, and the five boys, all in brightly colored hand-knitted sweaters.

Before my mother could be introduced to her mother-in-law, grandfather Beer stepped forward, doffed his silver grey homburg, disclosing a shock of white hair to match his distinguished mustache and beard, and took my mother's hand in his.

"I'm Edward Beer, my dear" he said warmly, "and I've been so looking forward to meeting you." At that moment there was an instant connection between them which would last the rest of our days in England, in contrast to my grandmother's cool dry kiss on the cheek, and firm handshake, and Esther's mixed look of curiosity and horror at Victoria's open-toed sandals in comparison to her own sensible brogues.

We were driven from the station in two cars, with a taxi for most of the luggage. How we all piled in I cannot imagine, but we did, or so the story goes when recounted by my brothers. We arrived at grandmother Brown's house, a dark old three story house that smelled of mutton when we entered the hallway. Almost immediately I was taken to one of the upstairs bedrooms and laid down to sleep after nursing from my mother.

Of course I don't remember any of this, but my sister Victoria's witty description remains in my mind as she told me the story when I was older. She said the only one in the whole family my grandma took to immediately was me, a cherubic blue-eyed little blonde baby. She described the supper that night as what was called a good hearty English meal: boiled mutton, boiled potatoes and turnips, and some sort of heavy pudding dessert. The boys, who at their ages would eat anything in sight, wolfed down everything, as did my father, reminiscing about his boyhood life and the good meals he had missed for all those years, clearly not a compliment to my mother's cooking. Dad's brothers then took us to our new home where Grandma had provided most of what she thought we might need for a few days before starting housekeeping. My mother went pale with her first look at the inside of the house, and clutched my sister's arm tightly. The silt-stained windows in the peeling window frames, the mildewed wallpaper, and the heavy brown doors all came at her in one blow and she thought she might be ill, but managed to stay silent. Grandmother Brown had offered to keep my brother Billy with her that first week while Mother settled down, but Billy started howling immediately at this suggestion. He was terrified they would leave him with the little gray-haired lady and the old bearded man. He grabbed our mother's skirt and wouldn't let go. However, again, I must emphasize how I now admire my grandmother's thoughtfulness, despite my mother's opinion.

I cannot even imagine how my family dealt with the first few weeks in that musty old house with very little furniture to sit on, no wardrobes to hang one's clothes in, and not even a mirror in the whole house, other than a small oval one in the upper bathroom. Somehow they survived.

My dad bought the newspapers the next morning and started to look for a job, but companies did not welcome an accountant who had only worked in Mexican oil or mining companies, even though he had the highest of recommendations. At first, he was offered a few crumbs with a starting pay that would not have supported a bachelor, much less a man with a wife and seven children, so after a month or so of eating up his hard-earned savings, he decided to sail back to Mexico. This proved to be a successful move, and from then on, the monthly check arrived promptly for my mother, who learned how to make it last until the next one.

Before my mother began to think of things such as furniture or curtains and rugs, she decided she did not want to live in that musty old house so she started to house hunt. She started out on foot until my grandfather--who by that time was a staunch ally--began driving her It wasn't long before she found a house more to her liking in Crouch End, and although it too had three stories like the rest of the houses on the block, there was a lovely ample living room with French doors overlooking a neat pretty little garden, which she mentally planted with all sorts of colorful flowers and greenery. Then came the battle between her and the landlord, when she tried to get out of the contract her mother-in-law had signed. He was furious, and maintained that the contract could not be broken, until she finally told him that her husband had gone to America and left her penniless, and she could never pay him his rent, nor would her in-laws. In the face of this he tore up the contract in front of her with a scalding warning that she and her family had to be out of the house by the end of the week. Mr Beer helped by hiring a moving van, and in a few days the family was out of the dreaded house.

My mother had still not advised my grandmother about the move, trusting Mr. Beer to do so. One morning my youngest brother, Bill, answered the door, and there stood Grandma Brown, dressed in a black dress with a little lace collar and a shawl across her shoulders.

"Hello dear, is your mother in?" was all she asked, and nine year old Bill slammed the door in her face and ran to get my mother. Horrified at his rudeness, my mother went to the door to apologetically usher her mother-in-law in.

"Come in, Mother, and welcome to our home. I'm so very sorry about Billy's rudeness. Please come in." She reached out to hold the old lady's arm, but Grandmother would have none of it.

She wrenched her arm away and said, "I can hardly believe your not advising me of your move, after all the trouble we took to find you a house and partially furnish it. I'm sure my son is not aware of your lack of courtesy toward me, but he'll hear about it, you can be sure!" And with that she turned and went down the three steps into the front garden. Only then did my mother realize that her second son, Alf, was with her, standing by the gate. Of course my mother followed her and tried to explain to Alf how the move was so precipitous that she had had her hands full settling down and was planning to call the family once she could receive them graciously. But by this time Alf had opened the car door for his mother and gone around the other side. They drove off without another word. My mother realized her mistake and now worried about my father hearing about the incident directly from his mother. To make a phone call was out of the question, for the cost would have been prohibitive, so she decided to wire my father to give him our new address, saying she would contact his mother that very day. He would then think that his mother had visited before his wife had had a chance to call her. Not a very likely story, but still, better than the real one.

Every month, my mother invested in one item. First was a large sofa in pale cream, at a discount, because no one was interested in a color which was so hard to keep clean. One would think that with growing boys, my mother would not have wanted it either, but she had a definite idea of how her finished living room should look, and although her vision of grandeur was anything but sensible, like so many of my mother's ideas, it worked out well eventually. Little by little and piece by piece she furnished what she began calling "the drawing room" and ended by making herself some elaborate pale green, silk damask drapes which hung long, in the English style, on either side of the French doors.

One of the first steps was to find a school for my brothers. This did not prove to be a problem, as children had to attend school in the same area where they lived. However each child

13

had to take an admittance test, and the result was that they were found to be below British school standards, so to my mother's disappointment, had to be put in lower grades.

Victoria had previously taken a business course in the United States and was checking the newspapers every day seeking employment. At the very first firm where she applied, the bosses found her so efficient and were so dazzled by her glamour that they did not hesitate to hire her. Besides, she was a great bluffer and said she was 21 years old and had held down a position for two years in the United States with an important company. They took her word for it, and as she turned out to be quick and competent, within three months she was asking for a raise in salary, which she was granted.

Little by little relations were patched up between the Browns and my mother, and when eventually the drawing room was finished and ready to receive the family, they were invited over for a proper English tea. Grandmother's only whispered comment to her daughter, overheard by my sister was "My poor son. He works so hard in that far-off country to support this pretentious life style."

My mother was very fond of Mr. Beer, and called him "Father" almost right away. Although she also called my grandmother "Mother", she never really became close to her, but by the time my father visited us a year later my mother had made the peace with her mother-in-law and even become quite friendly with her sisters-in-law. She had made friends with her neighbors too, and was gradually better accepted as a good English woman.

One of the friends she acquired at the local Catholic church was a French woman named Maud Moulton who had been living in London for several years, who took to my mother from the first time they met. She invited her to visit Paris to stay at her parents' home. Later on, when I was older and my sister was already married, Mother left me with her while she and Maud took the boat-train across the channel (this involved taking the train from London to Dover, boarding the cross-channel ferry, disembarking in Calais, and taking another train to Paris) and stayed for a week. Maud's mother was unable to walk for any distance, and Maud wanted to visit her girlhood friends, so my mother was left in the hands of Mr. Moulton, who had a glad eye, and who was more than happy to take her to all the high spots and be seen with an attractive English woman on his arm. In later life, that week was one of my mother's fondest memories.

I think it must have been my third Christmas in London when my mother gave me my first teddy-bear, whom I promptly named Teddy. That same Christmas my grandmother came over to have dinner with us and spend the afternoon, bringing me an almost identical teddy. I named this one Bobby, and got to love them so much that when I was a little older I told my mother that if I should die I wanted to be buried with my teddy bears. They were stuffed with straw, unlike the present day polyester-filled animals, and I have them still, although their eyes are no longer the original glass ones, but are embroidered by my mother with black yarn like their noses. Their little paws too have been thoughtfully mended with chamois skin patches so the straw cannot come out.

Meanwhile, my sister Vicki, as she came to be known to friends and family, had had a series of suitors who would visit on Sundays. The family album still holds photos of some of them sitting with us in the back garden, and funnily enough I can remember their names, perhaps because my sister referred to them occasionally in later life. First there was Freddy Clark who parted his hair in the middle and wore glasses. Despite this, he looks quite handsome in the photos, standing tall beside my slim sister, and when years later I asked her why she hadn't ended up with him, she said she had been embarassed by his rather "cockney" accent. She added that his family was far from upper crust. Cross off Freddy. Then there are photos of Henry Church, whose father was a blind minister. Vicki said she was fond of Henry, but when invited over to his home for a meal she was bothered when seeing Mr. Church senior drop his food on the tablecloth and fumble around for it with his fingers. Besides, Henry told her that if they married, they would have to live with his parents temporarily until his finances improved. Cross off Henry. Then came a handsome stocky sexy looking Swiss named Walter Bollman with sleek blonde hair combed straight back on his broad head. His sister Trudi visited us from Zurich, and shared Vicki's room for a week. My older brothers, Fred and Dick, both teenagers by then, were enchanted by her ruddy, healthy good looks, her Swiss accent, and her lack of modesty, as she used to walk between the upstairs bathroom to the bedroom in a tiny bra and skimpy underpanties. Once, when my mother saw her on the way, she rushed at her and asked her to please put on a robe, to the disappointment of my brothers. Later on, in reciprocation for this visit, Trudi and Walter invited Vicki to their home in the Alps to go skiing. The pictures show my sister, Trudi and Walter and their parents outside of their house and also on a snowy hillside with skis on. Vicki told me when I was already a woman, that she had shared a large four poster bed with Trudi, and the first morning Walter had come in early and crawled in between them. The three had giggled and talked until time for breakfast downstairs. Very open-minded family, who probably would have thought nothing of Vicki and Walter sleeping together, which never happened.

When she returned to London she decided he was not for her. Cross off Walter. She really had her mind set on marrying an Englishman, and started going out with David Bodimeade, certainly the most distinguished of all her suitors. He was an interior decorator, and came from a fine upper class family. By then she had learned about class distinction in England, and she never forgot it. When his family invited her with my mother and me over for tea, we went, dressed in our finery and on our best behaviour. We have a photo of the group in their front garden outside a fairytale ivy-covered house. The table was set beautifully for high tea, so Vicki tells, and I do remember the occasion because I was already five years old, and Mrs. Bodimeade senior offered me a scone asking if I would like some butter on it. I, finding the opening to be heard, answered in my loudest voice, "Oh no, thenkyou, mum, we only eat margarine in my house." Of course my sister and my mother were embarrassed, but everyone had a good laugh and it served as an icebreaker.

Vicky and David got married in 1936. They had a civil ceremony, and the photo shows David in morning coat and striped pants, and Vicky in a navy blue floral silk outfit with a large straw hat. My mother gave the reception at our house, and a neighbor of ours insisted on helping to make the cold buffet. The silver was laid out, our finest cloth, and the china and glassware glistened. I wore a pretty white organdy dress with a satin ribbon around the waist and one in my hair. We have a photo of me reaching into the car window as they were leaving, throwing confetti at the bride and groom as they drove away in a lovely little MG convertible. They went to Germany on their honeymoon and came back to settle down in a pretty little mews apartment which David had decorated to suit Vicki. He had painted above the living room chimney a Mexican indian and his wife in bright colors to remind his bride of Mexico, her country of birth.

You may think that my memory of these details is out of the ordinary. I wonder how many of you readers can remember back to when you were five. Perhaps, in my case, it is because of the photo albums which my mother kept methodically over the years, and which we referred to often, or perhaps because I heard the stories told many times later by my mother and by Vicki.

Shortly after Vicki moved out, my mother rented her front bedroom to Maud's brother who was living and working in London but was unhappy with his present lodgings. Willy Moulton was young and frail-looking but good humored. He spoke English well, although with a slight French accent, and worked as a telephone operator. Although he only took breakfast and supper at the house, he and my mother would have long conversations when he came back from work in the evenings, referring to snippets of conversation he had overheard when connecting important people on overseas calls. King George V had recently died, and Edward, his son, was in line to occupy the throne as King of England, but his subjects were worried about the liaison he was having with Mrs. Wallis Simpson, an attractive divorceé. Edward, had been warned by Prime Minister Baldwin that he was not going to be allowed to marry her. Divorce was frowned upon in royalty, and in any case Mrs. Simpson was quite unsuitable to be queen. Edward provoked a constitutional crisis by wanting to marry her and she had taken up residence meanwhile in Candé, near Angers in France. Several times a week she and Edward would talk on the phone, and Willy often put through the conference, when possible listening in for a while. He heard their endearing names for each other, and one night Wallis quoted the last lines of a poem by Browning (Confessions) which she had previously jotted down in a letter to him, but nevertheless recited on the phone. Willy had taken notes:

"How sad and bad and mad it was! But then, how it was sweet!" clearly referring to the obstacles that the British public had put between them, and the optimistic view that they would soon be united. We were still in London when Edward the VIII gave his famous speech, renouncing his throne to be with "the woman I love." My mother and sister and her husband stood in the kitchen with tears streaming down their cheeks. His brother, who took the title of George VI, occupied the throne and remained king throughout the war until his death in 1952.

When I was five my mother registered me in a nearby Catholic school, St. Peter in Chains. I remember Sister Anne, who was French, and a rosy faced Sister Mary, whom I took to immediately. I had already started reading at home because Bill my brother had started me out, so I fell in with the simple little books they dealt out in the classroom, and they thought me some kind of a child prodigy when I read right through them. I was put in the class band, and had to play the triangle, which I did with vigor whenever my green note came up on the music sheet.

I really enjoyed my class and classmates, and bragged about knowing America, which in reality I could not remember at all. The children asked me if there were wild indians there, and of course I embellished the stories which my brothers had told me. There was a cute boy named David, and another named Tom McCann, and I tried to make friends with them, but they would have no part of me. Disappointed, I had to make friends only with the girls.

In third grade, when I was seven, I remember two dark girls arriving at the school shortly after we started the term. They had stringy black hair, and wore odd clothes, and one day when my mother came for me after classes she saw their father with them, and commented on her way home that he must be from India. Just that. The next day, I whispered to my classmate that the girls' father was an Indian, and shortly after, I was confronted by the two sisters during recess.

"Did you say that my father was an Indian?" the eldest one said, hands on hips. I thought quickly, and couldn't deny it as the girl whom I had told it to was standing right by me.

"Oh no, of course not." I answered cooly. "I only said that your father LOOKED like an Indian." And with that, oddly enough, she seemed to be appeased and walked away.

There were two other girls in my class whom I envied tremendously. I think they were sisters and both had silvery blonde hair, cut in a bob with soft bangs. They were both extremely pretty, and wore beautiful clothes. I particularly remember Beryl's red wool dress with a white fuzzy wool edging, rather like a Santa Claus outfit, and her sister with an identical one in yellow. Thinking back, I can't imagine why on earth their mother dressed them that way for school. Beryl always carried a tiny leather bag, and at recess she would open it dramatically and take out coins for sweets or hot cocoa. I think they must have planted my first conscious desire to dress stylishly, which took me years to achieve after much trial and error.

I made my First Communion when I was six with the rest of

my class at St. Peter in Chains Church. My mother made me a lovely little white wool dress with short puffed sleeves and a Peter Pan collar. Father Coolheart gave us the Communion. For once, I felt I was dressed more stylishly than Beryl and her sister.

Meanwhile, Grandfather Beer and my Grandmother had decided to live apart. He was eighty-two years old, and they must have been having differences for several years because he finally told her " he'd "had enough" and went to live with his son. Shortly after, he invited my mother and me to spend a few days' holiday with him in Ramsgate, a seaport resort about an hour's ride from London. Mother was delighted, and so we three boarded a train, and when we arrived on the coast we went to a small boarding house where he had stayed before. I must have been five at the time, and Mother and I had our own bedroom but took our meals with Mr. Beer in the living room where three small tables were set for the guests. I remember vividly that on top of the mantlepiece I spied three little china pigs, one with a fiddle, one with a flute, and one with a drum. Anyway, they fascinated me so much that I felt I had to have them. One morning early before my mother awoke, I snuck out of our room and climbed onto a chair to take one of the little pigs, figuring I could take another one the next day. I hid it in our room in the open suitcase beneath my clothes. Later, while the three of us sat having our breakfast, my mother happened to look up at the mantlepiece, and immediately, without hesitation, looked at me, and said quietly, "Peggy dear, what did you do with the other little pig?" There was no doubt in her voice. She knew I was the culprit. I started to deny it, but then, crying, ran to the bedroom and retrieved the unharmed little pig. Wordlessly, Grandfather Beer rose from the table and placed it by the others. Nothing more was said.

After breakfast we would walk to the beach and they would sit in deck chairs while I played in the sand with my bucket and spade. There is a priceless photograph in the family album of the three of us, they two in the most unlikely beach garb, my bearded grandfather wearing a navy blue three piece suit and tie, watch chain showing on his waistcoat, heavy socks and shoes, walking stick held firmly between his knees; my mother in skirt and blouse, a silk scarf tied under her chin, hose, and sturdy shoes. Sitting on the sand in front of them, I sat, wearing a little wool bathing suit, the upper part which had fallen away from my chest, leather sandals, half squinting yet smiling at the camera. I assume this was taken by a beach photographer and paid for by my grandfather, as he paid for everything else. In back of us one can see another gentleman in gray suit and tie, and on the other side two ladies in frocks and cardigans, both with sturdy shoes and hose. Clearly the weather was not that warm, even though it was in summer. The hilarious thing is that when we returned to London, everyone commented on how sunburned we were despite the weak sun and cool breeze.

My brother Fred had started dating a young nurse named Nesta, and she and her friend Mary, another nurse, asked me whether I'd like to spend an afternoon with them while my mother went shopping. I said yes, and they kept me amused until, while they were making tea, I started jumping around on their bed. I happened to jump on Mary's new straw hat lying on the edge. The ribbon came off and I realized I had crushed the crown. Realizing what I had done I started to cry and Nesta had to hold me and reassure me that nothing terrible had happened. She straightened up Mary's hat as best she could and they both said it looked good as new. It was only a small incident, but thirty years later, my sister-in-law, Nesta, and I, remembered and laughed about it when we visited her at my niece's home on one of our many trips to England.

.The very first movie I ever saw was with my mother in London. It was "Captains Courageous, a 1937 film with the child actor, Freddie Bartholomew, and Spencer Tracy, based on a Kipling story, very appropiate for my age. I must have been seven, and I loved it and became hooked on movies for the rest of my life.

My mother had always written poems, essays, and articles, and sent them to a local newspaper when she lived in San Antonio in the United States, where some of them were published. Now, in London, she wrote a letter to Mr. Godfrey Wynn, a well known writer for a London magazine called Womens' Day. It was published and shortly after she was invited to join a writers' club, which she did gladly, and got to meet Mr. Wynn personally. After that she would regularly attend meetings once a week, and eventually started to invite a few of the writers home for a glass of port and what my brothers used to mockingly call "your high class literary conversations". Looking back I can see that my mother had finally found her niche. She was very happy, and loved living in London. I am sure she must have missed my father, but at the same time was enjoying her complete liberty to do all the things she had not had a chance to do earlier. She had become very independent, a quality not appreciated later by my father when they finally got together again in Mexico, and which became the cause of many heated discussions which usually ended with him turning on his heel and leaving the room.

During this period there was much debate in England as to whether or not there was to be war. Mr. Neville Chamberlain, the Prime Minister of England, had recently returned from a conference with Hitler in Germany, triumphantly waving a paper as he descended from the plane, in which it was stated that there would not be war between the two countries. He had desperately tried to prevent the slaughter on the battlefields as in World War I by appeasing Adolf Hitler and his Italian counterpart Benito Mussolini through negotiation, and his people wanted to believe him, but the situation looked ominous. Trenches were being dug in Hyde Park anyway. Officers were coming around homes passing out gas masks because it was assumed gas would be used like in the previous war if London were bombed. I remember trying one on and it being much too large for me, in which case, they told my mother, I would have to be evacuated to the country with other children if war should be declared. Of course

I was terrified that they would take me from my mother and send me to live with some family outside of the city, but my mother promised it would not happen. It was then that she made the decision to leave for Mexico with me. She called a meeting of her daughter, son-in-law and my brothers.

Dick had already joined the Merchant Marine and was convincing Bill to follow him. Ted and Bob had joined the Royal Air Force with the first whiff of war in the air, and Fred, the eldest, had decided to join the Grenadier Guards, but they were all there the day she broke the news of our leaving, urging them to remain in the forces and defend our country. That left me as her only responsibility. She decided to put the furniture away in storage, pack up, and leave with me for Mexico. Also, very importantly, she wanted to celebrate her twenty-fifth anniversary of marriage with my father, who had not come to visit us in England for over a year.

She was fêted by her friends, the writers' club, and of course, Vicki and David and his parents. To my mother's great sorrow, Grandfather Beer had had a fatal accident the previous month at his son's home while changing a light bulb in his room and falling and cracking his head on the mantlepiece. Mother had gone to his side at the hospital, not before giving his son and daughter-in-law a tremendous tongue-lashing about not caring for an eighty-four year old man the way they should have. She met with my grandmother at the funeral parlor, and told her of her plans to return to Mexico. I think that Grandmother must have thought it was about time my mother went back to take care of her poor husband, alone in that far away country.

The group that accompanied us to the train station the day we left day for Southampton to take our boat consisted of Vicki and David, Fred my brother and Nesta his soon-to-be-wife, and a few friends. Ted and Bob had just joined the Royal Air Force, and Dick and Bill had just shipped out. My mother kept a stiff upper lip, but there were tears in her eyes as she said her final goodbyes and took me by the hand to board the train. It was all a new adventure, to me, and I was excited that I had a new steamer trunk all my own where my mother had packed new clothes and some of my possessions not to be opened until we were on board the ocean liner. It was on the 29th of May 1939 when we left England, and I was not return until 1969, thirty years later with my husband Frank, on our first trip to Europe as tourists

MEXICO CITY

After arriving from Veracruz, we remained only a week in Mexico City at the Guardiola Hotel, across the street from Sanborns, the famous restaurant, known originally as The House of Tiles. After calling many of her old friends, several came to see us at the hotel, or invited us to their homes, happy to see the Brown family back in Mexico and eager to hear of their years in London. Everyone asked about Vicki, and was happy to hear she was now married to a fine young Englishman. They always referred to her as "la hermosa Vicki", the beautiful Vicki, and recalled her raven hair and large brown eyes. They would then compare me to her, adding that some day I would be as lovely as she, but as a blonde. She had been a vivacious teenager when they knew her, and had obviously charmed them all with her beauty and her personality, so I had begun to have serious doubts whether I could ever fill her shoes, either personalitywise or in beauty. My hair was what was known as "dishwater blonde" and although my eyes were green, my lashes and brows were so pale that they did not stand out. Also, I was very thin, and some of my mother's Mexican friends whose children were usually plump, would suggest that she give me a good portion of oatmeal with cream in the morning to put some fat on my bones. However my mother always reassured me that I was very pretty the way I was.

I particularly remember two elderly gentlemen who arrived at the hotel, whom mother entertained in the lobby. Dad had gone to the company offices to do some paperwork before our impending trip to Angangueo, the small mining town where he had been working for several years. Mother seemed very happy to see them but was dismayed to hear that one of them had had a serious operation which had necessitated a tracheotomy. I remember he wore a tissue tucked into his starched white collar and with each breath it would flutter. He insisted on pulling me toward him to sit on his lap, which I did very reluctantly, feeling the air blow at me from beneath the tissue, mixed with the odor of his cologne. After I let him smooth my hair and tell me that I was "muy bonita", I jumped off his lap and sat on the sofa by my mother. She later told me that this man had been in love with Victoria before they left Mexico, but she had not been interested in him because of his age. The other gentleman proudly presented my mother with his photograph taken in his youth, dressed in a Prussian uniform, spiked helmet and all. After duly admiring it, she thanked him profusely. I'll never know why he chose to be attired that way, or why he gave my mother his photograph, but I imagine he wanted her to remember him the way he used to be when she had first known him. Mother later explained to me that people in the past used to love to dress up to be photographed in various costumes, and now that I've seen sepia photographs of members of her own family dressed in various Welsh outfits back in the nineteenth century, I begin to understand it was a vain custom of my elders.

Another family we visited in the city was the Spanish family who had just come over with us on the ship, fleeing Franco's civil war which had started in 1936 when he became the caudillo leader, and lasted up to 1939. Maruja, the daughter, had recounted the atrocities of that war, brother fighting against brother, she herself fighting with the Resistance and proudly bearing a deep bullet wound on her shin bone. She was so attractive and vivacious that they had named her Queen of the Orinoco, the name of the ship we were on. I must add that I had been named the Little Princess of the Orinoco.

They had rented a beautiful house in the Lomas, a lovely

residential district, where we went to have supper with them and met other members of the family who had escaped to Mexico before them. Maruja remained my mother's friend for many years despite our travels in and out of the city.

During the time we were in Mexico City, my parents left me on several evenings with the house girl while they attended functions at theatres at the beautiful Bellas Artes opera house. I believe this is when they saw the soprano, Marian Anderson. There was no fear in those days of leaving one's child with a young maid at the hotel. They took me to the famous Chapultepec Park, where we climbed up to the Castle which one day had housed Mexico's Presidents as well as the Emperor Maximilian. Here I heard for the first time the story of the Niños Héroes (Boy Heroes) who one day, during the war with the Unites States, had defended their Military Academy and the castle from the American soldiers. They were all killed, and to this day Mexico venerates their memory. We rented a boat on the lake in the park, and Daddy rowed while I consumed a paleta de limón, frozen lemon sucker, which I found novel and delicious. I loved Mexico City!

ANGANGUEO, MICHOACAN

Early one morning we left by car for the mining town where my father had been working as Chief Accountant for several years at the American Smelting and Refining Company in Angangueo, in the state of Michoacán, about four hours from Mexico City. Today the town is famous for the winter arrival of the beautiful Monarch butterflies, and is frequented by tourists from all over Mexico and other countries to see the beautiful sight of the hills and fir tree branches covered with swarms of the colorful insects which start arriving during the first two days of November, coincidentally called All Souls' Day and The Day of the Dead. This convinces the local indians that they are people's souls returning to the place of their birth. With folded wings they can look quite drab, but when they flex to soak up the sun, they flash their orange and black inner surfaces and show their true beauty. Remaining during the winter, in March they start their long journey northward again. When we were there, either we were not in the right section, or the butterflies settled only in the nearby hills, but I do not recall ever seeing them. My loss.

Angangueo rests in a narrow valley between mountains, a mining village with cobblestoned streets winding up to the town square with its twin cathedrals. It was discovered by the Spanish in 1550, who never suspected the mineral treasure buried deep in the hills. It was not until two hundred and fifty years later that an avalanche of workers finally arrived to work the mines, first the Spanish, later the Germans, the English, and eventually the French and the Americans. The A.S.A.R.CO. mining company had built a lovely clubhouse in a gated area above the town, where some of the foreign employees lived. Inside, were a few red-tiled bungalows, already occupied by foreign families, so my father, being alone at the time, had been given a room in clubhouse. When he announced that his wife and daughter were arriving from England, they had hurriedly set aside two rooms with bathroom in the clubhouse for us until one of the houses should be unoccupied. This worked out very well, as my mother converted one of the rooms into a sort of den, using club furniture from their stock room. I slept on a couch, and my parents used the other as their bedroom. She also borrowed a card table and chairs to set up in the "den"so she could invite some of the other ladies to tea in the afternoons. On these occasions, she would ask the Chinese cook to make up little sandwiches and cookies with a pot of tea.

The Superintendent of the mine, a Mr. Edelen, lived with his wife in a lovely house on top of a hill, and my mother was often invited to their house for tea. A great coincidence was that the Manager of the office was also English, and was also named Mr. Brown. He was married to a Mexican lady and lived downtown with their two daughters, the youngest a year older than I, named Margarita, which is my name in Spanish. They called her Mague though, a diminutive for Margarita, and I was Peggy, so there was no problem differentiating between us when we were addressed. Margarita spoke both Spanish and broken English. She attended school in town, but as I did not speak Spanish, my mother thought it best that I not attend, but rather hired a Mexican teacher who would come to the clubhouse every morning to teach me Spanish. I remember her as a sweet lady, but I think I learned more of the language when playing with Margarita, although rather than correct her English, we spoke to each other in an idiom all our own, half English, half Spanish. For instance she'd ask me "What play today?" and I would answer "What want?" and from there we'd go on to "Vamos a jugar a tea party", or some other diversion. She had a beautiful little gray and white pony named Huesos which means Bones, because when they got him he was very skinny. He was well fed now, and while Margarita was in school they would bring Huesos to the clubhouse for me to ride. There was an old mozo who had a defect in his mouth and jaw, and whom they called El Mudo, the Mute One and he was given the job of leading me and the pony around the corral and sometimes up the hill to the Edelens' home. They finally brought me a little donkey to ride while Margarita rode her own pony, so that we could ride together, and as he was very skinny, I insisted on naming him Huesos also, which upset Margarita until someone suggested I call him Huesitos, which means Little Bones. Together we'd trot around the driveway together in the late afternoon after she was out of school and on weekends.

In September war was declared between England and Germany, the beginning of my parents' worries about the rest of the family in London and in the Forces. They had brief letters from the boys, who could never say where they were, letters which would arrive previously inspected by censors, with entire pieces snipped out or covered over with black ink, so that we never knew where they came from. I, unaware of the terrible fighting going on in Europe, continued to enjoy my days in that small town in Mexico.

My eighth birthday came up in November of that year, 1939, and mother gave me a little birthday party in the late afternoon so that my father could be back from the office. The Williams family had a darling little boy whom they called Zeppy, and who arrived at the party with a present of 4 boxes of Jello and one of Chicles Adams, a brand of chewing gum which I had never had in London. I had been at his house one day when his mother, Amy, had made Jello from a box in front of me. I had never seen this miracle performed by my mother and I was so amazed that this delicious dessert could materialize before my eyes that I wanted to make one too. She showed me how. Thus the present of Jellos. The Himboughs had a grandchild visiting them from a military school in Texas, who came to the party in uniform, and I was stricken by his appearance. Also the Lovelaces had a little girl named Sally who was a year younger than I, and of course she came to the party. My mother had set up a small table in the clubhouse living room, with finger food, followed by a large white cake with eight candles and of course ice cream which the Chinese cook had been making all morning in one of those ice buckets which his helper had hand-churned for hours. This was the first time I had seen how ice cream was made, and I was fascinated, and insisted on tasting it each time the helper lifted the lid to see if it was ready. The party went off well, and then came time to open my presents. I still remember the joy I felt when I opened one medium sized package which contained a white teddy bear, to add to my family of Teddy and Bobby which had come all the way from London. I promptly named him Sidka Rupert Whitebear, after a character in a book I had just read about a white bear in Alaska, and he too has remained with me all these years, along with Teddy and Bobby, although somewhere along the road he lost both his ears. A rather large box contained a little tea set from Margarita, to replace the one I had left behind in storage in London. Another neatly wrapped present that thrilled me was a set of clothes for my original two teddies, hand-made by a Mrs. Rowland, who also lived in the compound. I am still amazed that this dear lady who had only recently met me would have gone to the trouble of secretly measuring my teddy bears and making them such perfect little outfits. Other presents were sweets and chocolates, and books from my mother and father, who had sent to the American Bookstore in Mexico City for Hans Christian Anderson's Fairy Tales, and Louisa May Alcott's "Little Women. It was a wonderful birthday.

My mother's step mother had died years before when she and grandfather Hardy moved to the United States, where they retired in a small house in San Antonio, Texas. When Grandmother passed away, Grandfather Hardy was left to himself in his house, all alone. His only son, my mother's half-brother, John Hardy Jr., who lived in Texas, seemingly was too busy to take care of his father, so the old man gradually started to fade away. My mother and all of us were living in London at the time, unaware of the situation, but a young man who had been raised in Tampico by my grandfather, a Mexican worker's son whom he had raised almost like a member of the family, traced my grandfather, and made a special trip to San Antonio to visit him. He found him skeletal, hardly surviving the grief of his wife, and decided to take him back to live with his own family in Tampico. Thus, when we were living in Angangueo, one of my mother's first priorities was to make a trip to Tampico to see her old father. She and I took a bus to Mexico City and transferred to a "Carro Turismo" which was a limousine service which carried five passengers, all the way to Tampico. We arrived that night, and checked into the Hotel Inglaterra, where my grandfather had been waiting for us in the lobby since late afternoon. He was a dear old man, and very grateful to "Chepe" his "godson" for having him in his home in the best bedroom of the house. Grandfather told my mother that they treated him like a king, and fed him special food because he had never become accustomed to eating chili like the average Mexican. Chepe, and I never knew his full name, and his family lived outside of Tampico, in La Barra, so the next day we took a bus out to their home near a beach. We visited with the family who were humble but gracious, and Grandfather proudly introduced us to the various members and their grandchildren, of which he was quite fond, and showed us his room, very ample, and full of his memorabilia. He gave my mother many sepia-colored photographs and mementos belonging to her real mother from Wales, who had passed away many years before, and her ancestors. I treasure these photographs today in a little leather album.

On some of these trips,(because we made several during our time in Angangueo and later from Mexico City) my mother would rent a room at a nearby rustic hotel on the beach belonging to a bad tempered old Spaniard. It went with breakfast and supper, and we took our main meal at Chepe's house with Grandfather and the rest of the family. No one would start eating until "Don Juan" , as they called him respectfully, put the first mouthful of food into his mouth, at which time the rest of the family would commence. They had a well from which they drew their drinking water, and one day when they weren't looking, I could not resist pouring some sand into it, but Daniel the youngest boy spied me doing it, and told his father. My mother heard, and she and grandfather gave me a long lecture about how the well was their only drinking water, and should be kept clean. I was then banished from the garden.

Mother and Grandfather and I would walk on the beach near La Barra, and one day we saw the ship on which we had come out from England, the "Orinoco", forlorn and badly in need of a coat of paint. When we inquired, we were told that it was there for repairs and that all its crew members were in Tampico. Shortly after, we ran into the ship's German photographer, whom we had known while we were aboard, a handsome young man named Alvin Klüge. The Orinoco never went back to Germany and neither did Alvin, because Mexico entered into a "state of war" against the axis due to the cowardly sinking of two Mexican oil boats in the Gulf by German U-Boats. Alvin was taken to a detention camp in Perote, Veracruz, with other German long-time residents of Mexico, just as the Japanese-Americans were taken to detention camps in the United States after Pearl Harbor. This act disrupted many German families who already had businesses of their own and coffee plantations which went to ruin while they were detained in the camp. They were not released until after the end of the war.

Grandfather Hardy wrote beautiful poetry during his lifetime, and would tell me wonderful stories about fairies and goblins. He handwrote a long fairy tale story for me, which I still have, as well as some of his funnier verses, for he was a witty old man and always had something to say with wry humor. The beach at La Barra was full of tar and petroleum, so no swimming was allowed, but despite this, I would run barefoot in the sand, until one day I found something peculiar bothering my two big toes. My Grandfather looked at them knowingly and pronounced: "Niguas". Now, I have never heard that word again, nor have I ever come across such an insect on any beach, but looking it up in the dictionary I find that "nigua" in Spanish is a two-winged sand flea. These little fleas had incrusted themselves under my big toe nails and formed a little sack like a nest. My grandfather produced his pen knife, and without much ado, despite my mother's concern, slipped the tip of the small blade painlessly under my toenail and removed the whole small white bag, unbroken, with the tiny insects still inside. No blood, no pain. Miracle Man.

After about a week it was time to say goodbye. It broke my mother's heart to have to leave her father at Chepe's house, for although he was a good man doing his best to repay "Don Juan" the years he had had him in his own home while growing up, she would have wanted to take him to live with her, but our circumstances at the Angangueo club house would not permit it. Later, she thought, one day later I'll have him come live with us.

At this point, I must include something funny which

happened on one of these trips in the limousine that we took to Tampico. I had previously asked my mother pointedly, (I was eight years old) where babies came from. She finally told me that babies came from a little seed from the father's male "parts" and travelled into the woman's female "parts", where it nested and formed the baby during nine months. This usually happened at night while the couple were sleeping. No more explanation was required or requested from me. Well, after one of those long rides from Mexico City to Tampico, I fell asleep on the shoulder of the passenger next to me, a nice old fellow who made no effort to wake me. When we arrived in Tampico, my grandfather was waiting for us on the sidewalk outside the hotel, when I started tugging at my mother's elbow desperately. "What is it?" she asked, and I pulled her head down and whispered, "I think I might be pregnant!" She smiled and said "Why on earth would you say that?" To which I answered in a concerned voice that I had slept with the man next to me last night, and perhaps his "seed" had invaded me. My grandfather heard, his long nose starting to go to one side, the way it always did when he heard or said something humorous, and my mother refrained from laughing and explained quietly. "No dear, don't worry, that only happens when the man and his wife are in bed in pajamas." We then proceeded into the hotel, I, breathing a sigh of relief.

Angangueo and the clubhouse gave me my first introduction to Mexican maids. Of course in London we never had hired help, except for the old char woman who came occasionally to scrub the kitchen, as well as the coal man who came occasionally to empty a load into the cellar and to whom mother would always give a cup of tea in the kitchen before he left, leaving his black finger marks on the cup and saucer. But sometimes here I liked to watch the maids as they worked, mopping floors on their hands and knees in the days before we had mops on poles. I enjoyed pestering them with questions, although I can't remember how I made myself understood, and mostly they would just look at me and laugh. One maid in particular stands out in my mind because she was the one who taught me the words to a few Mexican songs which I still hum today. Her face was marked from small pox, and her strange name was Eduviges, a name I've never come across again. Other times I would go into the kitchen to talk with the Chinese cook who spoke broken English, and ask him what he was making for lunch. I loved the food he prepared and he did his best to please me when he found I especially liked some dish. This conviviality with the "help" has lasted throughout my years in Mexico, and I usually end up establishing a good relationship with anyone working for us.

I cannot forget to mention that there was a charming young Mexican company doctor, still a bachelor, who also lived in the clubhouse. He and my mother used to carry on long conversations in the evening in the club sitting room after dinner, and Dad, never a big conversationalist, would read his newspaper, excuse himself, and retire to our quarters. Dr. Ordoñez had spent a few years in the United States taking a post-graduate course, and wanted to continue practicing his English, while learning a little about life in England, which my mother was only too glad to relate. One summer an American friend of his from the U.S. visited him, and I was thrilled to have someone new in the clubhouse to talk to while the doctor was busy at the office infirmary. Apparently Dick enjoyed my company, and we would sit and talk and look at magazines together when "Doc" wasn't around. One weekend, my mother and father and Dick, the Doc and I drove to San José Purúa, the natural sulphur springs spa, where all of us dipped into the smelly yellow waters which are claimed to be healing and healthful. My mother took a mud bath and a massage, while my father and I and the two men spent time in the pool before driving back to Angangueo late that night.

Another time, the doctor who was eager to show Dick as much as he could of this area while he was visiting Mexico, drove the five us to Morelia, the beautiful capital of the State of Michoacán. The colonial city, that has retained an atmosphere of olden days, lies in a relatively fertile valley surrounded by pine covered mountains. People refer to it as "the Switzerland of Mexico" as well as being the city of orchids. We stopped on the way at Mil Cumbres (A Thousand Peaks), a natural mirador or viewpoint from which there lies an incredibler view of the wooded mountains of the western Sierra Madre.

During our time in Angangueo, my mother gave me a sort of "home schooling", today so popular in the U. S., so that I would not fall back in my studies. My dad, being an accountant, gave me arithmetic problems to solve, and I was amazed at his ability to instantly ad a seven or eight figure column by just running his fingers down the paper. He was very patient with me, but even then he must have realized that arithmetic was not my strong subject.

We had been in Angangueo one year, and the only time I had visited Mexico City again, aside from transferring to a bus there when we went to Tampico, was when my mother took me specially to see "The Blue Bird" with Shirley Temple, showing at a cinema. We drove with the Lovelaces, who were taking their little daughter Sally to see it. They stayed with relatives, while my mother and I stayed again at the Guardiola hotel. I loved the movie, although it did not have good reviews, but I enjoyed the story anyway, and Sally and I talked about it all the way home.

When we returned, we found Dad had had a major row with the Superintendent who had previously promised him one of the houses in the compound. Instead he had been offered a house in town, recently abandoned by a Greek family, which was in terrible condition. Clearly my father had taken it as a personal insult, this added to the fact that he had not been conceded the raise he had been promised, and in a moment of fury, he had resigned. My mother took it in stride, as she did all of my father's decisions throughout their marriage, but I was the one who was absolutely devastated with the idea of leaving Angangueo. I loved the place and my new life there, and started weeping bitter tears at the very idea of going somewhere else, so much so that the Crosbys who had become fast friends with my parents, now seeing my distress, promised me they would invite me back to spend time with them later on. I was still heartbroken and pleaded with my Dad to reconsider, but within the week we had packed up our belongings and left for Mexico City where Dad would seek a better position, as he had done so many times in the past. He was fearless, and confident he could find another job, as well as knowing that my mother would follow him as she had always done in the past. But the odd name of Angangueo has always made my heart quicken when I think back to those beautiful memories I have of our year there.

It was 1940, a year when the world heard of the terrible defeat of the British attack on the Germans in Dunkirk, a small village in northern France. The news about their failure to succeed was disheartening, and my parents were left wondering for weeks whether any of my brothers had been part of that attack. They finally had news from my sister that they were all well, and breathed a sigh of relief. My mother especially was shaken when she heard that 80,000 soldiers had had to be rescued and returned to the beaches of Ramsgate, where we had spent such happy days two years before with Grandfather Beer.

NACOZARI

In Mexico City my mother rented a furnished apartment for a month, and my father, before the month was up, true to form, had obtained a much better paying job than the previous one. This time, however, it was way up in the north of the republic, in the state of Sonora. So once again we started our trek toward unknown territory, by train, to a small mining town named Nacozari, which is very famous for a hero who saved the town in the year of 1907. A young man by the name of Jesus García Corona had been a machinist on the train that traveled between Nacozari and the mine, and on to Agua Prieta, on the border with the U. S. He had started from the bottom, doing odd jobs around the station, learning about engines, and being a stoker. Gradually he had worked his way up to being a machinist, the highly responsible job of driving the train that carried workers and dinamite from the town to the mine. On November 7, 1907, two train cars were being loaded with 160 boxes of dinamite, the detonators beneath them, to be used as explosives in the mines. Suddenly, the station master saw smoke coming from one of the cars. He started waving madly and yelling to alert the workers, but there was neither enough water nearby, nor loose dirt to drown out what was obviously the beginning of a fire. They could only stand by helplessly, resigned to the outcome. Suddenly, Jesus gallantly ran forward, saying, "Let me try my luck." He leapt on the train and proceeded to drive it full speed up the hill, hoping to reach the other side before the sparks reached the detonators and the cars exploded. He made it to the top of the hill, away from the town, before it finally exploded, rocking the whole town, but fortunately killing no one, except of course, Jesus, 24 years old, who gave his life to save his hometown. November 7, 1944 became Railroad Workers' Day, and in 2007, one hundred years after the young man died, a ceremony took place in the main plaza where there now stands a bronze plaque and bust of Jesus García Corona, the famous Hero of Nacozari.

Of course we were not aware of this when we finally got off the dusty train which took us to Nacozari and the mining company Dad was to work for. He seemed pleased with the offices, the salary, and the wooden house which was assigned to us, and as usual, Mother accepted her fate and made the best she could with everything. Within a few days she had made friends with the Manager's wife and other foreign ladies, as well as our Mexican neighbors. I too liked the camp, and when the Manager's three little daughters came to visit him in the summer from nearby Douglas, Arizona, on the border with Agua Prieta, Sonora, I made fast friends with them and they invited me for a week to their home. This was my first visit to the U.S. since I had been born there 9 years before, and I considered Douglas a sort of Disneyland, compared to the two previous towns I'd recently been living in. There were three girls, the eldest, Carol, was 13, and very pretty, then came Janet, my age, and little Donna, aged 7. Again, I promised myself that one day I would wear my hair like Carol, and dedicate time to my beauty as she did. It was summer and they did not have classes, so the three of us had lots of time to shop with their mother at the dress shops, grocery stores, and dime stores, which I loved. I immediately bought my mother some special combs for her hair, and my Dad a large ashtray that had a greyhound across the top where he could tap his pipe. He loved it, and used it for many years. Their father took us one day to the movies, where he purchased a giant box of popcorn bathed in butter, such as I had never tasted before, and individual disposable glasses of Coke with straws. Another day he took us to the drugstore where we had giant icecream sodas, another novelty for me. What a treat, and what a lovely vacation for me without my parents.

Back at home, my mother went back to home schooling me, this time with a Calvert Course which she had sent for from the U. S. She also obtained a Sears Roebuck catalogue, from which she ordered our clothes and Christmas presents. I remember I especially loved a gray tweed and green reversible raincoat which looked darling in the catalogue, so she sent for it, but ordered a size 10 for me although I was small for my age, so when it arrived it turned out to be huge on me, as well as being stiff and unflattering. I never wore it in Nacozari, where it seldom rained, but was forced to use it later in Mexico City when we returned. I eventually grew into it, but thankfully I finally outgrew it.

There were three huge black metal water tanks near the house about four stories tall, and I used to sneak over and climb up the ladders attached to the sides so as to peer into and touch the warm water inside. One day I bragged to our young gardener and begged him to go with me to watch me climb up to the top, but when we got home he promptly told my mother. She was horrified and told me I could fall and kill myself or fall inside and drown. I was forbidden to return, and carefully monitored after that.

I do not know what happened this time, but after about a year my Dad decided he'd had enough of Nacozari, so he quit, and we packed up and went back to Mexico City.

MEXICO CITY

Mexico City was founded by the Aztecs on a lake. They had wandered down from the north, looking for a sign given to them by their God, to find a place where an eagle stood with a snake in his mouth. This they finally found in the middle of Lake Texcoco. They built a magnificent city with canals instead of streets, and when the Spanish arrived in 1519, headed by the conquistador, Hernán Cortés, they were amazed by its immensity and beauty. The Mexico City of today is built upon the ruins of that city which was called Tenochtitlán.

This time my father found a wonderful job with the film company, Twentieth Century Fox, right in Mexico City. We rented an apartment in the Colonia Juarez, on Calle Londres, and my mother and father enrolled me in a small nearby school that belonged to a very old British lady named Miss Parmenter, who wore her long white hair knotted and held precariously by a large comb on top of her head. She always had a drop on the tip of her nose which she constantly blotted with a wrinkled old hankie she kept up her sleeve. I entered 3rd grade as I was already nine years old, and enjoyed my first formal school year in Mexico. The school was called The English School, of course, situated on Avenida Chapultepec in a run-down old house belonging to the lady, but after a few months my parents realized the classes were badly organized and the school not run efficiently, so at the end of the year, my parents took me out. They enrolled me in Garside School, on Calle Genova, walking distance from where we lived. This too was run by an older American lady, not as old as Miss Parmenter, but gray haired, and who smelled strongly of cigarette and had a gravelly voice. I entered the fourth grade, where I promptly fell in love with my English teacher, Miss Bertha. In this school one had to study every subject in English as well as in Spanish, so it was a heavy schedule. I was introduced by Miss Bertha to South America in the geography class, and was enchanted with the different cities, to the extent that I really wanted to go there. Out of kindness, and perhaps because she too was interested, she told me that one day when she traveled there, I could go along with her. I invited her to my birthday party where she brought me a lovely china pig with a slot in its back to insert coins, so I could start saving for our trip. Needless to say, the trip never took place, for she married the following year, and perhaps even went to South America on her honeymoon. But I still have the china pig, filled with centavo coins, and used as a paper weight on my desk.

One day we were ushered into the gymnasium for a treat. They showed us a film of a newly born volcano which had recently erupted in the state of Michoacán, yes, the same state I had lived in, but farther west. It started in 1943 and continued spitting out flames and lava for several years before it finally subsided. The story they told us about its birth described an old farmer plowing his field when suddenly he saw a tiny little mound of earth pop up. The mound continued to grow and sputter, so he threw his hat over it and backed off. When it started to discharge smoke and cinder he ran for help as it turned into a fiery hill. The name of the volcano is Paricutín, and the town it started in, now totally covered over, is, and here's a mouthful: Parangaricutirimícuaro. To this day. tourists can visit the area where a solitary church steeple can be seen peeping up from the black molten lava. I've often wondered whether the government ever reimbursed that poor farmer for his land, or whether he stayed around to charge fees for viewing his volcano when the tourists started coming.

We had moved to calle Dinamarca in the same colony, and to my parents delight they found friends whom they had known before they left for England, and with whom they had long ago lost touch. It turned out that the Humphreys lived right across the street from us now, so my parents started the relationship again. They had three children, a son my age, Roberto, a daughter named Marta, a year younger, and another little son about six, whom they called Tito. Roberto and I became fast friends, oddly enough moreso than with Marta. He and I were on the same wavelength, and whenever we could get together we would meet at his house or mine and think of something to do. We were both avid movie goers, and there was a small cinema nearby within walking distance, La Parisiana, where they showed second run movies, a year or so after being shown at the good theatres. We would get permission to attend, and thus saw many of the greatest films of the epoch. My favorite actor was Dana Andrews. We saw him in several movies, one, "A Wing and a Prayer", 1944, which takes place on an aircraft carrier in the South Pacific. As this was still during World War II, it was of special interest to us and I imagined one of my brothers in the part, even though they were in the Merchant Marine. But the actor dearest to my heart was Ronald Coleman, already a mature man, but who had something about him that made me love him and always make me cry at the end if he died, such as in Dickens' "A Tale of Two Cities", where he ends up at the guillotine. His last words spoken in that inimitable British accent of his: "It is a far far better thing that I do now than I have ever done; it is a far far better place that I go to than I have ever known!" still ring in my ears when I think of him, and I went around the house for days, dramatically reciting those words to my parents while tears rolled down my cheeks. However, as I grew a little older I began to appreciate the sensual French voice and half-closed eyelids of Charles Boyer. When his full lips kissed an actress, I almost swooned, and I believe I even wrote a fan letter telling him I had a crush on him, but it sounded so pathetic I ended by tearing it up.

Roberto and I considered ourselves expert tree-climbers, so very often we'd run over to the Paseo de la Reforma and climb some of the huge trees which majestically lined the avenue. We were lucky we didn't break our necks, and every once in a while a guard would tell us to get down or he'd report us to our parents. We also skated a lot in front of our houses, and rode bike, with little or no traffic on our street. Those were days when children needed little supervision from their parents. Roberto and I also rigged up a "telephone" between his house and mine, made up of two oatmeal boxes with a string tied between them. The string would become taught, and each one would yell into the box. I now believe that when we heard the other's voice it was because we were yelling so loud that everyone else could hear us across the street. We had an innocent friendship, and when we made contact fifty years later, he came to visit us in Torreón, invited by a local gallery to show his paintings. Over the years he had become a well-known artist in Mexico City. In the evenings, we would sit out on the terrace, having a glass of wine, while my husband Frank finished watching his unending baseball games on T. V., roaring with laughter while recalling our naiveté in those days.

As my dad now worked with Twentieth Century Fox, he was given free passes almost every week to the theatres, usually when the movies were Fox, but occasionally to ones released by MGM and Paramount. So on Saturdays we would leave the house in time for the 4 P.M. showing and see a movie, sometimes a double feature. From there we would walk downtown to Sanborns for supper, where I would invariably order chicken salad, followed by a most succulent chocolate éclair I will ever taste. They were filled with chocolate cream and covered totally in shiny dark chocolate. I have tasted many eclairs since, but never as wonderful as those at Sanborns in the forties. Years later, having heard this story, my thoughtful daughter-in-law one day brought me a little tray of éclairs in Los Angeles, but they were not even close, and one day, in the very same Sanborns, fifty years hence, I ordered a chocolate éclair, and the waitress looked puzzled. She said she'd never heard of them.

A little Fox Terrier was wandering around in front of our building. He didn't seem to belong to anyone, and he looked hungry, so I, ever the animal saviour, brought him in and fed him half a loaf of bread before he vomited. My parents said it was okay to keep him but not to feed him any more bread, so I named him Foxy and kept him. A few days later while I was petting him he suddenly started whirling around and around, frothy saliva coming out of his mouth. I hastily cleaned it off with a damp towel but a few minutes later he had a convulsion. Within minutes he collapsed and died, right before my eyes. I was heartbroken, and when my parents came home and heard the sad tale, they called the veterinarian who said he would like to autopsy the dog in case it had rabies. My father took the body to him and a day or so later the vet told us the test was inconclusive but there was a chance the dog had died of rabies, which to this day I doubt, the symptoms being more like a seizure or Parvo. Anyway, my parents took me to the pediatrician and he started a series of anti-rabies injections in my tummy, which I stood bravely, each time thinking of my poor little Foxy. Now, ten years ago, I found an identical Fox Terrier on the golf course, and when I saw the greenskeeper wanting to put her out in the parking lot, I brought her home. She has remained with us ever since. We called her Foxy.

I loved boys' clothes, and hated frilly dresses, so asked my mother to buy me a boy's shirt and pants, which I saved for Sundays. This, in a day when slacks were not popular for women or girls. In our same building there lived a Spanish family who had two little girls who were always dressed in frilly little dresses for church wear on Sundays, and whenever we met them leaving the building, they would look at my outfit and start whispering and giggling. No matter, I persisted, because my mother told me to disregard them and dress the way I wanted. Now in my older age, after years of wearing stylish skirts and dresses, I've reverted mostly back to the slacks and sport shirts of my childhood.

All through the war, my sister Victoria kept in touch regularly with my parents, and sometimes enclosed a special letter to me. We heard from each of my brothers too, from different parts of the world, France, North Africa, Italy, and other countries where they were temporarily posted. My mother joined a British group in Mexico called Work For Victory, whose women members got together to knit sox, scarves and blankets for the British forces. They published a little newspaper every two weeks, with information about whose son had received honors, or any first hand news received from abroad. They also had a column of obits, and sadly, some of the names listed belonged to sons or daughters of the Victory group. I did my share of knitting small squares of wool to be added to others to form large blankets. One day I wrote a poem, which my mother sent to the little newspaper and which was immediately published:

"Across the deep blue ocean, in England, far away, I have five brothers fighting, For freedom, and I pray, That when all this is over, and Britain wins the war, My Brothers will be waiting across the ocean far." I received many congratulations.

One day a telegram arrived for my mother from Chepe in Tampico, saying that her father had been ill and they had interned him in the hospital. She immediately took a bus to Tampico, found his condition very bad, and decided to bring him back to Mexico City to intern him in the American British Cowdray Hospital. They came back in one of those limousines we used to travel back and forth in, propped up in the back seat, and checked him in at the hospital. There he remained for several months, where we visited him after school every day. He was in a ward with several other men with whom he immediately made friends as he had a wonderful personality and enjoyed conversing with people in general. His lungs were bad, and he had been diagnosed with advanced bronchitis and emphysema. Then one day I found my mother crying at home and she told me her dear father had passed away. She buried him in the American cemetery in Mexico City because he had become a U. S. Citizen when they had taken up residence in the States many years before, although remaining British in his speech and manner till the end. He was a grand old gentleman and I missed visiting him after school, as he always had something funny to tell me or would show me an amusing new poem he had written for me.

One Sunday, my mother and father took me to see the famous "floating gardens", or Xochimilco, the indian name. Of course, they had been there previously, but no matter how often one returns, it holds a charm all its own, infusing a feeling of tranquility in the visitor. We chose a "chalán", a flat-bottomed boat with an arch of flowers spelling out a name, and I immediately decided on the one with "Luisa" on it, being my mother's name in Spanish. Funny, but I don't remember any of them with men's names, at least not in those days. We floated along, pushed by a boatman with a long pole, rather in the fashion of the gondolas in Venice, except that here, added to the pleasure of trailing one's fingers in the cool green water, we had music to accompany us. Another boat would come alongside with two or three musicians, two with guitars, and a singer, asking for requests. I always had plenty, as I've always loved Mexican music. Further on, we would be followed by long narrow canoes with women making tortillas and Mexican dishes, clearly not very sanitary, but delicious anyway. Perhaps this is why my stomach has built up a resistance over the years, and I seldom become ill when eating food at local restaurants. My present day friend, Sylvia, once commented that I could eat stones and not get ill because I had been brought up in Mexico City.

In school I did better in English than in Spanish, but held my own, and finally graduated from sixth grade when I was twelve. I received the honor of composing and reading a class poem on the stage during the closing ceremony. My mother had a seamstress make a lovely white organdy dress for me (we all wore long white dresses) and I had had my first hair permanent weeks before at the beauty salon where they rolled up my hair in metal curlers and connected them to heating unit. I swear I could even smell the hair or the curling liquid burning. I don't really understand

45

how my mother allowed it, but I had been adamant that I wanted curls. My dad chuckled at the result when I came home that afternoon, and started calling me "Fuzzy Knob".

I remember being on the stage on graduation night, poem in hand in case my memory failed me, reciting to the audience:

"Tonight while standing on this stage, About my class I'll tell, And also that we're here tonight To bid you all farewell…"

It went on for eight verses, and was my first time facing an audience. But I was shy, and my parents told me later that my voice was so quiet they could hardly hear me, a shame because only a few people in the front row heard the words of the poem I had worked so hard on. By that time I had already written many poems, and my parents were sure one day I would be a famous published author. I finally made it when I was 73, published, but still not famous!

I used to frequent the wonderful Benjamin Franklin Library, on Paseo de la Reforma, walking distance from our apartment. After I'd read just about everything that interested me in the children's section, I began to sneak into the adults' section and take out books. The librarian perhaps did not notice, but one day I checked out "The Stranger" by Albert Camus. Although much of it was over my head, I came to a part where it says something about the main protagonist being in jail, and as he had no females nearby he "had to do it himself". I wondered what it meant, and asked my mother, who said, "What on earth have you been reading!" When I told her, she prohibited me from going into that section of the library again, but still did not answer my question, so I had to wonder for years what the author was talking about.

The war ended in 1945, and gradually, four of my brothers and my sister came out to live in Mexico. My eldest brother, Fred, had remained in South Africa where he had remarried and was now living with his second wife. By some small miracle, all six of my siblings had come through the war at the front and the bombing of London unharmed.

At that time schools in Mexico followed a different curriculum from the ones in the U. S. They gave students vacations in winter, compared to summer vacations given in the neighboring country. I graduated in December from Garside, and as it was only a Primary school, started seventh grade in January at the American School Junior High. The school building at that time was on Avenida Insurgentes, where later on they built a Sears Roebuck store. Of course the Roebuck name was long ago dropped.

I was a shy girl, and did not make friends easily, and the only other girl who had graduated from Garside with me and transferred to the American School was my friend Alice Rhorer, so for many months Alice and I spent our recesses and lunch hours together and only started to break away and make new friends when our classes separated us. In one of my classes I sat by a boy named Robert Burnett who was often caught drawing comic strips during class. He would finish an entire page by the time the class was over. I assume he could master two things at the same time, because his grades did not seem to suffer. Mine did, as I spent a lot time doodling and writing stories and then had to study to try to catch up at the end of the week. Over sixty years later when my husband and I were visiting Cuernavaca, where Robert lives now, I called him up and he immediately came to meet us at the dowtown Plaza for a cup of coffee. We had been in contact by email for a couple of years ever since a class reunion in Mexico City, when my photo and email were published in the school newspaper. The minute he appeared amongst the tables, I recognized him, and he the same with me. It was only a short reunion, but we still keep in touch by email. And no, he does not draw comic strips anymore. He writes.

One day the teachers announced in each classroom that we should gather in the auditorium next day to hear a talk by the famous Babe Ruth. No one told me he had been a baseball player, and as my dad, being British to the core, did not follow American sports, neither of us had a clue as to who he was. The following morning I saw this corpulent man walk out on the stage and begin talking. As his name was Babe Ruth, I asssumed he had something to do with the chocolate bar, Baby Ruth. Well, he talked and talked about baseball, about how he had hit the ball out of the stadium, and all the homeruns he had made. I waited for him to start talking about his candy bar factory, which he never did. Bored, I was finally released from the auditorium. Only later when I mentioned my disappointment to a boy I knew, did he set me straight, amazed I had never heard of this famous sportsman who had made 714 runs in his career.

In 1946 there were two main candidates running for the Presidency of Mexico, both civilian, after many years of military presidents. Miguel Alemán was my father's choice, although, being English, he could not vote. He was very relieved when Alemán won, and followed his trajectory closely. The new president became the first Mexican president to travel to the United States to meet with President Harry S. Truman, and my parents were elated when their photograph together was published, riding in an open automobile during a parade in Washington. Amongst other accomplishments, he played a major role in the development and promotion of the city of Acapulco, so that it became one of the principal destinations in the world for the tourist industry. He later oversaw the diversion of the Lerma river, bringing an end to Mexico City's water problems, a big plus in his government. His son, Miguelito, slightly older than I, briefly courted a girl from the American School, and we used to see him at the skating rink with her. In those days, no bodyguards were necessary, not for the boy, and not for the President, quite a change from today.

I used to take the public bus to school, and one day I noticed a cute curly haired boy who had been following me from school to my bus stop to go home. He would board the bus also, and when I found he got off at my same stop I finally confronted him and said "Are you following me?" to which he answered yes, that he was, but that he lived only half a block away from me. It turned out he was an American part-time student from San Francisco, California, and as his parents were divorced he was obliged to spend certain months in San Francisco with his father who had remarried, and time with his mother in Mexico City, who worked at the American Embassy. He was a year older than I, and very good looking, with green eyes and light brown hair. Despite this, and now I wonder why, I never fell in love with him, but liked him as a friend and companion, and from then on that's what we became, constant companions until he had to return to California. His name was Cameron Wylie, but they called him "Sonny". We would take the streetcar on weekends and walk hand in hand around Chapultepec Park where we would ride the games and sometimes row on the lake. It seems that nothing was very expensive then, because I don't believe his mother gave him much spending money, but we made it do. After a few months of his allotted time with his mother, he would leave for San Francisco on a Greyhound bus, poor guy, returning home for the rest of the year. We wrote steadily while he was away, and the next year when he came to Mexico he showed me a picture in his wallet of a pretty little blonde girl who was the daughter of the woman his dad had married. Her name was Katrine, (I still remember) and of course they all lived in the same house. Instantly, I became jealous and made a big fuss. I was just possessive, I imagine, and perhaps fonder of him that I admitted.

One year when Sonny came from California in the summer he got a job as a bellboy at the Reforma Hotel on the grand Paseo de la Reforma. All the actors who filmed in Mexico (and in those days there was a constant flow) stayed at that hotel, so Sonny would let me know when one checked in, and tell me the room number. I was not only an avid filmgoer but an autograph seeker, so I would make it a point to go in the afternoons and talk with Sonny, who wore a cute green uniform with a bellboy's hat. When he had to lope around the lobby yelling "Calling Mr. So-and-so" I would follow him around like a little puppy dog. I would wait patiently for the actor or actress to come down into the lobby, and then accost them with my autograph book and pen or pencil. But sometimes I got desperate when they did not show up, and had the audacity to go up to their rooms and bravely knock on the door. I remember doing this with Joan Fontaine, one of my favorite actresses. When her secretary came to the door, I made my request, and she went back into the room where I heard her say in a British accent, "There's a little girl outside asking for your autograph." I heard a mumbled response and then to my surprise Miss Fontaine herself came to the door, and said "Hello" very sweetly, and when I repeated my request, answered, "Do you have a pencil?" Well, I just about fainted with joy. She signed my book and actually said "Thank you" to me when I thanked her before hurrying away. How gracious, and how beautiful she was.

Another time I obtained Myrna Loy's autograph, and was impressed with the amount of freckles she had all over her face. Also, Xavier Cugat, the famous orchestra leader, who started a conversation with me, and asked me why I was living in Mexico. Usually, they were not at all interested in anyone but themselves, but mostly they were complaisant, and I collected quite a few signatures. Where are they all now? Thrown away, I suppose, in a moment of tidying up drawers.

ACAPULCO

My Dad had always taken his vacations around Christmastime, and ever since we had been living in the city, we would travel to Acapulco every year to spend the holidays there, stopping in Cuernavaca, the land of eternal spring, on the way for refreshments, and then on to Taxco, the delightful little town known for its silverwork and immense mineral wealth. In Acapulco we would usually stay in a small hotel, walking distance from the beach, and spend all our mornings swimming in the warm waters at Caleta beach. In those days, the sand was pristine, and the hotels reasonably priced, including three meals. My parents would look for an unoccupied "palapa" which is a hut made with three posts and a palm roof, rent chairs, and settle down for a morning of reading. After a lunch of seafood back at the hotel and a short nap until the sun started to go down, we would head out to Hornos Beach, where the waves were stronger, and where I would to try to calculate their breaking point thus riding them onto the beach in a whirl of foam. Every kid did the same thing, so there was a lot of laughter after some of us landed occasionally upside down. No vanity in those days and I usually ended up with my hair in squiggles, my eyes and nose red, and my sagging bathing suit full of sand. The heat and the swimming takes it out of you, even if you are eleven or twelve, so after supper I was usually falling asleep and ready for bed.

One morning I saw a huge turtle in the front yard of the hotel, big enough for me to ride. I watched as it consumed a large amount of cabbage and pieces of watermelon. When he wasn't looking, I got on top of him, urged by the smiling gardener, and even stroked his head. Later I happened to see a huge cauldron of water being heated on a fire in the garden, but thought nothing of it. When we got back from the beach he was nowhere to be seen, although I looked for him. In the evening, after returning from Hornos, we sat down to supper where a delicious broth was being served. This is probably the only time in my life that I have had turtle broth but after supper I overheard my mother asking the waiter if this was the turtle that had been outside, and to my horror, it was. Just the thought of that lovely animal being put into the tub of hot water which had been boiling nearby made me want to be sick and gave me nightmares. I have never again had turtle soup. The idea of putting live lobsters into boiling water has always horrified me also, so only on counted occasions have I tasted the delicious meat, when I could not gracefully get out of it at a dinner party.

Another year we went to Acapulco when I was thirteen, and this time I became bored with swimming alone and sitting on the beach with my parents who were always reading. A family who was boarding at the same hotel, became quite friendly at lunchtimes with my parents, and their young son, nicknamed "Manny", started to pay special attention to me. He was a quiet boy of about forteen, and pretty soon we made it a point to go to the beach at the same time, where we would jump the waves and swim. He rented a surfboard one day, and he taught me to ride it. We'd paddle way out, almost to the island of La Roqueta, but when our watchful parents saw us so far out, they would start making wild signs with a towel to return to the beach. One day I ate or drank something that upset my stomach, and developed a high fever, for which I had to take medication and stay in bed. My Dad went down to the terrace and lay in a hammock reading, but my mother stayed with me, and who should come knocking at our door, but Manny. He told my mother he had heard of my illness, and asked permission to accompany me. When I told him I felt hot and dizzy, he knelt by my bed the rest of the afternoon, fanning my face and passing me my cool iced drink. He was so solicitous that I started feeling better, and by the time he left when my father returned, I was laughing and feeling well enough to eat supper. Next day I was up and around, and although I stayed out of the sun, he sat with me on the beach talking. What a sweet young man. Before we left, he wrote in my autograph book, a little rhyme in Spanish, "Corriendo corriendo, me dí un tropezón, por darte la mano, te dí el corazón." Running, running, I had a great fall; for giving you my hand, I gave you my heart." I only saw him once again in Mexico City when my mother invited him and his cousin over for tea with some of my friends, but it was never the same between us, and each of us went our individual ways. A few years later, Joaquín "Manny" Capilla became one of Mexico's most beloved sports heros, having won 5 Olympic medals for high diving, in three different olympics. I felt grateful that I had gotten to know him, if only for a short time. In a moment of inspiration, I wrote the following poem about him:

"Today, amongst a cheering crowd, I stand, applauding you: The man the people love, admire, So confident, so true.

My thoughts however drift way back, Back to the boy I knew. Throughout that summer at the beach, We laughed and talked and raced, Then when I felt so bad one day, Beside my bed you paced The floor throughout the lonely hours, And fanned my feverish face. You taught me how to ride the waves There on those golden shores, While summer softly stole away With memories, nothing more. The day we parted, in my book You wrote 'My heart is yours.' The boy who wrote that little verse, Is now a man of fame, And I am proud to have those words, Signed with his famous name!"

My mother had kept up her girlhood friendship with Evencia, an attractive silver-haired lady who had married a charming German man and lived in Atzcapotzalco, a suburb of Mexico City where there were many factories. Mother always turned up her nose at the district, but admitted that Evencia's old house was attractive. She used to invite my Mom, Dad, and me to lunch about twice a year, which meant arriving at around one, having little aperitifs until about three, with her, her husband and son, (an orange soda for me), and finally sitting down at her long regally set dining table to start a five course dinner. My Dad looked forward to these invitations and would always rub his palms and say: "Today we're really going to have a good meal." which irritated my mother, making her feel she never gave him enough to eat. When we sat down at the table there was already a stack of five plates in front of each place. That way one could calculate what was to be served. First her old maid would amble out with an avocado or shrimp cocktail. When we finished, she'd remove the plate and bring out a steaming tureen of creamed soup which Evencia would ladle out into each person's bowl, with croutons passed around. When we finished, the bowl would be removed, and Mexican rice would be brought and served on each plate, to be eaten by itself. Her son, Hector, would get up and open a bottle of wine, and go around the table serving everyone's glass. A platter of fish done with tomatoes and olives and tiny boiled potatoes would appear to be served on the next plate. She would look flirtily at my father and say, "Fred, tu favorito: Pescado a la Veracruzana"!" (Your favorite: Fish, Veracruz style!) When we had finished that, the "main course" would come, some kind of meat chopped or sliced, in a gravy. At this point I would tell her that I could not eat any more, but she always insisted I try a little bit as I was so "flaquita" (skinny). All these dishes were served accompanied by newly made hot tortillas, which the maid would bring intermittently to the table. After those plates were removed, a delicious dessert would be served, either a rich crown of "flan" (a creamy solid custard) or stewed fruit or perhaps a slice of pie. My Dad would eat every crumb and smack his lips when it was over, making us wonder how he existed on the one main plate my mother served every day. With the coffee, the "sobremesa" would begin, a very important part of the main meal at any Mexican table. The sobremesa which can only be translated as "on the table" means the conversation which takes place after the meal at the table, usually accompanied by a "copita" of something, such as cognac, anis, or something like a cherry brandy. It is sipped while everyone comments on the wonderful meal and then goes on to talk about news events, family matters, whatever comes to mind, but one NEVER eats and gets up and leaves, or even goes back to the sitting room. You stay at the main table chatting until it is time to leave, usually a couple of hours later. This rounds up a complete visit to your friend's home for a luncheon or dinner engagement. We usually got home at dusk, and mother would always get in a little dig such as "Did you notice Evencia never serves vegetables or salad?" to which Dad would look at me and wink, and say, "Well, actually I didn't even miss them, did you, Pegitus?", the nickname he called me occasionally.

My father had an old Scottish friend from the days when they had lived in Pachuca,named "Scotty" Forsythe. Scotty's life had been a sad one, never marrying, and sending money over the years to his younger brother in Scotland so that he could study at medical school. Whenever he came over he would smoke a big fat cigar, and when finished he would mash it into his coffee cup, which annoyed my mother no end. She thought of him as a bad influence on my father, because he was a heavy drinker, and would sometimes meet my father after work to go and have a little "copita" together. One day my Dad said he was going after work to buy a length of wool to have a gray suit made. That night it turned late and Dad had not come home. When he eventually did, he was "in his cups" and confessed that Scotty had met him after work and convinced him to buy a length of wool that he had at his house. Dad ended up buying it, to help his friend, but when he showed it to Mom, it was bottle-green wool. Mother was horrified. Needless to say, that suit was never made.

CHICKEN FARM

My mother, always an avid reader, had been reading a best-seller named "The Egg and I", by Betty MacDonald, a first-hand account of a housewife who had started a chicken farm and therein described some of her hilarious experiences. My mother mulled this idea over in her mind for several days and decided she would like to do the same thing. After consulting with my father and receiving assurance of his financial backing, she hunted around and found a lovely big house with a large garden and property on one side which would be ideal for chicken coops. It was further out from San Angel, a quaint village and residential area on the outskirts of Mexico City, and on the road to Desierto de los Leones, the Desert of the Lions, where no more lions roamed anymore and which is not even a desert, but a wooded area on top of a mountain. Dad would have to commute to work every day, and I would take the city bus for a 30 minute ride to school every morning. I was thrilled when I saw the lovely white house and its surroundings, and took in the possibility of hill climbing and inviting my friends for weekends. It had a fairly big reservoir at the back which was used mainly for irrigation, but which I knew we could clean and use for swimming. We moved in 1945 and my mother promptly sent for a catalogue showing the types of chickens, as well as a book describing their needs. She chose three types of chicks, Buff Orpington, White Leghorn, and a third I cannot recall. She had two workmen build and prepare the wire cages and coops for their arrival, and when they did and we opened the large ventilated boxes, we were thrilled at seeing the mass of fluffy little yellow chicks peeping loudly. As it was cool weather they were at first placed in a covered garage under a "breeder", a huge tin lid with short legs which kept the warmth in and which she had also ordered. She hired three gardeners, and in other sections of the property she had them plant corn, lettuce, spinach and alfalfa. Suddenly Mother was a farmer!

Dad, although amenable to this adventure, played no part in it other than to sit on the side terrace with a straw hat, reading his newsaper in the evenings, smoking his pipe, and on weekends drinking a cool beer. Some pigeons had come with the house and used to live on the roof and fly over us when we were sitting outside. Gradually, over time, they became fewer and fewer, whether because they died, or were eaten by nearby coyotes, or just decided to live somewere else, until eventually there was one lone fat pigeon that used to fly over us, occasionally perching on the the terrace balustrade. We never guessed how fond my father had become of it until one day, my mother, forever seeking changes in her menus, decided to grab the pigeon and take it to the kitchen. At lunchtime she produced roast pigeon, which my father assumed was chicken, and ate heartily. Nearing the end of the meal, my mother commented, "How did you like the pigeon, dear?" My father stopped chewing imediately, and said, "Don't tell me this was the lone pigeon that used to sit on the balustrade when I was reading in the evenings!" When my mother told him it was, he looked like he was actually going to cry, and his voice was thick as he said "Oh no! I used to delight in watching him as he flew into the skies, happy and free." We both remained silent as my father wiped his mouth on his serviette and left the table. We sat there, both of us feeling guilty.

When the the green vegetables and corn began to ripen, Mother made a contract with Sanborns Restaurant downtown to buy her produce, and twice a week a young German would come on a motorcycle with a side car to pick up and deliver them. The chickens grew and multiplied with the added help of an an incubator and were sold to restaurants in town. It became a thriving business.

Meanwhile, Sonny had come back from San Francisco and was a constant guest at our house every weekend. We would swim in the cement resorvoir where little tadpoles moved around us in the greenish water, hike up the mountain, and sometimes ride the bus up to the Desierto de los Leones where we would wander in the woods. We were both fourteen and considered ourselves buddies but still not sweethearts. Roberto Humphrey also came for weekends and perhaps there was a little jealousy between the two boys, but nothing much was made of it. Sometimes Roberto would spend the night, and at those times it was okay with our parents that he sleep in the upper bunk in my bedroom while I occupied the lower bunk. We were clearly very naïve, and we thought of each other as brother and sister, but it would probably be unthinkable today with the way teenagers are so sexually advanced.

One morning the gardener brought us a little puppy. His dog had had a litter and he thought I might like one. Like one? I loved it! She was snow white with longish hair, and her head was black. A beautiful puppy, probably part Border Collie. As she grew she became my constant companion and would sleep in my room at nights. She spent most of the day outside, but when inside, she left puddles wherever she went, so my mother named her "Puddles" and that name remained, even though we housetrained her later. We all adored her.

One memorable morning, my mother woke up with a tremendous pain in her back and legs. When she tried to get up she found she could not, and the doctor had to be called to see her, saying the only solution was to take her to the hospital for further examination. She was checked in at the Cowdray Hospital which is now called The American British Cowdray Hospital, or ABC Hospital, and the doctors pondered over her sudden paralysis. Her spine had been affected and they finally came up with the doubtful prognosis of something they called Meningismus, for lack of a better diagnosis. I do not know what medication she was given, but she remained interned for a almost a month, receiving dailyX-ray treatment. During these sessions I was allowed to sit by her side in the X-ray room, which, thinking back, was an unconscionable thing for the doctors to have allowed. Still, up to now there has been no obvious damage to me.

When my mother was allowed to go home to the farm she found things had not gone well. My father had been busy at the office every day, and the workers had let things go to the extent that she had lost her contract with Sanborns. The vegetables were rotting and the eggs were being consumed between the workers. She had recently bought two piglets which she had been fattening, and they, as well as the diminished amount of chickens, showed their neglect by looking underfed. As soon as she was well enough to go outside and inspect the damage, she fired the three workers and decided it would be better to move back to the city again. I was heartbroken. I had really loved life at the farm and the prospect of moving back into an apartment really devastated me. She sold the remaining chickens, and as her contract with the owner was finished and ready to be renewed, he luckily wanted his house back. It was all arranged in a few weeks, and we moved back into the city into a pleasant apartment in the Colonia Cuahtemoc a few blocks from the beautiful Paseo de la Reforma. Puddles came with us, of course, and took a while to be housetrained for life in an apartment, but eventually it worked out well and she was taken out for a walk on the leash three or four times a day.

My mother went about hiring a maid, and at that time there were a lot of indian girls from the state of Hidalgo who were seeking work. They were ignorant and uneducated, but with a bit of training sometimes worked out well. We had one who finally learned how to clean the apartment to my mother's approval, but when it came to serving table, she would come to the edge of the rug and try to hand us the tray from there. My mother urged her to come closer, but she replied that she didn't know if she was allowed to step on the rug! Poor girl. We had to reassure her the rug was for stepping on, and from then on she would tread gingerly. We used to laugh at the way she called Puddles, "Palos", that being the nearest she could come to pronouncing the name.

About this time my brother Bob, who was still in the Royal Air Force, had a few weeks furlough and decided to come out to Mexico from England to see his parents and his kid sister. He was tall and handsome and I was thrilled to meet him after so many years. All the boys had survived the war, and eventually, three of them came out to Mexico. My eldest brother, Fred, never came out because he had settled down in Johannesburg and remarried. Dick was living in New York by this time, with his second wife and the beginning of a family of three.

Bob got a temporary membership at the Reforma Athletic Club where English and American residents belonged, and he'd invite me to go swimming with him almost every afternoon after school. I noticed at these times that some of the older girls from my school who ordinarily never said hello to me would stop by when they saw us by the pool and linger to say hi, hoping for an introduction to my handsome brother. In the evenings we'd play Monopoly joined by a boy in the apartment next door, and it was such a treat for me to be with my big brother that when he left a few weeks later I wept bitter tears.

VICKI

Right before we moved away from the farm, my sister Vicki had arrived from London. It was 1945, and the war had finished at last with the ghastly explosions of the atomic bombs dropped in Hiroshima and Nagasaki. She had divorced her husband a few years before and my mother had told her to look up the storage company we had been paying to keep our furniture and belongings since 1939, sell the lot, and use some of the money to come to Mexico. When Vicki arrived in Mexico after taking a ship to New York, and then flying to Mexico City, she looked not like a survivor of war-torn London, but like a French fashion model, with lovely Schiaparelli suits and silk hose, beautiful shoes and bags. My mother, still using a walker, my father and I, were at the airport waiting for her with Maruja, her young Spanish friend who had come over from Europe with us in 1939. With her, was her handsome pilot boyfriend, in full uniform, who walked across the tarmac to the foot of the plane to receive Vicki. We were all bowled over at the sight of this elegant sophisticated young woman descending theatrically down the aeroplane steps. She took one look at the uniformed man, and said loftily, "Are you my mother's chauffeur?"

Further surprises awaited us, for although she was happy to see us after so many years, she did not want to be stuck out on the farm, so promptly found a wonderful job in the city and took her own apartment. Apparently, she was engaged to be married to an English Lord, and was supposed to return to him after a brief stay near her parents. I fondly remember her relating her experiences during the war years and the misfortune of having her husband declare himself a Conscientious Objector, one who refuses to take part in warfare because his conscience prohibits killing a fellow man. But the British army had many jobs in mind for the "C.O.s, one of which was to send them out to the fields to dig up potatoes. Being an interior decorator one can only imagine this hardship for David. The army then assigned him to be an ambulance driver, and later on he voluntarily joined and trained in the parachute squad and was dropped over France where his duty was to hunt for mines and take out the detonator pins. On one of these forays, he landed in a tree and remained hanging there for days, so that his left arm was rendered useless for the rest of his life. After he was released from the hospital, he and Vicki decided to divorce.

My father would often take Vic (I always preferred to call her Vic, not Vicki) to lunch on his own, introducing her proudly to any friend he happened to meet. She was truly a stunning young woman, still only 31, and causing quite a sensation amongst the foreign group of residents in Mexico City. Dad was still a very handsome man with silver hair and ruddy complexion, a typical Englishman. He often wore a blue tweed sport jacket, and always smoked a pipe, and it probably amused him that people who did not know they were father and daughter, took them to be an older man with his mistress.

I remember one day my glamorous sister looked me over and decided my mother was not taking enough interest in my appearance. I was skinny and still unmade up, with hair combed to the side, held up by a hairpin. She decided to treat me to a haircut, shampoo and set, a manicure, and a new sweater set. When I got home I felt like a princess, and from then on tried to take a little more care of my appearance. She also gave me a few of her own clothes, tweed skirts and jackets which fit me after alterations.

In a few months the Lord in London was forgotten, as by this time she had a series of beaux seeking her in the city, both foreigners and Mexican. It was not only her looks, but her charm and her worldliness and experience during the war which fascinated the men who sought her company for dinner or cultural events in the evening. I lived in constant awe of this sister of mine whom I was only beginning to know and emulate as time went by.

Vic finally decided to marry a persistent American suitor, one William Hasam, who had been smitten since first laying eyes on her. Unfortunately he had been married three or four times before, and was recently in the throes of a messy divorce. But she was crazy about him. In all fairness I remember his being a very attractive man, exuding masculinity, and I admit I was guilty for a time of having a bit of a crush on him. My father was furious that she had chosen this man, and stated that if she persisted in wanting to marry him, he would not attend her wedding, as he was sure it would end in disaster, which it did. They married, and had a small wedding breakfast at San Angel Inn. A few months later Vic told us she was pregnant, and Dad eventually came around and halfway accepted the father of his future grandchild.

Then, one unforgettable day in my life, I was at school when the Principal, Mr. Burleson, came into my class and whispered to my teacher. I was excused and accompanied by Mr. Burleson down the long school corridor, while he told me with a broken voice that he would be taking me home, as he had been informed that my father had just passed away. I was stunned, but quietly went along with him, not knowing what was awaiting me when I got home. We drove in silence along with a lady teacher, and when I walked into our apartment, I found the living room filled with friends of my mother, all trying to comfort her. Evencia rose from her side and hugged me before I could reach my mother, embracing me so tightly I could hardly breath, wailing "O, pobrecita, pobrecita niña!" Poor little girl. My mother opened her arms to me, and only said, "He's gone, darling, my Fred is gone!" I started to cry, and Vic came toward me and pulled me into the bedroom with her. She was three months pregnant, and we were later afraid she would lose the baby, but that day she was the strongest one there. She explained how Dad had had this terrible pain in his chest, and by the time the doctor was called and arrived, he was already dead. Somehow it had never occurred to my mother to call an ambulance to take him to the Emergency section of the hospital. I spent most of the rest of the day with Vic in the bedroom, both of us crying, while Bill her husband stood outside the apartment door receiving people and seating them. He proved to be a real asset to my grieving mother, both morally and financially. My father lay on his bed in his closed bedroom, wrapped in a sheet, and later that night I was able to creep in and kiss him goodbye. My mother refused to let him be taken to a funeral parlor, but the coffin was brought to the house next day and we all drove to the British Cemetery for his burial. My friend, Alice, and her parents were there, as were Roberto Humphrey and his parents, and many people I did not know from the English colony. My mother had called a minister from Christ Church, as my father was an Anglican, and when the minister started to wail in a high pitched dramatic voice, "Oh, Loooord, take this maaaan's soul with you to heaveeen, etc.", perhaps from nerves, I was suddenly overtaken with the giggles at this exaggerated goodbye, and could hardly contain myself. I choked and blew my nose and everyone thought I was sobbing, but I was totally overcome, half from grief but mostly from the minister's voice giving the stagey obituary. Also, I couldn't help but remember my Dad's voice saying, "There's no such place as heaven or hell. Both are right here on this earth; nothing but darkness after one dies." I was suddenly sad he had fallen into eternal darkness. I am inclined to believe his philosophy at times; on others, I almost feel the presence of a loved one who has gone before me.

Back at the apartment friends had brought us trays of sandwiches and hot food, and Vic had made tea and coffee. The rest of the afternoon went by with all these people around us. I will never forget that terrible day. Vic stayed on with us to comfort my mother who was devastated and in need of care. She had no will to eat or do anything but sit around with a resigned look on her face, wringing a handkerchief in her hands. Also, there was going to be the problem of money. My parents' funds had been almost totally depleted, first by my mother's long illness in the hospital, and then with the failure of the chicken farm. She had no idea how she was going to support herself and her teenage daughter. She had a little money to carry her for a while, but the problem had to be resolved. After a few weeks she decided she would take in translations.

First of all she talked to the Registrar at the American High School, and applied for a scholarship for me, which was only partly granted, she having to pay half of the monthly tuition from then on until I graduated three years later.

I particularly remember her typing without a ribbon in the machine late into the night, something called "stencils", directly onto carbon paper, harder to do than regular typing. The sheet of carbon paper would come out with the letters cut out, and I presume these were used to print copies. It was for the UNESCO, World Heritage Center, years before the photocopy machine was invented.

She had always been a good manager with money, so there was no scarcity of food at home, and gradually she found other sources of income such as giving English classes, and even making English marmalade for sale. Eventually she had the brilliant idea of renting another two apartments, furnishing them by buying on credit, and sub-letting them out to Americans who were constantly coming into Mexico to work with the "Aftosa", (Hoof and Mouth Disease) section of the U.S. Government. My brother Bill, who had been in the Merchant Marine during the war, had come in shortly after my father's death, and by a stroke of luck, had been hired for an executive position in the Aftosa offices. He kept my mother's apartments full of American couples who were contracted to stay up to a year or more in Mexico, so gradually my mother was able to lift her head again and think of a brighter future

Vic had her baby boy in March of 1948, and named him William Austin, like his father. Sometimes I went over to their house to babysit for little Billy. Vic and Bill were more or less getting along, but already starting with problems. He sold Hysters, and I remember he had one in the garage of their house, a huge monstrous thing which he said was like having money in the bank.

Once again, my mother and I were together, just like in England when Daddy was far away. I missed my father, but it was easier to take than if I had lost my mother, whom I worshipped and adored.

I was still in High School, and some of the boys had asked me to be their "novia", their "sweetheart". Somehow I evaded an answer, but enjoyed bike riding with them, skating, and going out for icecream to a nearby restaurant named "Kikos" where a group of kids would get together. I wrote a lot of poetry in those days, emulating my mother, who wrote both in English and Spanish, and had many poems and articles published in the Mexico City newspapers. Inspired by a skeleton which hung in our biology class, one day I wrote the following which was later published in our high school newspaper, The Scoop:

THE SKELETON

"Back in the classroom, stiff and dead, The skeleton hangs by its bony head. Its mouth is open in crooked grin, Its bones are yellow and bare of skin. Where eyes once twinkled, lies gaping space; Only structure is left of the once-full face. Its teeth are rotten, and falling apart; Its torso is hollow, where once throbbed a heart. The once-firm flesh has withered away And become a part of the soft brown clay, But the bones remain, though brittle and thin As proof that they held a soul within. So now as it hangs in a lifeless trance, And we sometimes throw it a careless glance, Remember that you one day might be In its place for other students to see!"

I was too timid to send it in under my own name, so invented a "nom de plume", Rusty Romaine. When I heard one of the teachers wondering who this person was, and how good the poem was, I felt like owning up and saying that I was the author. Too late!

By now, aside from renting her apartments, my mother had been hired to manage an elegant shop called Maya de Mexico, where they sold unique hand-painted Mexican skirts and blouses.

It was on Madero street where I would often meet her to walk over to nearby Sanborns for supper. The shop was almost in front of the Ritz Hotel, and one day I heard that the famous actor Errol Flynn was staying there while filming a movie. I had always loved to meet well-known actors and obtain their autographs, and he was certainly one of the most famous, so I set out one afternoon, rather late, and entered the lobby of the Hotel Ritz to wait for him. He finally came down from his room, dressed in a checkered suit, and clearly ready to go out to dinner. I bounded up to him and pecked at his elbow. He ignored me while carrying on a conversation with another man, so I said in a brave voice, "Mr. Flynn, would you please give me your autograph?" producing my book and pencil. He kept on talking with the man, and when I pecked again at his sleeve, he said in an impatient tone, "Just wait a minute, young lady, and I'll sign your book!" When he did, I all but curtsied, thanked him and ran out of the hotel. But when I told my mother about the incident later on, she was horrified. "You know the reputation that actor has with young girls? Why, if he had asked you to come up to his room for the autograph you probably would have gone, wouldn't you?" I nodded. She proceeded, "Never, never go <u>alone</u> again into a hotel to ask for an autograph. God knows what could have happened." Poor Mr. Flynn, he most probably would never have laid a finger on me.

Sonny (or Cameron as he wanted me to call him now) came back that year, and I noticed the difference in his physique and face, where one could see the beginning of a beard. He said he shaved everyday, and perhaps he did. He was sixteen, and I was fifteen, and this time our relationship took a different turn. We would go to the movies together where he'd put his arm around my shoulders and pull me toward him to kiss me every once in a while. My mother still thought of us as two little playmates, but there was definitely the beginning of physical attraction in our relationship. His mother, her name was Peggy, like me, had remarried an older man, and they had a home near where we lived. We stopped by one day to pick something up, and went into the upper den to play records. We were lying on the rug, side by side, listening to music when his mother came home and surprised us. Cameron started making excuses, because he knew he was not supposed to bring me home with him while no one was there, but his mother directed her anger at me, giving me a verbal whiplashing, telling me never to come into their house again unless she was there. Cameron walked me home, but I was so hurt and embarassed I told him that it was better we never see each other again. A week later his mother called and invited me to a goodbye dinner for him, from there to take him to the bus station for his return to San Francisco. Against my will, but begged by Cameron to attend, I accepted. They had other guests to whom I was introduced as Cameron's girlfriend but I remained quiet as a mouse throughout the meal. About to board the bus, he bent over tentatively and kissed me goodbye, saying he'd write me, but I don't know what came over me at that moment. It seemed so pointless to go on under these circumstances with his mother worried about our altered friendship, that I told him not to write to me any more, and that we'd better finish our friendship right then. He looked at me unbelievingly. I never wrote to him after that, although I really missed him, and he never wrote to me again. When his mother passed away a few years later I was tempted to drop him a note of condolence, but had second thoughts about it and never did. Over the years I have often wondered what ever happened to that sweet handsome golden boy.

I started going to the American High School parties with Carlos Centurión, a very nice boy I had met near the house. He was quiet and considerate, and would bring me tiny gifts, like charms for my silver bracelet, or chocolates. My mother used to organize little parties at the apartment for me so I could invite Roberto, his sister Marta, as well as a few other school friends. And always Carlos. She would put on records for us and we would dance and play games. I cringe to think of any mother today doing the same for a fifteen year old daughter with her friends.

Kids are so much more independent and sophisticated now. At the end, she would serve cake and icecream, and we would keep on dancing for a while. Carlos was an excellent dancer, and taught me how to do the "danzón", a dance done solely in one little square, very rhythmic, originating in the state of Veracruz. He wrote in my autograph book, "Whenever you hear the song, 'Girl of My Dreams', remember me." But our lives took us in different directions, and gradually we stopped seeing each other.

I don't even remember where I met Efrén Fierro. He was very handsome, around four years older than the rest of the boys, wore a mustache, sports jacket and tie, and hung around my apartment building in the evenings to talk with me. My mother was leary of him, and on one occasion when he asked me to go on a picnic to Lake Tequesquitengo with a group of young people, she refused to let me go because she did not trust his "motives". We had danced together at a couple of my girlfriends' parties and he was a marvellous smooth dancer, who did the dip at the end of each dance and made me swoon. I was disappointed about not being allowed to go to the lake, but a week later he came back to ask me to an elegant party at the country club in honor of a Mexican General's daughter who was celebrating her fifteenth birthday. In Mexico many people celebrate their daughters' fifteenth birthdays with a ball in the manner of a coming-out party. The girl invites her girlfriends with their "chambelanes", or "escorts". The obligation of the escort ends after the first few dances, when he may dance with whomever he wants. Well, Efrén was to be a chambelán, at the ball, and invited me to go with him so we could dance together after he had gone through the necessary routine. My mother told him she would not allow me to go with him alone, so he offered to take a friend, and I should invite one of my girlfriends as a chaperone. My mother halfway agreed. But later I think she must have had second thoughts, because when Queta, my girlfriend, arrived at our home that night to be ready for the two boys to pick us up, my mother decided she would come along with us to chaperone. Efren and his friend arrived and were taken aback when they realized my mother would accompany us. He pleaded that only a certain amount of seats would be available for invited guests, but finally had to give in and take all three of us. I was mortified, to say the least, but knew my mother would not change her mind. When we arrived at the ball, the tables were set for exactly the amount of people invited, so the General himself, seeing our predicament, very courteously invited my mother and us two girls to sit at his table with his family. Embarassed? I could have died, but my mother took it all in her stride explaining to the old General and his understanding wife that she could hardly have let her innocent little daughter go with a boy she hardly knew. They concurred, and my mother ended up by making great friends at the table, while I sat, miserable with Queta, and saw how our two dates ignored us the whole evening in punishment. We never even got to dance once. Needless to say, when Efren and his friend took us home, he never called me again. End of what might have been a torrid romance.

The Yacaru club during my high school years had long been one I had wanted to join, and finally, in my Junior year when I was sixteen they invited Queta and I to be members. That summer they organized a trip to Acapulco where we were to stay at someone's home and be chaperoned by the mother of one of the girls. My mother okayed the trip, and one morning early we gathered for the bus ride which would take most of the day to arrive. When we got to our destination, we changed into bathing suits and went to the beach. I noticed that several of the girls wore two piece bathing suits, and I ached to have one. The second day, this darling girl, and I can't remember her name, told me she had two, and I was welcome to use one of them, so I was thrilled. I promptly lay on the beach to sun, and found that several boys stopped by my side to talk. That night we all adjourned to Playa Suave, a nightclub, which was the place to go and have refreshments and dancing, and where I ran into one of the boys, who became my companion for the evening. After a while he suggested walking to the beach across the street to stroll in the wet sand, and the next thing we knew, the group I was with had left and gone home without me. I got panicky and said we'd better start walking down the highway in the direction of the house. Finally in the distance we saw the headlights of two cars coming, which stopped when they saw us. In one, was our chaperone, and the other car was full of girls who shared the house. The chaperone was very annoyed with me, as well as worried, and told me to get in the car. I crowded in, leaving my poor companion on the dark highway to find his way back. But I received kudos from the girls. I had been considered the little mousey one up till then, and they all looked at me with different eyes from then on.

It was fun belonging to the Yacaru club. They had a lot of activities, and once, Queta Quintero and I who had become fast friends, were invited to a tea party in the Lomas, a residential district in the hills of Mexico City, where lay some beautiful homes. We were not familiar with the names of the streets, but accepted the invitation and were asked to bring a cake between us. Queta's mother baked the cake and covered it with a delicious butter icing. Queta asked me if I knew how to get there and I said "más o menos" which means more or less, in this case less than more. Well, we started out at 4 o'clock in the heat of the afternoon, taking a Lomas bus and asking the driver to let us off near Monte Athos, the street we were looking for. At one point he told us to get off and said it should be nearby. Now Lomas is very hilly, so we started walking up one hill and down the next, turning and walking up another hill, all in the hot sun, as it was July. There were not many street signs, and no one in the streets to ask, so we kept on walking, looking for signs in vain. Finally a sleek black car came by with some boys hanging out the window asking us if we wanted a ride. They wanted to know where we were going, and of course said they knew exactly where it was. They eyed the lovely cake, the frosting beginning to melt, and insisted we ride with them to the party; perhaps invite them in for a piece of cake when we got there. I was hot and tired by this time and was ready to get in with them, but Queta, being less gullible than I, held me back, whispering that maybe they would try to "abusar de nosotros" (abuse us). They didn't look very menacing to me, just seeking fun and perhaps a slice of cake, so I argued with her, but she did not relent, and finally the boys drove off and we finally gave up when we saw a bus coming our way. Dejectedly, we got on and rode back home, cake and all. No tea party for us that day.

Two more of my brothers came out to Mexico after the war, one, Ted, the third boy in the family who had been in the Royal Air Force, still unmarried, and Bob, the fourth boy who had also been in the Royal Air Force. Bob was married, although he had left his wife, Lyn, in England until he was settled in Mexico. He was the one who had come out briefly on leave from the airforce before my father died. He took an apartment with a friend, but Ted decided to live with my mother and Bill and me in a beautiful house which she had rented in Polanco and where they three would share the rent. This turned out to be a real disaster, because Ted was so bloody English in every way. My mother had become lax about her British punctuality and when Ted, who worked nearby, would come home for lunch at 1 P.M. he expected it to be served at 1:10, no earlier, no later. Mother, who worked in town, would hurry home to find the maid only halfway through making the meal. No matter how much she would help her in the kitchen, we never had lunch on time like Ted wanted. He would finish and go up to his room to rest for a few minutes, quiet and sullen, before leaving for work again, until he told Mother it was not working out, and he would prefer to move out rather than have a run-in. Added to this, he had given our maid strict instructions not to clean his room because he had a pair of budgerigars in a birdcage, which he personally took care of and was teaching to "talk". A sure recipe for catastrophe. The maid decided one morning that his room needed a good cleaning, and while inside, opened the cage to clean it also. Out flew the birds, and off through the open window where they were lost forever. When Ted came home at noon that day he was furious with the maid, and acted like he had lost a dear relative. When he calmed down, he told me the little creatures had been beginning to respond to his lessons and could almost say "hello". I have always wondered how true that was, as I never knew "love birds" could talk. Anyway, that was the last straw. He moved out and rented his own flat. With Ted leaving, it was harder for my mother to meet the rent for the big house, so she and I moved back to the Colonia Cuauhtemoc into an ample apartment.

Right before that, my mother had been offered a job as manager of the Cosmetic Department at Salinas y Rocha, one of the best department stores downtown. She had a certain elegance and would be perfect for the position. She accepted, and found the job opened many doors for her, socially and financially. One morning while at work, she had a most unexpected surprise. When she was a girl, she had studied in Dallas, Texas, for a year, taking a business course, at which time she had met and become engaged to a young man named Stanley. She was fond of him, but when she returned to Tampico to her parents' home, she decided she wanted to break off the engagement because she neither wanted to marry Stanley nor live in Dallas. Shortly after, my Dad arrived in Tampico to work as an accountant for the oil company, and they fell in love and got married. However, my mother and Stanley continued to exchange Christmas cards over the years, and one morning, without previous warning, while she was reviewing the cosmetic counters, in walked a tall, heavy-set white-haired gentleman who came straight toward her and said, "Lucy, do you remember me? I'm Stanley!" Well, after the initial shock, she recognized him, as he had not changed much, only gotten heavier and now had white hair. They embraced, and he asked if she would be free for lunch, as his wife was across the street at the Del Prado Hotel. The three of them ate together, and his wife turned out to be a dear lady who did not mind at all that Stanley had carried a torch for his old girlfriend for over forty years. During lunch, they both urged her to accompany them on a four-day trip to the city of Oaxaca, south of Mexico City. Coming up was a long weekend, when the lst of May is Labor Day, and then the 5th celebrates the Batalla de Puebla, the battle where the Mexican army beat off the French army in 1863 in the city of Puebla. If there is a weekend in between, the majority of workers shirk off during the whole five days, and my mother knew she could get those days off from her boss, so she agreed. She came home with the news that night, and next day the Leesons picked her up in their car, (they had driven all the way from Dallas) and off they went to Oaxaca, which is a long road south with many sharp curves along the way. Perhaps by now, they have constructed a super highway, but in those days it would take them a full day to get to their destination. We were still living in the house in Polanco, so I remained with Bill and Ted.

When my mother returned, she was very descriptive about the city which is typical of southern Mexico, with nearby pyramids which are a "must" on any visitor's schedule. Besides this, what makes it a tourist haven are the many curiosities and handwoven goods, as well as pretty jewelry that the indians sell. Mother brought me back a lovely gold filligree chain with a locket, work from the artesans in Oaxaca. But on the side she told me that Stanley had given her trouble, trying to get into her room at night and misbehaving himself when out of his wife's view. She had asked him not to call her any more, and thankfully they were leaving for Dallas the next day. Of course I was shocked that anyone so "old" could behave in that manner. Both Stanley and my mother by that time must have been about sixty, and I thought of them as way past the flirting stage. How immature I was!

At school parties I was never attracted to any of the younger boys. They all seemed too baby-faced, and the older boys never looked my way. I mostly hung out with Queta Quintero, who was very pretty and popular, attracting a crowd of boys during recess. I brought her home one day and she met my brother Bill who was still working at the time with the U. S. Government for the erradication of the hoof and mouth disease in Mexico. They were both smitten, and started going out together.

FRANKIE

The same year, my Junior year, I went with my mother, under duress, to a Christmas party, which is called a "Posada" in Mexico. These Posadas take place every year during the last nine nights prior to the 25th of December, re-enacting the search for lodging for the Virgin Mary and Joseph. Posada, means "lodging", and partygoers walk through the streets, singing carols, each holding a candle, asking for a roof to shelter them, just as Mary and Joseph did over two thousand years ago on their way to Bethlehem where the baby Jesus was born in a manger. In the majority of big cities, these gatherings have degenerated into ordinary parties, where people might sing carols, but remain indoors, dancing and drinking and having fun. In smaller cities many people still go through the ritual of walking the streets at night with candles, singing carols, such as in Zacatecas and other towns. It is a beautiful custom.

In this case, the Posada was to be held in an adjacent building from where my mother rented her apartments, and a young tenant, Pedro Gallo, who had made friends with her, had been kind enough to invite her to the party and to bring along her young daughter. I looked much younger than my seventeen years, and perhaps he only included me as a courtesy, my mother being the one who had charmed him with her personality. He formed part of a group of students from the state of Chihuahua in the north, who all lived in the same apartment. I frankly did not want to go, knowing they were much older than I, and being timid about meeting new people.

We arrived at the party, and almost immediately Pedro came

over with a nice looking young man in a navy blue suit and introduced him as "Frankie" Balderrama to my mother and to me. He was about 24, and to my surprise starting speaking to us in perfect English. He told my mother they were all honored by our presence, and then began telling us about himself. It turned out he was from Los Angeles, California, where he had grown up, being of Mexican parents who had emigrated to the U.S. almost thirty years before from Chihuahua. When he was a teenager he had visited his grandparents in Mexico, in the state of Chihuahua, and was enchanted with life there. His uncle had described a wonderful Medical Military School in Mexico City, where perhaps he might be admitted if he was interested in becoming a medical doctor, and could pass the difficult entrance exams for which they were famous. Frankie, whose real name was Francisco, liked the idea, and proceeded to seek more information about the medical school. He travelled to Mexico City and found that although he had graduated from High School in the U. S., he would need to study two more years in "Preparatoria" which is equivalent to a prep school before he could present his credentials to be admitted for an exam. In Preparatoria he would have to make up missing subjects, such as Mexican history, geography, and literature, as well as perfecting his Spanish. After much discussion back in California with his parents, he decided to come to live in Chihuahua with his grandparents while studying for two years in prep school.

It was not easy being accepted into the highly esteemed and prestigious Escuela Médico Militar. Founded in 1917, it had already prepared 23 graduating classes by the time he applied in 1946, and the doctors who had gone on to practice their careers were known as the finest doctors in Mexico because of their strict training in medicine as well as in the military. In his case, after two years studying in Chihuahua, when he was finally allowed to take the entrance exam, it was with 500 other students, from which only 40 were accepted into the school, 20 of which were flunked out during the first year. In the second year of studies, more failed their exams, leaving a class of only 15. When they graduated after a total of six years, they would receive the rank of Majors in the Mexican Army, and would go on to serve six more years in a city which had been decided for them to pay the army back as military doctors. Of course I did not yet know anything about this, so was unimpressed when he told me he was finishing his second year of medicine and had four more years of studies before graduating. When we talked further, after dancing all evening, he told me he was planning to leave the next day for Los Angeles to spend the Christmas holidays with his family, and when he returned in January he would call to see me again. His father owned a large grocery store in L. A. where his two sons, Frankie's brothers, helped him. They had been in the U.S. Merchant Marine and in the Air Force during the war, but were now back at home safely, his younger brother married and with a young son, born the day I met Frankie.

The truth is, my mother was as impressed with the young man as I was. His quiet gentlemanly manner and respectful reference to his family had hit a high note with her, and she saw him as a serious and trustworthy prospect as a suitor for her daughter.

During Christmas school vacations, I had taken a part-time job in the children's department of Sears Roebuck. In January I was invited to a cocktail party for some of the employees who worked in my department. I was not accustomed to "cocktail parties" and felt very grownup that evening when I set out to a nearby flat where they were gathering. Someone had made up some mysterious spirited mixture which we were all supposed to try, and I loved it, so I had more than one. When I got back home, I was lying on the couch telling my mother about the fun I'd had, when the doorbell rang. My mother answered, and who should come in but the young man we'd met at the Posada, this time in full uniform, (perhaps to impress me) along with another friend to "back him up". I was still a little dizzy, and languidly got up off the couch to say hello to both of them. We listened to Frankie's relation about his family vacation in Los Angeles, and finally he ended by telling us he had to report back to school that night, where he was interned, but wanted to know if he could see me sometime the next week. I told him it would be fine, and we agreed on a date, and then, very formally, he and his friend shook hands and left. My mother commented that she had known he'd be around, although I didn't, and we both agreed he was a nice decent young man.

He came over a few days later, and we went out nearby for an icecream. We remained talking outside when Bill, my brother, arrived and invited us up to his apartment for a drink. Frankie accepted and I went up with them while Bill fixed some drinks. Bill had been in the Merchant Marine during the war, so was accustomed to hitting the bars every time they docked. Before long he was serving a second, and halfway through their third, Frankie excused himself to go to the bathroom. Time passed, and we wondered what had happened to him. Bill went in to look, and found that he had passed out on his bed, fully clothed. Bill came out and informed me we might as well leave him to spend the night, as he was totally "out". I looked in on him. His beautiful wavy hair was all tousled and he was sound asleep. I bent down to take off his shoes, and found that the laces were all knotted. For some reason this raised an enormous feeling of tenderness in me, looking at his helpless figure. We left him there and Bill told me later he had been up at dawn next morning, apologetically explaining he had to report back to school.

To make a long story short, I fell in love with Frankie, and he became the man I married four years later upon his graduation from medical school. In the meantime our romance grew, little by little, until I was sure I wanted to spend the rest of my life with him, despite the fact that he was so intensely jealous at times that he made me miserable with his false assumptions of my "infidelities". He was locked up in school most of the time, immersed in his arduous studies, perhaps unhappy because I was free in the outside world. When he phoned and I was not there as planned, he would punish me and not call again for days. My mother realized this as a major fault in his character and warned me I might be letting myself into a difficult marriage if that is what it was to end in. But by that time I paid no heed because I was head over heels in love.

Being Frankie's girlfriend was a delightful but unnerving experience in my young life. Although we enjoyed a majority of memorable moments together, I had never been exposed to what is known as a "macho Mexicano" male. The peculiar thing is, he had been born and raised in California, and had not received this kind of example of behaviour from his loving parents or his brothers. I truly believe he must have picked it up in Chihuahua, during those two years in which he was studying, dating local girls and forming friendships with young men his age who gave him the wrong advice. It was truly a terrible fault, and came close to ending our relationship many times when I would cry bitter tears after a row. He felt he "owned" me, simply by my being his sweetheart, and not even formally engaged. When he thought I might be attracted momentarily to some other young man, he would tell me not to look at him. On one memorable occasion, when a lady friend of my mother's visited from the States and was invited to dinner at our home with her son who had had a crush on me years before, Frankie imposed himself, uninvited, in full uniform, and had to be included at my mother's dinner table, right by my side. Throughout the meal I was not allowed to look up at the young man in front of me and hardly spoke a word to anyone because I was so much under his power that night. The next day, the lady called my mother and asked her how on earth she was allowing her daughter to go with a man who had her absolutely "hypnotized".

But of course, my loved one had his good side, and we would enjoy going out dancing together whenever he received his father's monthly check, always asking my mother to go along with us. Every year, perhaps twice a year, his school would give the famous Baile de la Médico Militar ball at the Military Casino in the Lomas district. At those times he would pick me up, looking terribly handsome in his white jacket dress uniform with epaulets and gold buttons, stripes on the sleeve, black wool trousers with a stripe down the side, and carrying his military cap. I usually wore my long white halter dress, and Frankie would bring me a lovely orchid to wear on my shoulder. He and I would dance every piece, and on a few occasions we had the pleasure of having the famous orchestra leader and composer, Luis Arcaraz, play his compositions on the piano, while we stood around him, requesting two of my favorites, "Bonita", and "Viajera". My mother, our chaperone, often took a male companion to dance with, and one time she even invited two, flirt that she was! Somehow or other she handled it diplomatically, and the three of them ended up having a fine time. These were memorable balls, everyone in their finery, and I do think my mother enjoyed herself almost as much as I did, but then she'd always had that unique quality of enjoying life under any circumstance.

Thinking back to our courtship, it is hard to believe the Frankie of those days has become my Frank of today, a sweet, tolerant, attentive and very dear husband of 55 years. I am glad I was able to stand his tantrums during that early courtship.

I had formed a close friendship with Mary Grimme briefly during my Sophomore year, before she left to live in Erie, Pennsylvania. When she returned to Mexico, we took up our friendship during my last two years in High School. She was crazy about a young man named Germán, and whom she called Herman. They made a darling couple, and were perfect for double dating with Frankie and me. Her mother also rented apartments, and many times Mary would use one of the empty apartments to give a party where we could play records, consume cokes and chips, and dance close till midnight. Both our mothers were perfectly happy with this arrangement, so it worked out well.

On other occasions Frankie and I double-dated with my brother, Bill, and my friend, Queta, who were living a torrid romance. They made a lovely couple and planned to marry, but Bill was drinking heavily at the time, and eventually, for this reason, Queta finally broke the engagement. But while it lasted we made a happy foursome. I remember stopping sometimes at the corner after having gone to the movies together, to buy "quesadillas" sold by an indian woman kneeling on the sidewalk who had her "comal" (black tin griddle with an indentation in the center for the hot grease) where she would fry the quesadillas. She would first make the tortillas from the dough, and while yet uncooked, fill them with cheese, or potato, or "flor de calabaza", (zuccini flowers) sliding them gently into the deep hot grease, probably pork lard, but oh, were they delicious! Bill would order some quesadillas, and when the woman would ask him "¿De qué las quiere?" What do you want them of? He would argue that quesadillas had to be made with queso, cheese, and if filled with anything else should be called by another name. Poor woman, she didn't get it, as quesadillas can have a variety of fillings, so she would just nod her head to humor him and hand over the order. I must say the ones made with flor de calabaza, were the best in my estimation. And they never taste the same when made at home!

Graduation from the American High School rolled around in 1950, and my mother planned on taking us to the elegant night club restaurant so popular in those days, "El Patio". Anyone living in Mexico City in the forties and fifties, and perhaps later, knew of El Patio, which although expensive, offered the best ambience and floor show in town. After the ceremony at the auditorium, my mother, Bill and Queta, and Frank and I, all adjourned to the Patio, where we spent an unforgettable evening.

I had decided not to go to The Mexico City College as my mother had wanted, because I knew I would marry Frankie when he graduated as a doctor in three years. How trusting youth can be. It never occurred to me that my boyfriend might tire of me or back out, so sure of our love was I. It turned out as I had planned, but I often wonder if I shouldn't have gone on to college to further my education and prepare myself for a career, but no,

I had my mind set on working at a profitable job until I married Frankie.

My friend, Mary Grimme, and her boyfriend, Herman, were going to marry right after graduation, and Mary asked me to be her "Madrina de Lazo", or "bridesmaid with the silk lasso" which I should put around their necks and shoulders at a certain part of the church mass. I wore a pretty peach colored voile dress along with a large-brimmed hat of the same material, and played my part at the church ceremony. I was a little envious she was getting married ahead of me, but I knew Frankie had promised his father he would not marry until he had obtained his medical degree, a very sensible idea, and being a good son, he concurred. I was patient, and sure we would marry, so I waited. Mary and Herman went on to have a long happy marriage and eight children, and fifty years later, after we had lost lost track of each other, she traced me in Torreón, and Frank and I went to Mexico City to celebrate their anniversary party. We renewed our friendship, and the four of us made a lovely trip together to Veracruz the very next year, which I will describe later.

My mother had been working for some time at the department store, Salinas y Rocha, when an opportunity arose which offered her a trip to New York City to visit some of the cosmetic departments of Bonwit Teller and Macy's. Eagerly she set off in style to New York, and while there, was lucky enough to personally meet the great Helena Rubinstein, queen of the cosmetic industry. She was wined and dined by the various representatives in the industry at some of the best restaurants, and invited to attend some popular Broadway shows. She came back riding on a cloud, singing "I want to wash that man right out of my hair!" from South Pacific, which I hear is again on Broadway. I was so proud of her and happy she had had a much deserved reward after so many difficult years.

Things went smoothly between Frankie and me because we were truly in love, but that terrible streak of jealousy stemming from his "macho" character would emerge from time to time.

I had found a suitable job with a travel agency, Aguirre's Guest Tours, right downtown, as an English-Spanish secretary, typing up endless itineraries describing Mexican sights for tourists. I enjoyed my work and felt very grownup and independent. Several times during my first year there, a handsome young American man often came in to visit the owner, and always stopped by my desk to chat. We laughed a lot together and I rather enjoyed his company, until one day he got my phone number from my boss and decided to call me for a date. Unfortunately, that evening Frankie was visiting when my phone rang, and when I heard John's voice I went cold. I didn't know what to say so that my boyfriend would not realize I was talking to a fellow. I answered in monosyllables until at the other end of the line he asked me, "Is something wrong? Can't you speak right now?" to which I muttered a negative and hung up. It was really embarassing, and of course Frankie caught on. The cross examination began, about who it had been, what did he want, where had I met him, why had I encouraged him to call, etc. It was terrible, and he finally left in a huff. Next morning at the office my boss called me in and apologized for having given John my phone number, inquiring if I had very strict parents, because the young man was upset at my obviously fearful answers on the phone. I reassured my boss, told him about my jealous boyfriend, and finally he let it go, although with a worried expression. For weeks Frankie gave me grief about that call and asked if I'd seen the fellow again at the office. I never did. He stayed away the rest of the time I worked there.

Shortly afterwards I found a better paying position with the Retail Credit Company which investigated clients applying for life insurance. Here I would type out the reports sent in by our field contacts, mostly handwritten, and in some cases, extremely colloquial language if they had not been educated up to literary standards. After a few weeks I learned how to rewrite their sometimes bawdy descriptions of the client's way of life, which assumedly affected the client's health or work, but some of the original reports were hilarious. I recall one of them writing that the man was not only a drunkard, but that he beat his wife and would fight off any neighbor who came to defend her because he was "hasta las chanclas" (an expression translating into "up to his old shoes" but meaning he was completely soused). I rewrote the report, tactfully saying the man was a heavy drinker and had had marital difficulties in the past. And so on. I would then pass these reports to the head of the department, a charming older man, who would smile at my interpretations of the rough report, and usually congratulate me. The years I worked with Retail were very pleasant ones.

I had previously taken modeling classes from an American lady who lived across the street from us in Polanco, and she put me in touch with a modeling agency, where I went to have my photograph and measurements taken. They dealt in filming commercials for television, which was just starting in Mexico. Shortly after, they began to call me to act in several television ads which in those days were live. If one made a mistake, it was there for all the public to see. I opened refrigerator doors, sashayed downtown in department store clothes, and even made an ad wearing exotic designed hose called "Medias Seducción" , (Seduction Hose) where I was filmed running around a fountain while the camera zoomed in on my legs and the pattern of the hose. Then they informed me at the agency that they had been asked to provide models for a movie in Acapulco with a famous Mexican comedian, "Tin Tan", and asked if I would accept. When I told my mother, she put her foot down. "You're not going alone to Acapulco to be filmed half-naked on the beaches with a film crowd! Definitely not!" So that ended a career I might have had in television or movies. Today, our son, Tony, kids me that I might have eventually been a star in the Mexican "novelas", soap operas, so popular all over the country. So be it. I'm sure I'm happier with my present life.

Vic and Bill Hasam's marriage had continued, sometimes well, sometimes very badly. They got along as the Mexican saying goes, "a machetazos y sombrerazos", which literally means "by machete blows and sombrero-swatting". It does not translate well into English, but means "on a bumpy road". They sometimes came by on Sundays for my mother and me, and Frankie when he was available, (many times he was on guard duty over the weekends) and we would drive out of Mexico City to spend the day in Cuernavaca, always stopping in Tres Marías, a roadside gathering of small foodstands, where one could order freshly made tacos which are famous, even today. The women hand-make the tortillas, cook them on the griddle, and fill them with barbecued pork or beef, a light chili sauce, and a mashed small black-skinned avocado, discarding the stone. There were other types of tacos, but these were the best of all. Other times we would drive to a wooded area surrounding the Pedregal de San Angel, covered in black volcanic rocks, and which in those days was uninhabited, but is now a beautiful residential zone. We would take a picnic lunch or stop at a wayside restaurant for Mexican fare such as tostadas or enchiladas. A few of these times my brother Bob came along, and the six of us would cram into Bill's big Chrysler. I don't remember little Billy being along on these outings because he was a baby, left in the care of his "nana" whom Vic trusted implicitly. It is a way of life in Mexico, where one does not lug along infants to grownup activities, but leaves them in the care of their maid or "nana", which works out better for both parties: the child gets his food on time and plays at home, and the parents are able to socialize without worrying. When children are older, they accompany their parents to places where they might enjoy themselves, picnics, birthday parties for their friends, or vacations.

When Billy was about two years old, the marriage finally exploded. Vic and Bill took him to San Antonio on vacation, where they had a big blowup which had been coming for some time. His father then kidnapped little Billy while Vic was shopping, leaving a note in the motel room in which he warned her not to follow him back to Mexico, as he was going to keep his son for himself, and would hire pistoleros (gunmen) to shoot her when she crossed the border. This was yet another case of Mexican "machismo", which I referred to earlier. Bill, although of American parents, had been born and brought up in Mexico, and had many of the worst traits of his paisanos. For this reason he felt he had the right to abandon his wife and take his son, and no one should cross him. Of course Vic was desperate, and actually afraid he would carry out his threat, so she called my mother from San Antonio, who advised her to keep out of sight while she hired lawyers in Mexico City to legally take the child away from his father. This turned out to be a nearly impossible feat, as the lawyers told her there was no way the child, who was born in Mexico, could be returned to his mother, who was a foreigner. The father had all the rights to keep him.

Meanwhile, Vic, desperate and alone, had found a job in San Antonio to have an income and be able to send Mother money for the lawyers. To no avail. It was to be two long years before they were able to find a hole in the law to recover the little boy, at which time Bill handed him over peacefully to Mom, and Vic was able to come to Mexico to recover him.

In the meantime, I went to visit Vic in San Antonio for two weeks, requesting leave from my office. She was sharing a tiny house with a girlfriend, and there was this nice fellow who came over to visit them, one Dan Tolbert, whom I thought was a personable, charming southern gentleman. I could see he was keen on Vic, but she had other things on her mind at the time, mainly getting her child back. Mary, Vic's girlfriend, and I, used to talk about him when Vic was at work, and we both agreed it would be nice if Vic and Dan ended up together once things were settled with Bill in Mexico. Eventually the judge took time to look at the case and ultimately actually sat little Billy on his desk to ask him whom he would prefer to live with. Naturally, the child chose his mother, and when the divorce was final, Vic picked him up at my mother's, and went back to San Antonio, where she married Dan Tolbert who turned out to be a wonderful husband and father to Billy. A happy ending to a sad beginning.

While visiting Vic in San Antonio, I decided one day to go into town by myself to shop. Vic told me where to take the bus, so I set out in a cute skirt and blouse and high heels to walk around the corner. My heels were metal spikes, and how I could walk in them I cannot imagine, but walk I did, right around the banked corner lawn, over the carefully tended grass of the neighbor. A young man was backing his car out of the garage, and spied me. He started yelling at me through the car window, and making wild signs, but I could not decipher what he was trying to tell me, so I just smiled and waved back. He persisted, and finally from his expression I could tell it was ugly. He finally rolled down the window and yelled, "Get off my lawn, stupid girl!" at the top of his voice, till I finally got the message, but still had to dig my heels into his grass while I got off the hill. He was clearly furious. When I told Vic about it that evening, she was horrified that I would do such a silly thing and told me of the pride people take in their lawns in the States. Well, live and learn. Today, I too have a beautiful lawn, but I don't yell at people if they traipse across it! Besides, women don´t wear those terrible metal spiked heels any more.

Frankie's mother and father were coming to Mexico City to see their son, along with his sister, brother and wife. He wanted me to meet them and told me they would be arriving on the future weekend. I had already made plans with Mary and Herman and two of Mary's American girlfriends, visiting from the U. S., to go with them to Acapulco. I promised I would cut short the days spent there, and would return on the bus instead of waiting for them to return. Frankie was very upset and said that once I got to Acapulco I would not return in time, but I promised. Mary and Herman were just starting out their marriage, and were very short of money, so off we went in this old car which belonged to a friend, and as soon as we arrived and drove by Hornos, the first beach you hit on the road into Acapulco, we stopped, donned our bathing suits in the car, and ran into the ocean. It was dusk, and we rode the waves until dark, having a wonderful time. Oh how wonderful to do things on the spur of the moment, not thinking of "the right thing to do" or having any vanity about coming out all salty and sticky and half-dressed into the little hotel where they had made reservations for all of us. After the next day at the beach, we all went to Playa Suave at night, the popular place in front of the beach where one could drink and dance and where I had been a couple of years before with the Yacaru club. We ran into two of Herman's friends (one always ran into people one knew in Acapulco) and he invited them to the table to meet the two girls, but one of them preferred to come over to sit by me and chat for the rest of the evening. He asked if he could see me the next day, but I told him I'd be leaving on the bus. Then he asked if he could see me in Mexico City, and I finally told him I had a "novio", a sweetheart, but that did not discourage him. It was a known fact that when in Acapulco, everyone found a romance which usually ended upon their return to the city. Anyway, next day we all enjoyed ourselves at the beach, and at 9 P.M I took the overnight bus, and arrived the following morning, in time to meet Frankie's family.

He came by for me that evening with his sister, Irma, and we went to the Patio to meet the rest of the family. Frankie's mother and father, a handsome couple still in their late forties, were very formal with me, and I with them, but I did enjoy his sister, Irma, his brother Hank, and Sally his wife. I felt in my heart that his parents had wanted him to find a nice Mexican girl, but were politely smiling and accepting their son's choice. Only after our marriage did his mother and I come to know each other well and really like each other.

Finally, four years after we had met, Frankie received his medical diploma and with it the rank of Major in the Mexican army. Then would come, first, his year of practice in the province, and later, two years in the Military Hospital for postgraduate specialization. The plan was for him to go wherever they sent him, prepare the terrain, and then obtain his permit to come back to marry me and take me with him. His orders came through:

Campeche would be the city where they were sending him, way down south, almost to the tip of Mexico, for his one year service. He was disappointed of course, as he had hoped for a post up north, nearer to where he could visit his family. Again, trustingly I waited for his return, never doubting he would come for me. He left Mexico City on the train, not knowing what to expect at this post, and left a tearful girfriend behind.

Before receiving his final orders, Frank commited an unforgivable error, at which time he learned the hard way about the ritual of going through the chain of command in the army when making an application. On vacation with his parents in L. A., he was assured by a friend of his father that he knew a man in Mexico City who could give him a personal card to present to a General who could influence his transferal upon graduation. Frank was elated, and obtained the calling card, which he presented to the secretary of the General and was granted an appointment. On the cited day he presented himself at the Defense Ministry and was ushered into the sumptuous office of the General, who was at that time the Secretary of Defense. As he went in, he noticed several generals sitting in front of the man's desk, and Frank, a lowly Major, felt intimidated by their presence. However, bravely, he went through with his intention, after saluting the General, and firmly told him the purpose of his visit was to be granted a position in one of the border cities such as Tijuana or La Paz in Baja California, from where he would be able to visit his parents who resided in Los Angeles. The General looked at him, probably incredulously, and said, "Of course, Major, I understand. We'll see what can be done." Frank was then dismissed. When he received his orders to go to Campeche, at the other extreme of the Republic, he realized his error. Shortly after, he was called by the Colonel in charge of giving out the positions, who told him sternly: "When you have a request, never forget the chain of command in the army. If you are a Major, you ask your Lt. Colonel, who asks the Colonel, who asks the General. Keep this in mind, and NEVER forget. Dismissed." Frank never forgot.

Queta had broken up with my brother Bill, and was dating a young man from Des Moines, Iowa. She called me up one afternoon when Frank was already in Campeche, and asked me to join them and a friend he had brought along, for dinner that night. I hesitated, but she urged me, saying it was only that one night and they already knew I was engaged to be married. They picked me up, and I almost fell over when I saw the handsome young man who would be my companion for the evening. He resembled the popular actor Robert Wagner, although he was only nineteen years old, Queta had previously told me. His name was Morrie, and we four went to the 1-2-3, a well-known restaurant Frankie and I could never have afforded. I was delighted, always having loved fine food and ambience. The young man was impressed with my conversation and knowledge of Mexico, and knowing I was two years older than him, was a bit in awe of me all evening. I lived it up, and when they left me off, he asked if I would accompany them to the Pyramids the next morning. I accepted, having found him very agreeable, and so off we set the next day in their convertible and climbed all the way up to the top of the Pyramid of the Sun. There he tried to take my picture, but I pleaded that the wind had messed up my hair and I didn´t want any pictures taken. The truth was I didn't want him to have any proof we'd been together that day, or ever! At night we all went out to dinner again, and he told me if I ever went to Des Moines I should remember his father was the owner of the biggest department store there. My goodness! We said goodbye that night, and as I've never been to Des Moines, I never found out what department store he was referring to.

OUR WEDDING

The months passed, and finally Frankie obtained his permit to come in August. My mother had already had the invitations printed, some in English, some in Spanish for our Mexican friends, and it was settled that she and I would fly to Los Angeles where the wedding would take place and where the rest of his large family were waiting to meet me. Frankie arrived in Mexico City full of tales about Campeche and how he had already rented a tiny house near the ocean where we would live for the remaining four months of his term. He was to fly to Los Angeles ahead of me and wait for me there.

I was having my dress made by a seamstress, from a model in Bride's Magazine, and was thrilled we were finally getting married. The dress was white faille, halter top, with a lace fitted jacket over it with rear train to the floor. Frankie's mother and father had made all the reservations with the church, the banquet, which was to be held at their newly built home in Baldwin Hills, and the brief honeymoon which would be in nearby Catalina Island. Of course, they were paying for it all, having realized that my mother was a widow in no financial situation to pay for a big wedding. I was like a robot, accepting all that was presented before me, and not ever having been to Los Angeles, gladly leaving it up to them. Bless his mother's heart, she accepted me like one of the family, and as I had to fly there ahead of my mother who could only get a few days off from her job, was ensconced in his sister Irma's room, who moved into her kid sister's room for the time being. Everything in the house was new, and it was truly what I had imagined as a Hollywood dream, except that this home was in upper Baldwin Hills.

I arrived in Tijuana, which is on the Mexican border with San Ysidro, California, this being a cheaper flight than the one from Mexico City to Los Angeles. Frankie's brother, Hank, and his cousin picked me up and drove me through San Diego and on to L. A. They explained that Frankie was busy picking up some papers he needed for the marriage, so they tried to converse with me all during the long drive home, but I was disappointed, of course, that he hadn't been there to meet me with open arms. When I got to his parents' home he still wasn't there, but off doing some errand or other. His mother and father made me most welcome, and told me to get comfortable. We were to be married three days later. When Frankie eventually got home he seemed happy to see me, but things had not started off on the right foot, and I was having misgivings. I think he was too.

My sister Vic surprised me by arriving in L. A. with her little boy, Billy, from San Antonio, Texas. The minute she was present the atmosphere picked up. She looked so attractive and had such a vivid personality she took center stage, which was fine by me, as I didn't want any more attention centered on me. Everyone was delighted to meet her, and although she had checked into a downtown hotel to await my mother's arrival, she spent the day with little Billy in Frankie's parents' house. My mother arrived in Los Angeles and they both shared the room in the hotel, but then she decided she should spend some time with a half-sister she had living in L. A., so moved over there the second night. She and Vic and I met next morning for shopping downtown though. Mother and Vic looked stunning, both in white suits and hats, very Mexico Cityish, making everyone turn, as these were improbable outfits for casual L.A. Mother insisted I move from Frankie's house to her relatives' home so I could leave from there for the church. She said it was bad luck to leave from the same house as the bridegroom. Against my will, I did as she wanted.

The morning of the wedding dawned. I asked Irma to make a hair appointment for me in a nearby salon, which she did, and I came out totally dissatisfied with the result. I called Frankie's house so that he could come for me and his mother answered and said he'd gone to have a haircut. I had to wait over an hour at the beauty parlor before he finally got the message and came by to pick me up in a bad mood, grumbling that he still had a lot of things to get done. Neither of us was very happy that morning.

Vic told me later she had heard his mother reprimanding him and telling him to be more patient and calm down. I believe now he had the last minute jitters, which was natural, as he was taking an important step in his life. I was too, and felt things weren't coming out the way I had visioned.

Finally, the time came, and I dressed with my mother's help and was driven to Holy Name Church (Irma had had to change the church at the last minute because of something happening at St. Joseph's, (which had been specified on the invitations). My three bridesmaids were already waiting with the rest of the family. They consisted of his sister, Irma, Hank's wife, Sally, and Zulema, his older brother Armando's wife, decked out in beautiful peach-colored voile dresses and tiny hats. How thoughtful of them! I had not even stopped to think of bridesmaids. I must have been in a cloud throughout all the arrangements. As my father was dead, Frank's eldest uncle gave me away, and Frankie was at the altar in his white jacket dress uniform, looking very handsome and smiling at me. I knew right then everything would be alright. The photographer took photographs, and off we went to the Balderrama home for the wedding banquet and lots of good champagne. His family had really done themselves proud, and only now can I appreciate the pains his parents had taken to make things turn out so perfectly. I met all of Frankie's uncles and aunts, his many cousins, and my own two cousins, Joanne and Carlos, son and daughter of my mother's half-sister. My mother was the star, I must say, in a silver-gray lace dress and a large gray hat with pink lining. She stood for a while in the kitchen with all the uncles, talking and holding court and being admired, until Vic went for her and told her to mingle and keep close to Mrs. Balderrama, who discreetly stayed with the ladies. I really enjoyed the party, and finally Irma came up to me and suggested it was about time for me to go into the bedroom and change so we could leave on our honeymoon. I had had a good quantity of champagne by then, so was ready to leave. Frank also changed, and we said goodbye, not before throwing my bouquet to the girls gathered outside down the steps.

We took off in Frank's father's new car, and drove to Long Beach, where we checked into a motel for the night to take the boat next morning for Catalina Island. Next morning, the boat ride took about an hour to get toAvalon, the main city on Catalina. When the clerk at the desk in our hotel saw our names, he smiled and said, "Oh yes, the honeymooners. We have a really private cabin for you." This was true: it turned out to be at the top of the hill, too far for us to trudge up today.

During the daytime there, we walked around the island, poking around in little shops and eating in the various restaurants. The first day we went to the beach, Frankie ran into the waves bravely, not realizing the water was so terribly cold, in comparison to the warm waters we were accustomed to at Mexico's beaches. He came out trembling, and never went into the water again. One day we went to the Bird Park, where I was enchanted with all the types and colors of various birds, and another afternoon we went to the movies. In four days our honeymoon was over and we took the boat back to Los Angeles and back to the Balderrama home.

My cousin Joanne called to invite us out that night to stop at some clubs along Malibu beach. She and her Scottish husband picked us up in an old Cadillac, and we drove along the Malibu coast, stopping at several bars where the surf sprayed the windows I was impressed. At each of tour stops I had trouble getting an alcoholic beverage because the waiter would take one look at me and say I did not look over eighteen and could I produce a credential. Of course I hadn't thought of carrying one that night, so only took sips of Frankie's drink all evening. Even doing so, I got high. They finally drove us back about one o'clock in the morning, and upon trying the key in the the front door, we found Frankie's father had remained awake to open up for us. I walked in very straight, and promptly tripped over a stool in the den to my utter embarassment. But we'd had a wonderful time. I never got to see Joanne again, but she later visited my mother in Mexico City, and we now correspond by e-mail. She long ago divorced the Scot, remarried, and is now a widow, living in Bodfish, California, where she has become a well-known artist and sculptor in the area.

Time finally came for us to return to Mexico City, where we stopped briefly to say goodbye to my mother before leaving by plane for Campeche. Looking back, I am amazed I did not feel bad about leaving my mother, whom I had always been so close to. I suppose I was just so thrilled at finally being married to my Frankie. We had waited so long. So off we flew, to begin the grand adventure.

CAMPECHE

When we arrived in Campeche, we went straight to the hotel Frankie had stayed in previously. He had rented a darling little "chalet" close to the ocean, but we were not able to move in until a few days later, when our mattress would be delivered. Frankie had been sleeping on a military cot the whole time because (get this) no one slept in beds there because it was too hot. They slept in hammocks! When one was invited to a house, one would only see big hooks on the bedroom walls where hammocks would be slung at night. Naturally, Frankie had shopped around for a bed, but not finding a large one in the stores, had ordered a double bed made, which was to be delivered before he left to marry me. But ways being what they were in Campeche, and Mexico in general, they did not have it ready until after we arrived.

A jeep was brought to him from the battalion and we eventually drove to the house. I thought it was precious. Actually, there were two little houses together overlooking the ocean, one for us, and one where a German engineer and his wife lived, who were to become our closest friends there, besides her being my guide for the remaining four months of our stay in that city. When I walked in, I saw a small marble topped sideboard, a small table, also with a marble top, and a bentwood sofa and chairs with willow woven seats. These had been lent to us by the Commander of the Military Zone, and were the entire furnishings of the living room. In the dining/kitchen area, a wooden table stood with four wooden chairs, also borrowed. In the bedroom there was the bed that Frankie had ordered for us, period. Mercifully, he had bought sheets and towels, although no pillows. In the kitchen, there were two little electric hotplates to cook on, sitting on another wooden table. And there was a sink and a small icebox. Any other bride might have backed out and gone home, but I was as delighted as if it were a fully furnished mansion, and immediately mentally rearranged the furniture, adding cheesecloth tacked to the two bedroom window frames where there were no screens. I had heard so many tales since childhood from my mother about making "do" under primitive conditions in the south of Mexico when she and my father were newly married, that I was delighted that I too would now have a chance to make a little home out of nothing. What I did not count on was the occasional scorpion appearing, when least expected, on the floor or bathroom walls. They were of the large dark brown variety, and I was told they were not as poisonous as their "cousins" in the state of Durango, where they were called "güeros", or blonde ones, and can be very poisonous. Not very comforting to us, as we were both scared of insects, and it became a constant concern the rest of our time in Campeche although we were able to prevent visits from some of them by using insecticide.

Someone had advised Frankie to tie rope around the legs of the bed to prevent scorpions and the occasional snake from crawling up. (He later told me had encountered a snake in the house when he first moved in.) We did this before we went to bed that first night. He told me proudly that one of his civilian patients had promised him two rocking chairs of the local redwood, which would not be ready until next month. When they eventually brought them we were thrilled, and they were the only pieces of furniture we took back to Mexico City when we left. I noticed he had lost no time in placing a tin plaque with the words printed: "DOCTOR Francisco Balderrama Ruiz" by the front door. (the maternal name is always added in Mexico after the paternal name.

He then took me next door to introduce me to our neighbors, the German engineer whom we respectfully called by his title, Ingeniero, and his Mexican wife, Beatriz. She immediately ran into the back patio and produced our "wedding present", and I can't think of more useful gifts under the circumstances: a bucket, a tub, a broom and a mop, all items which I would need desperately to start to do chores the next day. Beatriz was fat and dark, much younger than her husband who was in his late fifties, perhaps closer to sixty, and who had previously been married to a German woman who had passed away. He had then married this delightfully appealing woman who became the joy of his life. Two daughters and son who lived in Mexico City were from his first marriage and he was expecting his young son to come visit them in a few days.

Beatriz and I hit it off from the very beginning, and she was a boon to my existence in this foreign environment. I believe my life there during those months would have been harder to adapt to without her, and I found a true friend who gave me advice in every aspect. First of all, I found to my dismay, the water coming from the taps was mixed with sea water because the ocean seeped into the wells and polluted them. The only drinkable water was one which was sold in tank trucks which blew their horns every time they came around. By then I had already tried cooking potatoes in tap water and was very upset with the result. I consulted Beatriz, as I learned to do about everything, and she explained this point to me. The water in the shower was the same way, so after washing my hair I had to rinse it out in a bucket of fresh water.

I became very frustrated with the electric hot plates. The heat could not be regulated, and I had to learn to hold pans up if I wanted eggs to fry slowly. Also, at least once a week, the coils would burn out and Frankie had to call in the batallion electrician to fix them. Mostly, I burned things, but my young husband was a brave soldier who ate my overcooked offerings. I really did not know how to cook at all, so Beatriz came to my help, walking with me to town in the early mornings to buy what was needed, and then giving me detailed instructions as to what to do with the purchase. I bought a lot of canned salmon or tuna fish for casseroles that first month, but eventually she taught me how to make enchiladas filled with cheese, although she was the one who would make the red chili sauce to dip the tortillas in before filling them. She also taught me how to choose and fry fresh fish, as well as the many ways to prepare chicken, which we would buy in the marketplace, with or without feathers, the former being cheaper than the latter.

One day, probably being tired of casseroles and fried fish and meat, Frank asked me to make him some "chiles rellenos", or stuffed green chiles. I had not the vaguest idea of how to start, and told him so. "Oh, my mother makes them often, so it can't be that hard", he offered. "I think that what you have to do is to grab each big chile, cut it open, stuff it with hamburger meat, and put it in the oven." Something did not ring right, even to my naïve ears, so I decided to ask Beatriz for instructions. She was horrified that I would undertake such a complicated job. It turned out that what I was supposed to do was to first toast the chiles over the flames. (I didn't have any flames on my electric heaters, so she said she'd toast them on her gas stove.) Then, one had to put them in a little bag, paper or plastic, to "sweat" before undertaking the peeling, no easy job. Once peeled, one should slit one side, and fill each one with grated cheese, (Jack type) with a toothpick inserted to keep the slit closed. They could alternately be filled with browned and condimented hamburger meat After that one should dust each one with flour, and dip them in salted frothy beaten egg whites, frying each one separately in hot grease on all sides. After they sat, golden, on a paper-covered plate, the making of the tomato sauce would begin by frying chopped onion and juicy peeled tomato, mashing it together, and spooning over each chile on the serving plate. Well, I was lost halfway through the instructions, so she took pity on me and told me that next day we would be invited over to her house for lunch, and she would serve the famous "chiles rellenos". We accepted gladly, and although they were a little hot for me, Frank smacked his lips and said they tasted as delicious as his mother's.

My husband had been living in Campeche for a little over seven months by the time we married in California, taking most of his meals at the barracks, but at night going out with a group of young single men and women. This group liked to get together almost every night for a "fiesta" in someone's house, where they would put on records and dance and drink a mixture of rum and coke and guayaba (guava) juice, which sounds ghastly but was really very tasty. Beatriz and the Ingeniero were invited to some of these parties even though they were older. I was introduced to the members of the group, and they accepted me, although some of the girls eyed me with resentment at first because they had previously tried to get their claws on the handsome young single military doctor who had arrived in their mist. We fell into the habit of getting together with the group almost every night, and I remember that when we came home in the dark neither of us wanted to reach inside the doorway for the light switch because we were afraid there might be a scorpion on the wall. If we had to get up in the middle of the night to use the bathroom, we put on the light, scared of stepping barefoot on some insect.

A few weeks after we arrived in Campeche, the Ingeniero's son arrived from Mexico City for a visit. His name was Hansi, a very tall Germanic looking boy who had just finished his studies and wanted to have a few months vacation before looking for work. I imagine he was about my age, so fell right in with us and the party group. At first, knowing the way Frankie had previously responded to other young males around me I thought he might show some jealousy, but he saw from the very beginning, that Hansi and I had no interest in each other aside from a platonic friendship.

My husband had to report every morning early, in uniform, for duty at the batallion, to care for any soldier or officer who might be ill. He would return around two o'clock for lunch and was free for the rest of the afternoon. Once in a while he would borrow a jeep from the Commander and put about three pesos of gas in it, and he and Hansi and I would drive out by a nice beach to swim, or visit the old Spanish wall on top of a hill with its cannons pointing out to sea. These used to protect the city against British or French pirates who continually attacked and ransacked the town in the past. I imagine that after their attack and conquest, the pirates spent some time in town enjoying the delights of good food and the ladies' favors. For this reason there were many fair-haired inhabitants with light eyes and European names such as Gladys, and Myriam, and Jacqueline, and some of the young men were fair and long-jawed like the English. Beginning in the 17th Century the port of Campeche was involved in many cutthroat battles with the pirates, so the Spanish had built the stone wall around the city to protect it from takeover by the marauders.

Right below our chalet, there was a tall statue made to the memory of Justo Sierra, one of Mexico's beloved poets, writer, and founder of the National University of Mexico in 1910. Close friends of ours, Peggy and Porfirio, recently went in the year 2000 to visit Campeche and told us the statue remains overlooking the sea, but there are no remnants of the little chalets. Instead, modern buildings have taken their place. How sad.

Frankie occasionally had a few clients from the local residents, fishermen or other humble people who would stop by the house and ask for a consultation. Of course the young doctor welcomed them, first for the experience, and second for the small amount of money he could charge. Some of them were only able to pay a few pesos, but others would pay him the next day by bringing a bucket of shrimp, or a live squid in appreciation. Naturally I had no idea of how to deal with these offerings, so would immediately seek help from Beatriz, who would either give me advice, or cook the item herself, and we would share the food.

Looking back at that time, I realize this was our real honeymoon, which lasted the four months we were together in that little chalet by the sea. We were very much in love, and a less demanding husband, one could never find. He even accepted my poor efforts at ironing his military shirts and pants. Holding the rank of major, he was entitled to have a soldier's help whenever he might need it, so we had a boy come over for a few days every week. He would mop the floors, empty the big trashcan in the back area (where scorpions always ran out from beneath) and even do errands in town. Evenings, when we didn't join the group, we adjourned next door and played poker with our neighbors, using black frijoles as chips. We'd never lose more than a few centavos a game, but we bet as if for hundreds of pesos. Or we'd go together to a small restaurant in town where they served delicious fresh crab. Once in a while Beatriz would invite us over for southern tamales, totally different from the ones in Mexico City, which have a more doughlike consistency, and very little meat in the center, or the ones in the north, which have less dough and more meat in red or green chile sauce. These were larger than both, wrapped in banana leaves instead of corn leaves, and very moist inside, with a tasty marinated chicken filling. I enjoyed them then, but have since tasted them elsewhere and now much prefer our northern tamales with chile colorado. Sometimes we'd make "sincronizados" which were ham and cheese sandwiches pressed between flat tongs and held over the gas fire for a few minutes on each side, an equivalent of today's cheese toaster machine.

Frankie and I went over one afternoon to meet his Commander, a distinguished old General and his wife. She served us a lovely merienda, a light repast of "panuchos" which are slightly fried tortillas with the edges turned up all around, filled with refried black beans spread between the top skin and the lower part, and vinegar-marinated fish with purple onions on top. Really delicious, although they might not sound so. Before we left, the

General's wife gave us a precious little kitten from their litter. I was thrilled, as I've always loved animals, any kind, so went home happy that afternoon, and my husband immediately said, "We really should invite them to our house". I agreed, and one day the next week we invited them to come over in the early evening, along with our next door neighbors.

Now, I cannot imagine by what stretch of imagination I thought I should offer them tiny sandwiches filled with carrot salad as a kind of hors d'oeuvre. I was familiar with my mother's cucumber sandwiches at her tea parties and assumed that grated carrots would do just as well, perhaps because they were what I had handy. Also, I made them ahead of time, so that by the hour the guests came, the sandwiches were already soggy. Anyway, I added a bowl of potato chips, and 7 miniature cold beers, one for each of us, thinking they would be enough before they took their leave. Beatriz and the Ingeniero and Hansi came over before our other guests and I had to give them one beer each, realizing I only had enough for two more guests. I decided I would not drink any. We dragged out our two rocking chairs and the four kitchen chairs to the porch, and placed a small table in the middle. I would be waiting on them, so no need for another chair. They arrived, looking very happy to see us, and were introduced to the Ingeniero and Beatriz and Hansi, and then Frankie told me very grandly, "Kiddo, (he had started calling me kiddo) bring out the drinks and the food." I went into the kitchen feeling a little desperate, and brought a tray with the two beers served in three glasses so that they would go further. The General said immediately, "I'll have mine in the bottle please, if you don´t mind. It's colder that way." My heart sank as I watched him guzzle the last bottle of beer down in a few gulps. I then brought out the platter of sandwiches with their corners already turned up. They graciously had one each and a fistful of potato chips, and then Beatriz, seeing my despairing face, jumped up and ran next door, returning with a half a dozen regular-sized cold beers in a bag and a package of potato chips. She placed them in the

101

kitchen, whispering to me, that she had more in her fridge if we needed them. It turned out that we did, as the General and his wife relaxed and started talking, clearly enjoying themselves, to the delight of my husband, who did not know the agony I had been going through. The soggy sandwiches disappeared, with no comments, and Hansi went for another bag of chips and more beers. Thank God for good neighbors! This was my initiation to entertaining, and I've never forgotten it, nor have I ever made carrot salad sandwiches again.

The Ingeniero and Beatriz asked us if we'd like to go with them to visit Mérida, the beautiful Mayan city further south, known as La Ciudad Blanca, or The White City, in the upper part of the Yucatán peninsula. It is known for its beautiful vegetation, mild climate, which encourages an unhurried way of life, and has retained its very noticeable provincial charm, a heritage from its Colonial past. We were thrilled, especially to celebrate my twenty-second birthday there, so the next weekend we started off in their pickup truck, the five of us. We took turns, at first the two ladies riding in the cab with the Ingeniero, and Frankie standing up at the back with Hansi, and then Beatriz and I standing up in back while Frankie rode with the Ingeniero and Hansi. I think back now at how undignified we must have looked, our hair flying in the wind, our eyes bloodshot, our clothes sweaty from standing in the hot sun when we finally checked into the Gran Hotel. But we were having a good time, and vanity played no part in either of us. We immediately went down to the bar and had cold beers before going out to visit the rest of the city and look for a place for lunch. The majestic Avenida Montejo, will always remain in my mind as one of the most beautiful and unique Mexican avenues I have seen, with its white mansions facing the street. Horse-drawn carriages waited in the Plaza for passengers, and the whole atmosphere, perhaps because of the contrast with backward Campeche, impressed me greatly. We drove by the Palacio Montejo, built in the sixteenth century by the family of the same name and still occupied by the descendants, the grand Cathedral on the Plaza Mayor, the main plaza, as well as the Gran Cenote, a large water reservoir in the ground, made by the Mayans, and perhaps used for sacrifices. Beatriz and I insisted on visiting the marketplace, one of the most fascinating in Mexico, where one can find henequén goods, (sisal), particularly hammocks, (she bought a matrimonial-sized one) as well as embroidered "huipiles" a type of square wool sarape with an opening in the center, to wear as a cover-up. The hotel was one of the best and most central, and I'm surprised now we could afford it, but we were living it up that weekend, so enjoyed it to the hilt. Next morning we drove to the port of Progreso, where ships were being loaded with sisal, one of Yucatán's main exports to the world, used for cordage or rope; and chicle, extracted from the chicozapote tree.

We regret now we did not include a trip to the Mayan ruins of Chichén Itzá but that would have taken another whole day, and we only had that one weekend at our disposal. Frankie had to report back to the barracks on Monday, and the Ingeniero to his job as Manager of the electric plant. Recently, I finished a marvellously gripping book about the true story of a famous romance between the Governor of Yucatán, Felipe Carrillo Puerto, and an American newspaper woman, Alma Reed, who first encouraged American anthropologists to visit the site of Chichén Itzá in 1922. Tragically the Governor was consequentially assassinated because of his backing and promotion of the backward Mayan indians, whom the government preferred to keep subdued. But his name lives on as a city in the neighboring state of Quintana Roo.

We returned to Campeche, and started preparing for the coming Christmas season. Beatriz decided we should give a Posada party at her house where we could serve tamales and have a piñata for everyone to take turns to hit and try to break. She insisted that both of us should decorate the piñata. I had not a clue, but together we went to the market to buy an "olla", a large earthenware pot. We bought "papel de China", tissue paper, in various gay colors and proceeded to decorate the piñata. First she showed me how to make glue with flour and water, then she put me to cutting long strips of tissue paper which we folded in half and snipped halfway down. We stuck different colored rows to the olla, all the way around, and when it was fully covered it looked fatter and gaily decorated. We wrapped Mexican candy and lots of unshelled peanuts, filled the pot, and added a thin rope through the holes at the top, ready to be strung up on a tree in her back yard. I believe now that she and the Ingeniero must have paid most of the money for the beer and cokes we bought, but we did contribute partly, and gave our ideas and enthusiasm. All the invited guests came, as well as a few more, and each person brought a platter of something to eat. The party was a great success, and we even sang "Posada" songs while carrying candles around the garden, ending the evening with a great bash, literally, which was the breaking of the piñata by one of the blindfolded competitors. Everyone talked about the Posada for weeks afterwards. A good time was had by all.

Beatriz then invited us to have our Christmas meal with them on the 24th at night, which is when Mexicans celebrate the Birth of Christ. The Ingeniero's mother was to come from Mexico City to spend the Christmas Holidays with her son. She was introduced to us when she arrived, a very tall, stern, plain looking German woman whom the three of them called "Muti", which I gathered meant Mother in German. She took over the kitchen, presumably to make all her son's favorite dishes, and used a large recipe book witten in German. Beatriz told me later that when she finished using it she would put it on the highest shelf so that no one else could read the recipes. As if Beatriz could read German!

It was hard to buy presents in downtown Campeche, and although I went from shop to shop I found nothing I'd like to give my new husband, or buy for my friend Beatriz. I finally ended up at a store that sold cosmetics, and bought Frankie aYardley aftershave lotion . At a small bookstore I bought Beatriz a book of poetry by Amado Nervo, one of Mexico's beloved poets, and ended up buying the Ingeniero and Hansi some handkerchiefs. Not finding anything for "Muti", I decided to give her my prized lace-trimmed handkerchief that had been given to me to carry in my wedding dress, and was yet unused. Christmas eve we went over in the evening and had a drink, followed by the scrumptious dinner that "Muti" had fixed. She said she had wanted to find a goose for the main dish, but could not find any, so settled for turkey, which she stuffed with bananas and fruit. My mother had always made a bread and celery stuffing, and I thought I would not like Muti's, but it was delicious. She accompanied it with potatoes and many other dishes for which she gave me German names, so I did not know what we were eating, but everything was wonderful. This was the first Christmas I had ever spent away from home, and I kept thinking of my mother having my brothers, Bill and Bob and his wife Lyn, over for her traditional Christmas meal. Frankie had already spent two Christmases away from home when he was studying in Chihuahua, while he was living with his grandparents. Later when he was already studying medicine in the military medical school in Mexico City, he had always gone home for the holidays. But we were so lucky to have close and dear friends to spend that day with, and I'm still grateful for their friendship during that first year of our marriage. They have long since passed away, but their memory still lives fondly and vividly in our minds.

The New Years' Ball was coming up at the old Casino, which had seen better days, but was still the best entertainment salon Campeche had to offer. Beatriz asked me if I had a long dress, and yes, I had brought along my wedding dress, the part underneath the lace, with a halter, so I took it to a seamstress and she cut it and made it ankle length. Beatriz decked herself up in a strapless dress, and her husband actually wore a white tux coat. Frankie wore his beige uniform (he had left his dress uniform in Mexico City with my mother) and we went to the Ball. Hansi decided not to go because he said none of the girls in Campeche were pretty enough to date, not true, so we four attended and had a fine time.

By now, Frank was eagerly awaiting his orders to return to Mexico City, and we were worried about our little cat, whom we were crazy about and had named Bobo. We did not want to leave him as we were both too fond of him, and still did not know our method of travel, plane or train. When the orders finally came, tickets were for the train, so I decided I'd send Bobo to my mother a few days before on the plane in a little crate. I think daughters believe their parents are there solely to help them through thick and thin, and I never stopped to think of the inconvenience it would cause my mother to have a cat in her apartment for four days before we arrived.

Beatriz and the Ingeniero decided to give us a goodbye party, and invited all our friends to attend. It was a happy event, but tearful at the end, as we had made good friends among the local "Campechanos", and they were sorry to see us leave. We danced until past midnight, and then Frankie did his usual "exit", where he disappeared to go to the bathroom, and did not reappear. Everyone accompanied me to the front door of our house, and sang "La Barca de Oro", the Golden Boat, which is a sad goodbye song which ends with "Adios, para siempre, adios", Goodbye forever, goodbye. By the time I went to bed, Frankie was already fast asleep. The next morning Beatriz and Hansi and the Ingeniero took us to the train station, and we waved goodbye tearfully, promising to write. The long train-ride lay ahead.

We had to change trains three times on the return trip. Frankie had already made that same journey when he first travelled to Campeche, but we had flown there together after our marriage and I did not realize how far down in the peninsula or how deep in the jungle we had been. The train had to push its way through dense tropical foliage, and workers in the engineer's cabin would often descend, with machetes, to whack at the thick weeds and limbs which had covered the tracks. We were thankful for Beatriz's thoughtfulness of making us a supply of sandwiches, for the train carried no dining car. The second train was a small one which we boarded in Jesus Carranza, already in the state of Veracruz, and the third train was named "El Mexicano" , lavishly furnished during the time of President Porfirio Diaz, with red velvet seats and tassled curtains. This train had a dining car, so we were able to finish our ride in style. It took us two days in total to arrive in Mexico City, and my feet were so swollen from sitting down that I could hardly walk off the train. They lasted that way for several days, but of course by that time I was home with my mother who got to baby me a bit, while Frankie had immediately checked in at the Military Hospital for duty. Bobo had raised havoc in my poor mother's apartment. He was not house-trained, the doors and windows having been kept open in Campeche where he could use the yard for his "necessities", but indoors, he had chosen her plants to "go" in, and scratched the dirt onto her impeccable floors and rugs. Bravely, she tolerated him, and when I got there I was so ecstatic at seeing him, that she merely smiled and did not complain. I finally got him a sandbox, but could not find sand, so we put in folded newspapers, which worked just as well. Amazing how quickly he adapted.

MEXICO CITY

My mother and I began checking the newspaper ads for a small apartment for Frankie and me, and when he got leave that weekend from the Military Hospital where he had already started his internship, we went together to look at some of the more interesting ones. Almost immediately we found what was the ideal apartment for newlyweds in a small building in Polanco, where I had lived with my mother a few years before. It was new, had one bedroom and a small living-dining area, kitchen and bathroom. It could not have been more appropiate for our needs and we fell in love with it at first sight, signing a contract for two years. We only had money for the basic things, and started with a sofa bed for the living area. We had brought our two red cedar rocking chairs from Campeche, and these went well with the wood on the arms of the sofa. We bought a gray shag rug and my mother lent us a small coffee table. For the first month we slept on the sofa bed, but then my mother asked if we'd like a single bed which she had in the guest room where my brother, Bill, had slept when he was living with her. We promptly accepted and put it in the bedroom, which up to this time we had only used for our suitcases and boxes. As Frank (around this time I started calling him Frank instead of Frankie) spent most of the week at the Military Hospital, and only came home for weekends, this worked out fine for us and we enjoyed sleeping together in a single bed. It kind of reminded me of my mother's old joke about the five children who slept in one bed with their parents. When asked how they managed, the youngest boy replied: "It works fine, 'cause when Pa turns, we all turn." The same applied to Frank and me.

My mother also donated a large round kitchen table, which we had a local carpenter adapt into a double drop-leaf table to fit against the very attractive black rock wall. We painted it black and, voilá, we had our dining table. I hung a large Mexican tin-framed mirror over it, also from my mother, and then one night we happened to go to the Jai-Alai, or Fronton court where Spaniards play handball with a scooped basket and where one bets on the players. We were very lucky and won a few pesos, enough to go to the Lagunilla Market next day and purchase two wooden Mexican chairs with wicker seats. We painted the wood black, and they went well with our table. That night at the Fronton court when we were leaving, we saw Rita Hayworth with her husband, Ali Khan, exiting at the same time, and I asked her for her autograph. She looked very glamorous, and although cordial, regretfully was unable to comply because neither of us had a pen or a pencil.

Bobo, our cat, adapted well to the apartment and used our bathroom for his necessities. He would wander out onto our little narrow porch overlooking the street and walk along the railing. One day he fell onto the porch below where no one lived, so we had to call the owner to lend us a key to get into the apartment to retrieve our cat. He was not happy about it, and neither was Bobo who had to spend all day there before we rescued him.

There were only six apartments in the building, two on each floor, one on the ground floor, and a small penthouse at the top where a mysterious bachelor lived. We discovered that on the ground floor two women lived together, obviously lovers, who maintained constant rows and shouting matches. One night they had a tremendous row and one locked the other in the tiny bathroom. However she yelled so much, and for so long, that someone finally called the police who came and tried to get her out through the barred window which looked on to the stairwell. They finally managed to pull her, feet first, through the narrow opening and as she came out, her nightgown was pushed over her head by the middle bar, while the policemen and anyone peeking over the stairs got a good look at her bare body. She could care less, and continued to scream ugly words at her companion, while pounding on the front door, until finally the other woman had to let her in. The police entered with her and somehow pacified them both, because when they left we heard no more from that apartment. I happened to see them next day leaving by the main door, laughing and looking like a couple of lovebirds.

From our balcony I could see the house in front, and noticed that early every morning, the lady of the house would come out, in a saggy old evening dress, to sweep the sidewalk. In those days, women in Mexico sometimes used their old clothes, or worse still, their robes, while doing morning chores, instead of donning slax and a t-shirt or something casual. I saw a variety of her old dresses over the two years we lived in that apartment, some with spangles, some with drapes, all with bulging shoulder pads which had been in style before. I imagine that when she had worn them enough, rather than throw them out, they would be relegated to the hamper as workclothes. In most houses maids did this work, but in instances where they could not afford one, they had to do it themselves. I stop to think that in the States I have never seen a housewife out sweeping her sidewalk. Perhaps it is not necessary because people do not throw trash in the street there, but in Mexico, someone, be it the maid or the owner of the house, always waters and sweeps the sidewalk in the mornings. Just a small observation.

A few months after we moved in, a young couple rented the apartment across from us on the same floor. The young man immediately came over to see us both and introduced himself as Salvador Alvarez, a lawyer, and told us his wife would be arriving from the States in a few days. He was movie-good-looking, as was his wife when she showed up, making a beautiful couple. Her name was Pat O'Connell, and she was from Grosse Point. Frankie later told me that this was a wealthy district in Michigan, and it must have been, because I imagine her parents, and perhaps his, helped the newly married couple to furnish their flat beautifully, starting with wall-to-wall carpeting, drapes, and fine furniture which I'm sure a young lawyer could not have provided himself. Our apartment in comparison to theirs looked very rustic, to say the least, but they were very friendly toward us and Pat's mother, a silver-haired glamorous lady, visited them and was brought over one day to meet us. She was sweet enough to compliment us on our ingenious decoration. Although we made friends with the couple from the very beginning, we found it impossible to accompany them to the many social functions they constantly attended, first, because we did not have the money, and second, because Frankie was only available on weekends, and not always then, for sometimes he had to stay at the hospital on guard duty. One evening they invited us to a party at a friend's home, and to our surprise it was held in the cellar of the house, in almost complete darkness, lit only by scattered candles. The host, an elderly gray-haired American, was the disc jockey, and stood on a raised podium directing music with a lighted baton. He was really into it, and obviously enjoying himself while we all danced and drank some sort of punch. There was a large crowd, and apparently these soirées took place once a month, but this was the only one we were invited to. When we arrived, who should I meet but my old flame, Efrén Fierro, who was obviously impressed at how sophisticated I looked -- I had just had my hair cut and coiffed and had on full makeup, -- and came over to ask wonderingly, "Peggy?" He looked just as handsome as ever, but I acknowledged his enthusiastic greeting very cooly, and we only exchanged a few words. He slunk away, and I never saw him again throughout the rest of the party, but I felt redeemed from that unforgettable night years before at the Ball.

My sister Vic and her husband, Dan Tolbert, arrived in Mexico City with son Billy, now seven years old, to have a meeting with Bill Hasam, her previous husband, about getting permission from him for Dan to adopt Billy legally. She was nervous about seeing Bill again, and they met in the gardens of Shirley Courts, a nearby motel where many American tourists used to stay, with a lawyer and all the necessary papers ready to sign. Bill arrived, stiff at first, but later showing some of the charm with which he had originally wooed Vic before their marriage. Surprisingly, he agreed for the adoption. He too was remarried and had another son by then. When Vic and Dan and Billy came over to my mother's apartment after it was over, they were ready to celebrate with all of us. Little Billy had been calling Dan "Daddy" anyway, ever since he had gone back to his mother, and a wonderful father he was.

That summer of '54 Frank said that he could probably obtain a free military plane ride to Tijuana, on the border, from where we could take a bus to Los Angeles to visit his family. He was granted the permit, and we flew from Mexico City in a small plane which had one long wooden seat along each side of the walls for the troops. Rather uncomfortable, because with each dip or rise we would slide, but it was free, so neither of us complained. It made its first stop in La Paz, which means "The Peace", Baja California in the Gulf of California, where we found that we must spend

111

the night before leaving next day for Tijuana. I was delighted. La Paz is a lovely town facing the sea, and we were out walking that evening on the " malecon", the dock where the sailboats were anchored, when we saw a handsome couple walking toward us. The man wore a navy blue blazer with an emblem on the pocket, and the woman was tall and silver-blonde. Frank whispered to me, "That's Clark Gable!" and sure enough it was. We smiled at them as they went by, smiling back at their obvious admirers. We followed them into the hotel bar where they had ordered drinks, and Frank went up to the actor and asked him for his autograph. Gable grinned and said, "Sure boy, gladly" , and I produced my calling card which he signed on the back. It was several years after he had lost his first wife, Carol Lombard, and later we gathered from movie magazines that this wife must have been Lady Sylvia Ashley.

When we arrived in Tijuana, we crossed over to San Diego and took a Greyhound bus to Los Angeles where we spent almost two weeks with the family. One day we were invited by Frank's brother, Armando, and his wife, Zulema, to spend a day at Knott's Berry Farm. A cute incident took place when we visited the set of "The Old School House" where what we thought was a very old teacher showed us the classrooms. He had white hair, pince-nez glasses and a white beard. Frank and I were so naïve that Frank actually respectfully asked him, "And how old are you, sir?", to which he winked and replied, "Twenty-eight! And how old are you?" We had both been taken in.

We also had time to go nightclubing with his other brother, Hank, and Sally, his wife, and Irma, Frank's sister. When we were ready to return to Mexico, his parents said they would drive us to Tijuana, along with his kid sister, Margie, to take our plane there. We chose Tijuana because the flight to Mexico City came out a lot cheaper than flying straight from L. A.

While visiting the family, we had asked Irma, who is my same age, if she would like to come to spend some time with us in Mexico City. She was thrilled with the idea, so that same year she flew in, and stayed with us for six months until her visa expired. Most of the time I was living alone, with Frank at the hospital, so she was a good companion for me and we became very close friends. Often we would go to visit my mother, who always invited us to stay for a meal. Neither Irma nor I cooked very much so we were always grateful for the invitation. Lord knows what else we survived on those months. I don't recall ever going into the kitchen to make a meal, but I do remember that Irma was amazed we had not bought an icebox, much less a refrigerator, and that I only had a big metal tub in which the iceman would dump a small block of ice three times a week. In it stood the milk, and a wrapped bar of butter floating around in the chilly water. Mexico City is seldom hot, and houses are generally very cool, so there was no problem with the bread and other staples I might have had. But Irma was horrified that I would let the butter float in the water, so graciously bought me a little plastic box to keep it in, and we let that float around instead. Not much of an improvement.

Frank's aunt Emma, his mother's younger sister, lived in Polanco, not far from our apartment. She had two unmarried daughers and a teenaged son, and often Irma and I would visit them and attend the parties the girls gave. Irma had more spending money than I did, as her parents sent her a monthly check. Frank, of course, only received his army wage while doing his internship, just enough to pay the rent and utilities, with a small amount for our food. As he always ate at the hospital, and I usually ate with my mother before Irma came, that money was usually used to attend an occasional movie or have a snack downtown. But when Irma was there she often treated me to breakfast at Sanborns, or sometimes we would meet my mother after work and the three of us would have a cocktail of our favorite Cinzano vermouth and taquitos with guacamole dip at the Ritz Hotel Bar.

One night Frank invited all the boys who had lived in the apartment where I first met him. They came over and were happy to meet Irma, and one, his best friend Pedro, squired Irma around for the rest of her visit. Right before Irma returned to L. A. Frank decided she could not return without seeing Acapulco, so with very little money in his pocket, we boarded a bus and took the seven hour ride there. We found a small spartan boarding house not far from the beach, which provided us with two rooms and three "meals" a day. For breakfast they would serve us coffee, a sweet roll and a few beans; for lunch, rice and a thin piece of tough meat, always ending up with beans. For supper, the very popular "café con leche" which is strong coffee with milk, and a sweet roll. What did you want for $15 pesos a day per person? It was enough to keep you alive, but we were only interested in going to the beach anyway. All morning we would spend on Caleta beach, where the waves are mild, and in the afternoons we would take a bus and go to Hornos to ride the waves. There was a tent-like nightclub on Caleta beach called the "Boom Boom Room" and not having enough money for the entrance fee, we would stand right outside the door and listen to the orchestra and watch the people dancing barefoot in the sand. Years later, my husband, who has always remembered the past through rose-colored glasses, when recalling the story of our youthful trip to Acapulco, would say we had been to the "Boom Boom" often, seemingly not remembering how we had only stood outside listening to the music. We had fun despite our lack of money, and the last afternoon, before we took the bus back we only had, between the three of us, enough money for a bag of "pan dulce", Mexico's famous sweet bread. We bought six pieces, and ate them in our rooms with our bags already packed.

Time came for Irma to return to L. A., and she cried so much at the airport I thought she would collapse. We knew we would miss her too, and those days have always remained a fond memory in all our minds.

During our second year in Mexico City we were surprised I had not yet become pregnant, and Frankie decided to take me to the Military Hospital for a checkup with a gynecologist. The doctor, after studies and X-rays, diagnosed me with obstructed fallopian tubes which carry the ova to the uterus, and suggested injecting air into the tubes to clear them up. I went that same week and had the fairly simple procedure done, the only uncomfortable outcome being that I had an acute pain in my shoulder area for a few days.

That same year, in July 1955 we returned for a visit to L. A., this time by commercial airline. Frank's parents had expressed a desire to drive to Mexico City, so we knew we would drive back with them. They had just bought a large, new, beautiful '55 Buick Riviera, and wanted to stop in Chihuahua to see Mrs. Balderrama's parents and family. Frank's father also had family there, so after spending a happy week in L. A., we six started out on the long drive back: Frank's parents, his sisters Irma and Margie, and the two of us. When we were packing the car, I remember Frank's Dad putting a large watermelon in the trunk. Shrieks ensued from Irma and Margie, who said we could always stop at restaurants on the way to have refreshments, but he insisted that for the long hot road through the desert we would all enjoy the watermelon. He prevailed, and as it turned out, in the middle of the Arizona desert we stopped briefly to add water to the motor, and he took out his penknife and cut open the watermelon which had remained cool under all the baggage. Each of us had a luscious piece, and never has watermelon tasted so good to us since then, cool and dripping with juice. We had to admit it had been a terrific idea.

We spent the night at a Travel Lodge in Arizona, and started out for Chihuahua early next morning. When we arrived, we went straight to Frank's grandparents' home, from where I met his aunts, his uncle Dustano, and many of his cousins. He had been the apple of his grandmother's eye while he was studying there for two years, and she lost no time in telling me how popular he had been with all the girls in Chihuahua. I was not charmed by this, as one can imagine, but smiled bravely and remained quiet. She was a short pink-faced, silver-haired lady, with a twinkle in her eye. His grandfather was old and feeble, and sat most of the time in his rocking chair in their enclosed patio. We also got to meet one of Mr. Balderrama's brothers, a sister, and more cousins from his side. His other brothers had all emigrated to Los Angeles shortly after him, his older brother being the one who had given me away at the altar. Frank introduced me proudly to his Uncle Dustano, Mrs. Balderrama's brother, who had been the one who had first encouraged him to study medicine at the military university in Mexico City. I was grateful that he had convinced him!

We only stayed for two nights, young Margie complaining that she hated the smell of the sheets, because they were washed with "cortadura", the large white bar of soap which people still use for spots on some materials. We left early for our trip to San Pedro, near Torreón, where Mr. Balderrama's other sister and family lived. Frank had vacationed there while living in Chihuahua, and I had heard much about how he had enjoyed his stay. San Pedro is in the state of Coahuila and forms part of what is known as "La Laguna", The Lake Area, which years ago was full of water, reason for which it is still called La Laguna, although it is now dry as a bone. It comprises Torreón, Matamoros, Gomez Palacio and Lerdo. We had to drive over a long expanse of " terracería", gravel road, to get to San Pedro and I was worried the paint of the pretty new Buick would get scratched, but the damage was minimum. Never had I seen such a welcome. Frank's aunt Concha, her husband, Don Jesus, a perfect gentleman who had been at the entrance of the city to welcome us, and his cousin, Yoyo. They gave us the main bedrooms, and treated us to some of the famous home cooked dishes from that region, machacado con huevo for breakfast, (dried shredded beef mixed with scrambled eggs), guisado con chile colorado, (stew made with red dried chiles) for lunch, of course, accompanied by hand-made flour tortillas. It was a pleasant little town, arid, but with a large plaza surrounded by shady trees.

We left for Mexico City, passing by Torreón, where we drove by a beautiful country club and golf course on our way through.

The city looked new and clean, and I was very favorably impressed. Little did we know we would shortly be coming to reside there, and spend the rest of our lives in that city.

Frank's family spent a few days in Mexico City and then wanted to visit Acapulco, so we drove with them and spent a restful week in a lovely hotel near the beach, not at all like the other poor little place we had stayed at the year before. I remember Frank's Dad, resting in a hammock at the hotel, enjoying the sea breeze, and commenting, "Esta es Vida!" This is the life! Acapulco was truly a haven before it became so overcrowded.

Back in Mexico City, they loved our apartment, and we invited them for a meal, my first experience with cooking for his family. I decided on meat balls in a tomato sauce, which my mother had shown me how to make, adding a tiny bit of "albahaca", (sweet basil) to the ground meat, and Mexican rice. Everything came out very tasty, and Frank's parents complimented me on the meal. I was pleased as punch.

Shortly after they left, I realized that I might be pregnant, so, telling Frank nothing, I asked my girlfriend Queta to do me the favor of having her uncle, a doctor, test my urine at his lab. The result came back positive, so I visited my husband at the hospital and surprised him in his room. I smiled as I handed him the analysis, and waited for his reaction. He was so surprised he let out a whoop of joy and picked me up and kissed me. No child would be more eagerly awaited than ours! My mother and the rest of our families were thrilled for us also.

Frank did not know yet where he would be posted for his six year medical service to the army. He had studied two years by then at the hospital, specializing in Gynecology and Obstetrics as well as general surgery, and they would send him to a Military Hospital in the provinces, to take care of military personnel and their families at that station. There were several places being given out to the doctors who had graduated along with my husband and I heard that one of them was to be on the Islas Marías, the island where there is a prison. I don't know why, but I was hoping we would be sent there, perhaps having a vision of another chalet by the sea like in Campeche. But when my mother heard me express my choice she was very upset with the idea of her grandchild being born on a prison island. As it turned out, they chose Torreón for him, in the state of Coahuila, the city we had driven by the previous year on our way to Mexico City from our visit in Los Angeles. Immediately, the vision of the country club came to my mind, and I was thrilled we would be going there.

I had a marvellous pregnancy, only a few early mornings with sickness, and a larg appetite every time I visited my mother. I knew she had had seven healthy pregnancies with no problems,

and I expected mine would be the same, and so it was. Frank and I were convinced it would be a boy, and he even bought me a pocket book about how to take care of babies, and wrote on the front page, "For the care of our dear son". He foretold the future! He was pleased we were going to Torreón, and knew his departure date would be at the beginning of January. Before we left Mexico City we made it a point to go to all the landmarks and take each other's picture. We did not know whether we would ever live there again, as the army frequently changed their doctors to other cities, mostly in the provinces. We stood in front of Bellas Artes, the beautiful Palace of Fine Arts, in front of the golden Angel of Independence column, the National Palace, the Cathedral, the Hotel Del Prado, the House of Tiles, and of course in front of the entrance to our apartment building. We did not need to pay that month's rent. Instead I moved in with my mother, and we sent our few pieces of furniture to Torreón to the Battalion headquarters where it would await our arrival. Frank stayed on at the hospital meanwhile.

He left with only his suitcases on the train, our goodbye tearful but assuaged by the knowledge that we would be together shortly, as soon as he found us a place to live. During those years the trains had Pullman sleeping cars, and good dining facilities. He met some fine people on the train, the Diaz de Leon ladies, who were thrilled to have a new military doctor going to their hometown, and who treated him to delicious "tortas" (individual French bread loaves, usually filled with sliced pork or ham and avocado, tomato, onion and lettuce) from their hamper of food. The two elderly ladies were known in that region for making "ates", bars of solidified fruit jelly, mainly from guava or quince, which they exported all over the country.

When Frank arrived in Torreón he reported immediately to the Battalion where he was posted, and checked in at a central hotel. He looked at several apartments before he settled on one, not far from the very center of town, across from the lovely little Plaza Juárez, in front of the City Hall. A Mexican flag flew on a pole in the middle of the Plaza, and every afternoon at 6 P.M. the bugles would play the Mexican military version of "Taps" while they lowered the flag.

Back in Mexico City I prepared for the train trip, and when Frank let me know that he had rented an apartment and had had soldiers put our belongings in place. I said goodbye to my mother, my brother Bob, his wife Lyn, and Bill, my youngest brother, who had recently married a lovely widow from Guadalajara, and boarded the train on January 17th, 1956, seven months pregnant. I had sent our cat, Bobo, to Frank by plane the day before. My mother had promised me she would join us before the baby was due in March, and I was confident I would have her at my side. The train trip was uneventful except for the old conductor reaching through the curtains to my bed early in the morning and tapping me on the stomach to advise me that we were about to arrive in Torreón. When the train drew up at the station, Frank was waiting, accompanied by two doctors with whom he had made friends, Dr. Angel Aguilar, and Dr. David Cruz, who have remained our friends throughout the years. He took me to the apartment, on the third floor, and I was surprised at how well he had arranged the furniture and made everything as cozy as he could. Our first night together, on our little porch overlooking the Plaza, was a happy romantic one. The rest of our married life lay before us.

TORREON

We arrived in Torreón in January of 1956, our baby being due in March. Our pleasant apartment was on the third floor of a building on the corner of Avenida Morelos, one of the main and prettiest avenues in the city, and consisted of three bedrooms, one overlooking the plaza, as well as a porch running along the side, living-dining room, a long hall with a bathroom, and a large kitchen. It did not have an air conditioning unit although each room had vents for one, so I had to leave the windows wide open for the breeze, which was almost non-existent. When there was a dust storm, which was frequent, a cloud of dust would fly in and cover our floors and furniture immediately before one had time to close all the windows. However, Frank was alotted a young soldier to clean up, who would arrive early every morning, dressed in olive green khakis and wearing heavy boots, to do the heavy chores such as mopping the floors of the apartment and the porch. I would also ask him occasionally to do errands. There was a market nearby which I hated to go into as it was full of flies, and the floors were always wet from the vendors spraying their fruit. Later on I would have the money to hire a maid, but at the beginning I only had the soldier, and thank God for him!

The day I arrived, Frank and I decided to walk to a nearby restaurant to have lunch, where they served mostly tacos, tostadas, light meals, sandwiches etc. As we were leaving our apartment, a light wind was starting up. By the time we got to the end of the block, the air was white with dust, the wind blowing it all in our faces. I remember cars passing us by with people peering at us through the windows as if we were mad to walk in the dust storm, which I later learned were called "tolvaneras". This is a local word, as it does not exist in the dictionary, and should be called "polvareda", polvo meaning dust. Anyway, this was our initiation, and we found that later on, especially during the month of March, there were to be many more "tolvaneras".

Torreón is about seven hours, by toll roads, from the border with El Paso, Texas, and about eight or nine hours southwards, to Mexico City. I am talking about today's divided highways, but before, it used to take us twelve hours to drive to Mexico City, and at least ten hours to get to El Paso. Frank would leave early every morning for the Battalion, in the lower part of an old house on a hill , referred to as "The Wulff House", to consult the soldiers. The more serious problems were taken to the Military Infirmary downtown, where he took care of all the surgery. His obligation was to dedicate two hours every morning to the army, unless a surgery took longer or he had too many consultations. The rest of the day he was free for his private practice.

Torreón, Coahuila: desert, sun, sky. A young city, looking forward to its fiftieth anniversary at the time. Located along the border of the Nazas River, it is at the center of the Laguna region, which I referred to before. The weather can be extreme, and temperatures can rise to 100° F in summer, and mostly very cold during winter, but it has snowed only twice in the fifty-two years we have been here. Very few rains are registered, and those which fall are almost always preceded by severe dust storms.The old Wulff house, where the batallion was now located, had been the first elegant house built in Torreón by a German engineer named Federico Wulff in 1905, two years before Torreón had become a city. In the mid 1800's, men with great vision had come to this hot arid area, bordering the great Nazas River, finding the terrain favorable for farming cotton, amongst other crops. There were swamp areas in places, result of the river overflowing into the lowlands. They bought farm land from its original owners and proceeded to build the first dam. The Torreón Ranch was the first one where a tall Torreón (tower) had been built to protect the ranch against the Apache indians, still fighting against development of what they considered their land. Thus, the name of Torreón remained as the name of the city. Other cotton farmers soon built around it. Eventually, thanks to the visionary Don Andres Eppen, an important business man associated with a cotton company, the railroad tracks were built in 1883, connecting with the central railroad four years later. Cotton farmers could now export their cotton bales all over the country. In 1893 Torreon was designated as a Villa, and in 1907 it was finally named a City. Mr. Federico Wulff, a German engineer who happened to be visiting Lerdo, a small nearby city, was requested to map out the streets in the downtown area, starting from the railroad track, which he did, despite the fact that he had not brought his working tools with him. He measured the width of the city streets in "varas", a Spanish measure, which did not coincide with the meters he had in mind, reason for which the streets in Torreon are much wider than intended, an asset in later days. He decided to build his house on the hill overlooking the railroad crossing. It took two years to build, and when finished, had all the conveniences, made out of brownstone, wooden floors, tiled kitchen, seventeen rooms and a cellar. He even built a large cement water deposit which could be used as a swimming pool. He and his family lived in the house for many years, after which it was occupied by his many descendants, and much later used as headquarters for the Military Battalion. This is where Frank reported for work, but eventually the army moved, and the house was abandoned, falling into complete decay. Ultimately, in 1991, a new municipal government decided to refurbish it, and after extensive work, it was opened to the public as a Museum known today as La Casa del Cerro, The House on the Hill, a fine example of one of the first elegant houses ever built in this city.

We knew no one when we first arrived, but Frank met a few of the military doctors, who in turn, introduced him to various established civilian doctors. One, an obstetrician, invited him several times to be his assistant in surgery, a most welcome opportunity, which provided us with a little extra money. Of the two doctors who had accompanied him to the station to meet me, one was a pediatrician, and the other was an anesthetist, and they suggested renting an old house downtown between the three of them to consult. Frank was game, so they rented a house on Avenida Juarez, one of the central avenues, and opened shop. Frank's exploration table and implements, as well as other necessary furniture for his office, were ordered by Frank, but paid for by his generous father. Now Doctor Balderrama was set to start consulting. Some of his first patients were sent to him by the family of the lady whose food hamper he had shared on the train, and they in turn sent him other patients, so that in a few weeks Frank was earning enough to clear his two rents and our expenses. Of course added to this, was the base wage the army paid him every month.

One day I was walking down the palm-lined Avenida Morelos, when I spied a small curio shop across the street from the Nazas Hotel. I stopped to look in the window, and almost immediately, an elderly American lady came out and started to speak to me in English, it being obvious that I too was a foreigner. She informed me that her name was Mary Elizabeth Goddard de Botello, but that everyone called her Mary Lib. She asked me to come in and meet her mother, which I did. Her mother was a white-haired, sweet old southerner, and they both encouraged me to sit down and talk. I told them my husband was a new doctor in town and that we lived on this same avenue, across from the Plaza Juarez and the old City Hall. She was thrilled that there was an English-speaking doctor in town and told me about a large foreign colony of residents, many working for cotton companies from the United States and Switzerland, as well as for John Deere and other international companies. She said she would like to have us over to her apartment soon to meet them as she was sure they would all be interested in Frank's services as a doctor. I liked her instantly, and she and her family remained our friends for the rest of their lives.

Meanwhile, Frank had met and was charmed by the pediatrician at the Military Hospital, a Dr. Tinajero, who had a bombastic, humorous personality, and Frank wanted me to meet him and his beautiful wife. He brought him home one night without letting me know, and I'll never forget I was sitting at my old sewing machine, making a loose cover for the sofa bed, (yes, I actually used to sew!) when they walked in the front door. Our apartment was still very barren, and I felt like Little Nell out of a Charles Dickens novel, mending clothing. He lost no time in exclaiming, "Oh, so you like to sew? Well, my wife prefers to read!" making me feel completely illiterate. His visit was short, but he invited us to go with them the next evening to meet some other doctors and their wives in the adjacent Gomez Palacio, which is in the state of Durango. I learned that Gomez Palacio and Torreon are twin cities, although in different states, only separated by four miles and a bridge over the now non-existent Nazas River. He and his wife picked us up, and yes, she was quite beautiful and very friendly. We went to a Dr. Galindo's house, who was married to an attractive American girl who welcomed us to the group. There was another American girl there, Laura, married to another doctor, but I soon learned that these two girls did not mix with the foreign colony, but only with the locals. I remember I first tasted Chile con Queso that night, which is a typical dish in the north, and I loved it. It consists of strips of large green stuffing chiles, sautéed with onion, and then added cream and grated Chihuahua cheese, similar to Jack cheese. This is put in the oven briefly until it melts. Tortilla chips were passed around, and we all gorged ourselves on the casserole. On the way home I realized there were speed bumps on the bridge and that he was driving over them so fast I was afraid with each bump that it would bring forth the baby I was carrying. However we arrived home safely.

We had not had a phone connected yet, but on the street corner below us there was a taxicab stand where the drivers did us the favor of lending us their phone and even ringing our bell if Frank had an urgent phone call. Well, that night they had received a call for Frank. He was asked to report to a doctor he knew to help him in an operation. It was already about 2 A.

M., but off he went, eager to be of service. I realized the beauty of living in a small city, when complete strangers were friendly enough to take calls for you! I cannot complain about those first months in Torreon. People were extra nice to us and we have continued to be friends with many of the people we met at the very beginning.

Dr. Aguilar, who shared the office building with Frank, and his wife Tere, were two of the first people who invited us for dinner at their house in Torreon. They lived nearby, and so we walked over at the specified time, eight o'clock. We knocked on their door, but only after knocking several times did he finally come to the door. The hall was in darkness behind him, and Frank asked, "Did you say this Friday, or did we make a mistake?" He smiled, "No, no, come on in. We didn't expect you so early." (We had yet to learn that guests usually arrived about half an hour to an hour after the time one is invited.) He ushered us into a dark living room and turned on the lights. His wife was nowhere to be seen. I did not know her, so was looking forward to meeting her. The doctor said he'd get us a drink, and left the room. We waited and waited. Finally he came back with some little aperitif, and sat and talked with us. Still no wife. Another couple came about a half hour later, he a short dark doctor, she a tall, lovely, young, beautifully coiffed, sophisticated wife, Loló. We were introduced and made stiff conversation while our host disappeared. Minutes later, Tere, our hostess, burst into the dining room from the kitchen, apron still tied around her waist, laughing and apologizing for not having received us, but saying she had had to finish making the soup. She was a short, pretty blonde lady, speaking with a definite Spanish accent, as her family had all come over from Spain in the thirties. We finally sat down at the table, and had the afore-mentioned soup, which was delicious, well worth waiting for. She was an excellent cook, and the rest of the meal went off fine, with highbrow conversation, as Loló was into Mexican literature, politics, and travel, all of which I yet knew nothing. I did not say much that night, but was spellbound by Loló. Later I learned that she often performed in local stageplays, and was considered an exceptionally good amateur actress. Any wonder, she was clearly so self-confident and beautiful.

A few days later, Mary Lib Botello came by to invite us to a cocktail party at her apartment, fairly close to ours. Frank had purchased a second hand car, a 1950 blue Mercury coupé, six years old, but our very first car! We arrived at the address she had given us, a large apartment on Avenida Colón, another important avenue. Here we were welcomed on time, American style, by Mary Lib and her husband Rafael Botello, who started presenting us to over a dozen couples. We were very young, and they were all a little older than we were, interested in the young doctor and his bride, asking many questions about how we had met and how long we had been married. The Botellos had a son, whom they nicknamed Pachal, although his name was like his father. He immediately asked me how old I was and when I told him I was twenty-four, he told me I was twice his age, twelve. Now, fifty odd years later, the joke between us is that I am still twice his age when he refers to me!

I remember several outstanding couples we met that night: the Bombardiers, both tiny people, she, talking with an exagerated southern accent, he, talking and looking like "Mr. McGoo"; the Edelens, she, a striking tall ex-Powers model, he, a fair, handsome bespectacled man; the Fordes, he a large portly English gentleman, she a sweet southern gal from Tennessee; the Barnards, she, a tall, striking blonde from California, he, a good looking, young, part-time artist who worked at the Electric Light Company; the Withingtons, he, a tall talkative American who had been born in Hawaii, and she, from Washington state, quiet and cultured; and last but not least, the Barboglios, he, a tall good looking cattle rancher, and she an attractive tall woman, both from Texas. Quite a group! Later on, at another party, (and there were many parties in those days) we met the Barnetts, both English brought up in Mexico much as I was; the Hubers, he, Swiss, she, a red headed glamorous American woman; the Pochés, both from New Orleans. In all, Torreón had a large, diverse crowd of foreigners.

By this time we had been in contact with Frank's aunt and uncle who lived in nearby San Pedro, and whom we had visited two years before. They were thrilled to have us in Torreón and immediately offered to lend us their daughter Yoyo's bedroom set, which they had previously intended to sell. They sent it over, a dark wooden headboard and double bed, as well as a dressing table with a big octagonal mirror. It was not to my taste but who were we to refuse a kind offer when all we had was the single bed my mother had given us two years ago. We put Yoyo's furniture in the main bedroom, and left the single bed in the other bedroom, ready for my mother's imminent visit.

Our social life took a giant leap forward, and when my mother arrived in the middle of March, she couldn't get over the amount of acquintances we had made. She said we had to do something about the baby's room, for all we had was the bare room which I had decorated with little cutout animals on one wall, and two long wooden medical boxes which we had painted, and for which I had made a pleated cotton skirt with a mirror over it. Frank's uncle's sisters had lined a beautiful basket with blue satin and little pink rosettes around the edge, and a mattress stuffed with cotton, covered in the same material. Very unappropiate for placing the baby in a hot climate. My mother had embroidered two little white sheets, and knitted a pink sweater. I had started a yellow sweater, but never finished it. I was definitely not a knitter!

OUR BABY'S ARRIVAL

One morning early I woke up with a pain in my lower abdomen, and I knew the baby must be coming. I rose while Frank was still sleeping and went to the bathroom to comb my hair and put on lipstick for I did not want to be taken to the hospital without my mouth painted. That's about all I did paint in those days.

Shortly after, when I came out, my mother saw me wincing, and she said, "Tell Frank the baby is coming!" But I had heard about false alarms and insisted I had better wait. She knew the signs however, and woke Frank herself. When he saw me recoiling, he hurriedly dressed and told my mother and me to ready ourselves and get in the car with him to drive to the Sanatorio Español, the Spanish Hospital. We had previously decided on a veteran doctor to attend to me as we had assumed that Frank would be too nervous at that time to attend to me himself, despite the fact that this was his specialty, obstetrics! We checked in at the hospital and when I got to the room, my water broke and all hell let loose. The pains were suddenly terrible, and I remember telling my mother between moans and yells, "How could you have gone through this seven times?" Frank would look at me with an ashen face and leave the room to talk to the doctor, and the nurse would examine me again. Finally I was wheeled into the delivery room and they gave me a shot to relieve the pain, and voilá, my baby was born, four hours and a half from start to finish. The next thing I knew I was resting in bed with Frank and my mother at my feet, and my tiny baby in a crib by my bed. In those days they used to leave the newborn baby in a high small metal crib by its mother. I peered at him, and saw he was wrapped tightly like a little taco, all red in the face, and looking precious to me. I felt so proud that I had a son! Unbelievable that I had produced that little mite. I got a lump in my throat when I saw Frank looking proudly at his son and my mother crying with relief that it was all over. Frank kissed me and we choked up together. I can't remember how long it was until the nurse put him to my breast, where he started nursing immediately. I lay back and rested when they put him back in his crib, and people started arriving with presents. I think all the foreign colony came to see me that day or the next with little presents, stuffed puppies, teddy bears, hand knitted sweaters, booties, etc. No disposable diapers! In those days one had to wash their supply of diapers every day. How I would have enjoyed the advantages modern mothers have today!

We would have named him Frank, for Francisco, like his Daddy and his grandfather, but there was already a Frankie in the family, the son of my husband's brother Hank, having been the first grandchild in the family. We decided on Anthony Francis, Saint Anthony having been my favorite saint for years, and the name which I had chosen when I was confirmed in San Antonio, Texas, right before I was married. So our little son was called Tony from then on.

I believe I was in the hospital for three days, and when I got home I relied heavily on my mother for everything. She did the shopping and the cooking until we hired a maid, a woman who had worked for the family that Frank had met on the train, and was highly recommended by them. She was an older woman, Lola, sweet, sympathetic, and helpful. Her cooking wasn't bad either, so things went along successfully until my mother had to return to Mexico City. Before she left, she went downtown and bought the baby a lovely blue baby bed with a screen cover to go over it at nights. After she had gone, I entered a sharp depression, which I imagine is what is referred to now as post-partum blues. I was exhausted from having a baby who cried all day and all night, only quiet when he was at my breast. Frank and I were desperate, not knowing what the matter was, until he called in Dr. Cruz, the pediatrician who shared his office building. The doctor took one look at the baby and declared "This child is very undernourished and clearly not getting enough to eat! I suggest you add three half-bottles of this brand of powdered milk mixed with boiled water to his diet, along with your breast milk". Abra-cadabra, like a miracle, the baby began to sleep well and gain weight rapidly. The poor little fellow had been crying from hunger. I felt pangs of guilt for not having enough milk in my breasts, and Frank felt guilty he had not recognized the clear symptoms of hunger. Now little Tony gained weight so quickly that a few months later, Chavela, a dear friend of my mother, arrived from Mexico City and came over to visit me. She bent over the crib and exclaimed that his eyes looked Chinese because he was so fat. True, his brown eyes were almost like slits above his fat little cheeks. He continued to grow, and would sleep the whole night after his last bottle, letting us rest after having had so many sleepless nights.

Our friends all belonged to the country club in Gomez Palacio, and urged us to become members so we could enjoy the swimming pool, where they would congregate for lunch a few times every week, taking sandwiches and refreshments. Frank and I would leave Tony with Lola for a couple of hours while we joined the group. Later, when he was older, we used to take him along with us.

Frank had made two investments when he started having a little spare money, one in a mine with another doctor, and the other in a small drugstore with two other doctors. The mine never paid off, and he lost his money, which had not been very much to start with, but the drugstore paid for itself during a few years till he finally sold it. Another investment, and probably the best one we ever made, was the lot our house sits on today. It was five blocks from the Campestre Lagunero country club, and sat in front of a house belonging to some friends of ours, the Kangases. Also, Frank had sold his little blue coupé and bought another second hand Ford '53 from a friend. We were doing quite well financially, and all because his patients had found Frank to be a very good physician and surgeon.

I had seen in a magazine a lovely bedroom set consisting of a headboard with room for books, side tables, and a large chest of drawers, in pale gray wood, and asked Frank if we could afford to have it made. We looked around and found a responsible cabinet maker only two blocks from where we lived. He gave us a price to make it in mahogany, we gave him a downpayment, and he promised to have it ready in three weeks. Of course, it took a lot longer, more like two months, but he made it just like the clipping from the magazine, and gave the wood a pale gray sheen, with the grain showing through. Beautiful finish. We were so proud of it. But before we could move it into our apartment, we had to move cousin Yoyo's loaned bedroom set out. She was disappointed, for I believe she had thought we would eventually buy it from her. I had a seamstress make a pale gray counterpane just like in the picture, with two pale pink pillows to top it off. When it was done, I invited every guest we had to come see our bedroom!

Frank's family came for a visit from Los Angeles in August, especially to meet their new grandchild, and fell in love with him. The bond between Tony and his grandfather was instant, and lasted for the rest of Abuelito's (Grandpa's) days. Frank's sisters, Irma and Margie came with them and slept on the sofa bed, while the parents slept in our bedroom and we stayed in the guest room. The family brought with them boxes of all kinds of groceries to help out, and I let my mother-in-law take over the kitchen while she was here, poor woman, but she did it gladly. I would take Irma and Margie to the country club in the mornings to swim, leaving little Tony with his grandparents, and when we got back, lunch was made and Frank was home. I now realize how selfish it was on my part to leave them with all that responsibility. Years later I told my mother-in-law, whom I called "Mamá" from the very beginning, how I regretted my irresponsible actions, but being the best mother-in-law a girl could ever find, she was sweet enough to answer that I was young and had done it to entertain my sisters-in-law.

While they were in town, we took advantage of their stay to baptize our son. We chose young Margie as his Godmother, and I wanted Ted, my brother in San Francisco, to be his Godfather by proxy, so Frank's father stood in for him. Tony was so cute at the ceremony, sitting in Margie's arms and trying to grab the flame on the priest's candle while gurgling with joy. The priest asked us why we had waited so long, as most families baptized their children while they were still tiny babies, but we explained we had been waiting for the family to arrive.

We spent our first Christmas in Torreón. There was a round of cocktail parties which started weeks before, given by many couples in the foreign group, and it seems we attended most of them. On Christmas Day we were invited to have dinner with the Botellos, Mary Lib, Rafael her husband, Mrs. Goddard, her mother, and their young son, Pachal. I think she invited another couple, as Mary Lib was always kind enough to invite people who were alone without families in town. I'm sure she invited Sonia, who was an attractive Russian widow, a longtime resident of Torreon who lived in a beautiful house of her own. Sonia spoke with a pronounced Russian accent, and had an eye for attractive males. Mary Lib was an excellent cook, and decorated her table beautifully with all her crystal and old silver, belonging to her mother. Her father had been an American doctor in Chihuahua years before, married Katherine Goddard, from Missouri, and lived first in Chihuahua, where he practiced medicine for many years. After Mary Lib was born, he became the company doctor for a cotton company in the town of Tlahualilo, near Torreón, where many foreign families lived, so Mary Lib had grown up in Torreón.

We had had someone take our picture with our little boy at our apartment, and integrated it into our Christmas cards, which we sent out to family and friends. Frank and Tony gave me my first portable typewriter, a Lettera, which I used until I bought this computer three years ago, and on which I wrote my first book, "Bilimbique", in 2003. How much easier it is to write on the computer! Friends, and especially my son Tony, had encouraged me to buy one for years, but I was stubborn and said my trusty old typewriter was all I needed. How dumb!

In 1957 Tony was one year old in March, and I invited one little boy who was his same age, and his mother, and we had a little cake at the dining table with Daddy present, and my dear friend Mary Lib. The little boy, Jaime Poché, became Tony's closest friend throughout the first 7 years of his life, until the Pochés returned to the States. My mother arrived for a few days' visit, and was féted by our group of friends, who always commented how attractive and charming she was. Later, my always glamorous sister Vic came, and then Frank's sister Irma and her husband, Fred Dalton, passed by Torreón on their way back from Acapulco and Mexico City for their honeymoon. We had not been able to attend their wedding in Los Angeles as intended, because at the last minute, Frank did not receive his permit from the army to leave the country. This was the story of every vacation while Frank was in the army. He would request certain days' leave and then wait breathlessly till the permit arrived, sometimes only hours before we were supposed to leave! On one occasion, many years later, on our way to Europe, he still had not received his permit by the time our plane left for Mexico City to make our connection. From there we were to fly out to London the next day. He told me to go ahead the night before, so I flew off and checked in at the airport hotel. I advised them at the desk, before I went up to my room, that my husband would be arriving in the middle of the night, or early the next morning. They nodded, uh huh, but it sounded like a lovers' tryst. Frank arrived as promised on the early morning flight, but they scrutinized him at the desk with raised eyebrows before letting him up.

At the end of July 1957, Mexico City and Acapulco suffered one of its worst earthquakes. Parts of buildings fell off, and one of Mexico City's beloved landmarks, the beautiful Golden Angel, which sat atop a slender column inaugurated in 1910, came crashing to the ground. Residents saw it as an omen of worse things to come. My mother's apartment fared well, as did Bob and Lyn's, but my mother was terribly frightened. She told me later that she had been in the bathtub at the time, and the water had started to slosh out of the tub. Trembling, she got out and dried herself, preparing to run into the street, but it turned out that by that time it was over and there was no need. Still, it left her nervous for months, like most of the city's inhabitants.

In September of that year, Torreón celebrated its Golden Anniversary as a City. They conducted a contest among the young society girls to see who would be the queen, and there was a grand Ball held for the winner, where she would be crowned.

A local committee organized a wonderful style show of period dresses, worn about fifty years ago, and I was asked to model a wedding dress which had belonged to Mrs. Katherine Goddard during that epoch. She told me I was the only one who could possibly fit into her beautiful old dress, and I modeled it with pride. The show was a sensation with songs and dances from the beginning of the century, and I must say that it was all coordinated very professionally by local society ladies. There was a lot of local talent in the city, and Frank and I attended many stage shows at a new theatre they were building, where the residents acted and directed. I could hardly believe how professional the actors were. One would think they were off the Mexico City stages, where my mother and I had been avid theatre goers before I was married.

Another Christmas in Torreon arrived, after the usual round of cocktail parties. I remember going over to Sonia's house for a lovely party that year. She met her guests at the door with a shot of Vodka in her hand and a small tray of caviar on little buns held by a waiter at her side. "This is a Russian pahty tonight" she said, so we drank Vodka all evening until she served a lovely dinner at the table, starting with a delicious Borcht, which I had never tasted, and which I did not taste again until we went to Russia in 1990, at which time I did not like it as much as Sonia's. The crowd we had joined was an international one, and we were the benefitted ones, for they afforded us the opportunity to see, through their example, how to entertain, being from various countries such as Switzerland, England, Russia and the United States, and most of them being a widely travelled bunch. We were invited to brunches where they served us oysters Rockefeller, eggs Benedict, Bananas Foster; luncheons with Lobster thermidor, dinners with Indian curry or Chicken Kiev or Goulash, and many other dishes which we had never tasted before. My mother had always been a roast beef or pork loin with mashed potatoes type of cook, and Frank's mother made mostly Mexican-style food with an American accent, so these dishes, and the savoir fare which we encountered, were educational in our young lives. They were all older than we, which put them at a definite advantage, and they accepted and treated us as the "kids" of the group, expecting little in return.

Frank's mother and father had urged Frank to return to the United States once his obligation towards the Mexican army was over in six years. They knew an old Mexican doctor in Los Angeles with a large clientele, who was planning on retiring in a few years. They were sure Frank could pass a Board Exam and be free to practice there, perhaps even take over this doctor's practice. But we were doing too well, and having fun doing it! Frank would not even think of leaving Torreon because of the amount of patients he had accumulated, not only from the foreign colony but from local society residents. For the moment we were satisfied with the status quo.

FRANK'S ACCIDENT

At the end of February of 1958 my mother visited us again, which turned out to be a lucky event, because the morning after she arrived, Frank left for work very early, and about an hour later, I had a phone call (yes, we finally had a phone!) telling me to come to the Red Cross Hospital in Gomez Palacio, the neighboring city. They said my husband had had an accident but told me nothing more. I asked my mother to stay with the baby, and took a cab to the Red Cross. On the way, as we crossed the train tracks, I had an erie feeling that the accident might have involved the train, as he had commented to me a few weeks before that when crossing the tracks a train had barely missed him. He had always been a distracted driver, and when I saw him laid out in the hospital I realized with a sinking heart that this had been a near-fatal accident. His left ear was almost entirely cut off, he had lacerations all over his face, and his arm was obviously broken. The doctors commented on how miraculous he had not ended up with more broken bones or a crushed torso. He was only semi-conscious and they told me they were going to transfer him to the Sanatorio Español in Torreón for surgery. I was stunned, and did not want to break down in front of the staff, so I only hugged him and told them I wanted to ride along with him in the ambulance, which I did. They informed me that the accident had taken place on the tracks, on a back road leading out of the residential colony where we had our lot. The train had hit his car and carried it for about 100 meters, where it fell off the track into a ditch. Needless to say, the ride to the hospital was a terrible one. I kept thinking what would happen if he should die and leave me and our little son, but he started mumbling and my hopes rose. He was young and strong, and with the right medical care he would come through. I was sure of it. When we got to the hospital, the two doctors with whom he shared his office building were already there, and somehow, two American couples we knew had heard about the accident and were waiting for us. In a small city like Torreón in those days, news spreads quickly. Actually, it still does, fifty years on.

I called my mother and she immediately called Frank's parents in L. A., describing his accident, and then joined me at the hospital. Having her by my side I felt strong enough to face whatever might come. By this time Frank was in surgery, and when he was finally brought to his room several hours later his right arm was in a cast, and his head was all bound up. The doctor told me he was suffering from severe concussion and had to be kept lying completely flat. Several doctors came to see him, but one, his friend, Dr. Aranda, an osteopathic surgeon who had put his arm in a cast, became his main doctor, and I am eternally grateful to him. When Frank eventually came out of the anaestesia, I realized his mind was very disturbed, as he complained dreadfully about the cast, and pleaded with me to go to his car and bring him his surgical scissors to cut it off. I had to humour him, and the cast remained on for six weeks. His parents called me several times a day, and wanted to speak to him, but I could hardly connect them, first because the phones were only in the administrative offices, and second, their son was too confused to have a conversation with anyone. I hesitated to tell his parents his mental condition, and complained instead about the lack of phones in the rooms. They were terribly worried, as they should have been, and asked me if they should come, but feeling that he would soon come around, I reassured them and told them to wait a while. Every night I would leave the hospital late and go back to the apartment where my mother would be awake and my little son fed and peacefully asleep. There was always some friend visiting the hospital who would take me home where my mother held the fort tirelessly. The following morning I would take a cab to the hospital and remain there the whole day.

One morning a doctor whom I knew only slightly, approached me and informed me that several doctors had gotten together and decided to ask me if I needed financial help while Frank was in the hospital. I thought this was an astoundingly kind offer, especially since our time in Torreón had been a short one, and none of them were close friends of ours, but told him that luckily our savings would carry us through the ordeal. The truth was that Frank had been so exraordinarily lucky with his consultations and operations, that we had recently bought the aforementioned lot in Gomez Palacio, near the country club, and were making plans to build our home on it in a year or two. This, after only having been established for less than two years! God had been good to us, and now this. Never feel too sure of your luck was a lesson I learned early. The American colony rallied to our side too, and visited us at the hospital almost daily, sometimes bringing me food. Our dear friends, the Botellos, invited my mother to their home often, and offered to bring her and take her from the hospital whenever she wanted. Thinking back I do not remember what she did about her job in Mexico City. I imagine she left that job and found another one when finally she returned over a month later. I was not thinking of anything else but Frank's health during those days, confident that my mother was taking care of our little boy.

The weeks passed, and finally they released Frank from the

hospital. It was difficult for him to manipulate anything at home with his left hand, and he needed help for bathing and dressing. Luckily, his mental condition had improved, and he had accepted the cast and told me more about his almost fatal accident. It seems that the morning he had visited a patient in the Las Rosas colony, (where we had bought the lot) he found their daughter in need of an emergency appendectomy, instructing them to meet him at the Sanatorio Español, and going on ahead, taking the shortcut over a back hill and the railroad tracks. He said he had the radio on, listening to the morning news, and his windows were all closed, so he never heard the train hooting at him. The train hit him full broadside, and carried the car for about a hundred meters, finally pushing it off to one side into the ditch, but his mind blanked out since the moment of the crash. Someone must have called the Red Cross, for they immediately went to the site and pried him out from the car, not without difficulty. From his identification papers they found our telephone number and called me to go to his side. The car was totally destroyed. It was a second-hand four-year old Ford which Frank had just bought from a friend to take the place of our original little blue coupé.

Right before my mother returned to Mexico City, I decided I should give a little party in appreciation for the people who had been so nice to us at the hospital. My mother was doubtful of Frank's condition and did not think the party was a good idea. He had not returned to work yet, and was suffering from a terrible depression. But foolish girl that I was, I went through with the plan. About twenty people came, and I had made a big pot of chili con carne and rice, plus dips and other snacks. I made martinis and daiquiris, but found that most people asked for Scotch, of which I had only bought one bottle, so they all ended up drinking my mixed concoctions. I had borrowed two army cots for extra seating, covered them with army blankets, and prepared to receive the crowd. It was to be a real stand-up party, not at all appropiate for my menu. At one point, two of our male guests decided to both sit on one of the army cots, but being big men, their weight caused the poor flimsy cot to come crashing down! Everyone started to laugh, and it only added to the fun. Looking back, they must have been a most forgiving lot for I did not have enough of anything, and this included liquor and glasses and plates. I think I must have bought some plastic ones, or cardboard ones in those days. How awful! But everyone seemed to have a good time, and were happy to see Frank at home again. My mother was the belle of the ball, as usual. Her personality was vivid, and everyone still found her very attractive. She was about 65 years old at the time, with a good figure and a smile for everyone. As far as I was concerned, the party was a great success. Only now, after so many years of entertaining, I cringe to think about how I had the nerve to host such a celebration. There's youth for you! Eventually Frank went back to his consulting, arm in a cast and all, and his depression gradually lessened every day. My mother left for Mexico City, and our days went back to almost normal. Naturally we had to have another car, so this time he bought a '58 Opel, our first NEW car, small, but pretty.

March 24th came around again, and our Tony became two years old. The best present of all was to have his father back from the edge of death. He never knew how close he came to being left fatherless. Every evening I would take my little son out onto our porch overlooking the plaza and hold him in my arms to watch the lowering of the flag and hear the bugle play its sad tune, ta-tán ta-tán ta-tán. Since he was learning to say his first words, he would raise his little hand, and look at me and say "Ta-tán!" So it became known as the ta-tán hour to us.

In July of that year, one of Frank's patients gave him a goat. Living in an apartment, it was a most unwelcome gift, but I decided we would tie it up on the roof above our apartment and feed it for a day or so until we could have it killed, to cook it in the oven. But of course I had never tasted or cooked a goat before, and did not have the faintest idea of what it entailed. I consulted with Tere Aguilar, Dr. Aguilar's wife, an excellent cook herself, and she told me I should first inject the dead goat (I had the soldier take it to the market to be killed and skinned) under its skin, with olive oil, all over, then salt and pepper it and roast it for I forget how long in the oven. Well, I did what she said, made a scalloped potato casserole to go with it, a green salad, and invited the Aguilars and the Tinajeros over for supper. It went off well, except it was kind of difficult to cut up the roasted goat at the table. (I served it whole!) Aside from that, it tasted pretty darned good, poor animal. Today I would never think of having it killed, loving animals the way I do, but would either give it away or keep it as a pet until it died of old age.

One of the best things that happened that year was our move from the apartment to a nice little house in Colonia Las Rosas, four blocks away from where we had bought our lot, in the adjacent city of Gomez Palacio, which is in the state of Durango. Some friends of ours had moved away into a larger house, and this one met all our needs, with four bedrooms, bath, dining area, living room and kitchen, as well as nice back and front gardens. What more could we ask? Our furniture was lost in it, until some other friends moved away shortly after, and we were able to buy their two den couches, coffee table, and two side tables, as well as two arm chairs. I forgot to mention that our dear friends, Harriet and John Gilman had recently moved into a gorgeous newly built company house and decided to get rid of their dining set, so she GAVE it to us right before we moved. What a generous gift! We were so grateful. It was made up of the table, six chairs and a sideboard. Now we had a furnished dining room, a complete living room, and our new bedroom furniture in the front bedroom next to Tony's. We still had the one single bed my mother had given us, so we had an identical one made with the furnituremaker and voilá, we had another bedroom set for the guest room. We also put the sofa bed in the third bedroom, along with a piano our friends had left us, to sell for them, when they moved away.

A few months after we moved in, we three were invited out to some friends' house for Sunday lunch. She served us a delicious but heavy meal which we enjoyed, and afterwards, they all decided to go to the movies. I said I had a slight stomach ache and would prefer to rest, but told Frank to go on with them. He left me at home resting and taking some medication. Luckily I had a maid in the house. (In those days, maids worked on Sundays, and were given a day off during the week. Don't even think of it now!) She was amusing Tony, so I laid down and fell asleep. I awoke to the most excruciating pain, and immediately asked her to call the movie theatre to have Frank paged, knowing that the administration at the theatre would insert a message on the screen, paging the person involved, in this case, "Dr. Balderrama call home, URGENTE". Within a few minutes, Frank was by my side with our friends. I was rushed to the Sanatorio Español and had blood taken for an immediate analysis, and yes, I had an acute appendecitis.

This time, my husband took charge and performed the apendectomy himself. I was glad my husband was a doctor, because on Sunday it might have been harder to find one in a hurry. Within a couple of days I was back home and feeling fine. When I walked into the front garden, still bent over from my healing incision, I saw Toña the maid feeding Tony at his little table which she had set up at the entrance. He seemed happy as could be, eating applesauce which she had made for him specially. I was so grateful for her competence and her warmth toward our little boy.

Christmas 1958, my sister Vic, and Dan, and her ten year old son visited us. They stayed in theuest room, and I borrowed a cot for Billy.Then my mother arrived, and I put her on the sofa bed in the extra room. Mother would get up early and play the piano, and the morning would start out very festively every day with so many guests, accompanied by background music. Tony was happy to be doted on by his grandmother Brown, aunt and uncle and cousin, whom he called "Cassan Billy". I think it must have been an unusually cold winter, because my sister, with her usual wit, commented that our guest room was so cold there were icicles hanging from the ceiling. I didn't believe her, but sure enough, when we checked, we noticed a small leek in one corner, from which hung little icicles. We put a small electric heater in their room and another in my mother's, although she had not complained.

Frank and I decided to give two Christmas cocktail parties to accommodate all our friends, the first on the 21st of December, and the second a week later. At the first party there would be 24 guests, and at the second there would be 26, because unexpectedly, my brother Bob and his wife Lyn had driven up from Mexico City to spend a few days with us. They stayed at the nearby Motel, but spent most of the time at our house. I have no idea what I served for food at the parties, but I do remember that everyone seemed to have fun. Must have been the martinis! Christmas day, we put extra extensions in the table so that we all fit, and Dan carved the turkey. Lyn, my-sister- in-law, had thoughtfully brought two cans of Crosse and Blackwell English Christmas Pudding. This has to be the most delicious pudding one could ever find, concentrated and heavy, with lots of dried fruits and suet. After the meal, she and I remained at the table after everyone had finished, and polished off the remains of the pudding, smacking our lips afterwards. I've never had one since, despite our many trips to England where I always forget to purchase some.

We went to California in March 1959, and while visiting Frank's family, Vic and Dan invited us to visit them in San Francisco. We left Tony with Frank's parents, and it tore me apart when he cried as we were leaving, but we knew he couldn't be in more loving hands. I can't imagine a more complete brief stay than the one which my sister Vic, with her usual efficiency, had planned for our two and a half days in that beautiful city. After they picked us up at the airport, we drove around down town, went over the Golden Gate Bridge to Sausalito, and back to Fisherman's Wharf, where we stopped at a delightful bar called the Buenavista Café, packed with people, where they invited us to taste our first Irish Coffee. I paid strict attention to the bartender's method of making it, and have tried to copy it since, exactly the same, but never as good as that first time. We went from there to pick up Billy, now a handsome eleven year old young man, and over to my brother Ted's. I had not seen Ted since he left Mexico City in 1952, and he had just married Rita the month before. Next morning after breakfast, Dan went to work, but Vic took us and Billy to board the famous cable car. We met Dan for a drink at The Top of the Mark, after which we met Ted for lunch in Chinatown. He insisted on ordering from the Chinese waiter a plate of "pok-flied-lice" (that tired old joke, which did not amuse the waiter). After lunch he drove us over Bay Bridge to the University of California in Berkely, with its impressive buildings and campus. That evening Vic and Dan took us to the famous transvestite show at "Finoccio's", where we were astonished when seeing the beautiful "women". Later we met Ted and Rita at their favorite restaurant, and on to the Papagayo Room, ending the evening again at the Buenavista Café. Next morning we flew back to Los Angeles, where we found that Frank's parents had gone to church with Tony. We met them there as they were just coming out. I leapt out of the car and ran toward Tony to pick him up, but he turned away from me and put his head against his grandmother's skirt. I was so hurt, but obviously, he was the one who was hurt for our leaving him. After the car ride home, things went back to normal and the next day we celebrated his third birthday party with the family.

Frank's parents visited us in our rented house that summer. They always drove from California, a two-day trip, Frank's dad being a cautious driver who never sped, a fine example for Frank, who drove too fast wherever he went. His mother had been suffering with pains in her legs for some time, and after examining her, Frank found she had varicous veins. To protect her from ulcering, he decided to perform surgery, a procedure called a saphenectomy, which consists of stripping the veins in the legs. It is a major operation, and Frank, who had been trained at a military hospital, and was accustomed to taking care of all types of general surgery on the military personnel, performed the operation at the Sanatorio Español with another military doctor to help him. She remained resting at our house for several days until she was able to walk around painlessly. My mother came to visit us at the same time, and Frank did a minor gynecological surgery on her. So we had the two mothers in rehabilitation at the same time. One day, at noon, three year old Tony came home from play school to find both women in their robes, and uttered in surprise, "¿Qué pasó? La una y ustedes todavía en bata!" (What happened? One o'clock and you women still in your robes!") We all roared with laughter. Frank's parents were really impressed with Tony's ability to speak in both Spanish and English without any accent whatsoever from the moment he began to articulate. I find this is common with many children brought up in foreign countries. Frank and I have always spoken to each other in English, and Tony could switch languages with ease, just as we could. When Frank's parents left, his mother had recuperated thoroughly, and both were proud of their son's excellent surgical ability.

Our friends, the Mcguinesses invited us to spend a weekend with them at the company house of the Light and Power Company at La Boquilla Dam, which was finished in 1916, for irrigation and supplying the north with electricity. Jim was the General Manager, and Kay, his wife, an attractive, agreeable woman. We drove to Camargo city, in the state of Chihuahua, and south from there to the dam. The first night after we arrived and had supper, Kay told us not to dress for breakfast next morning. "We'll have breakfast in our pajamas" she said. As they had told us it would be cold in the house, Frank and I had packed our old flannel pajamas and robes to wear, so we showed up for breakfast in our much worn attire and found, to our dismay, Kay looking very glamorous in a red lace peignoir and Jim in silk pajamas and robe. We felt like a couple of country bumpkins! We visited the hydroelectric plant at the base of the curtain as well as the offices, received a talk on how Torreón was supplied with electricity, thanks to this dam, walked around and admired the pecan trees, and left for Camargo city, still in Chihuahua, to have lunch. It was an uneventful but instructive weekend, but we enjoyed it and were flattered they had thought of inviting us.

Frank and I had previously begun to play tennis at the country club before his broken arm and shoulder, result of the accident. He found it difficult to swing a racquet after that, so we switched to golf, urged by our group of friends who nearly all played. We took classes from an attractive professor from Buenos Aires, who had all the ladies wanting to perfect their swing. He told me I had promise, and when I won my first local tournament, I was sold on golf and continued to play for the next forty years.

Next year I was invited to one of my girlhood friend's wedding in Mexico City. Tere was marrying a Mexican millionaire, and although she was only my age, he was at least thirty years her senior, and had already been married and divorced twice. I imagine he painted her a pretty picture of their future life together, travelling royally and owning a gorgeous home in Mexico City, because she was bowled over with the prospect. Frank said I should attend and take Tony with me, so I decided I would also take the "nanita" to take care of him while I joined in the festivities. I immediately had a fine seamstress make me a fitted lavender wool dress with satin cuffs and cummerbund, and borrowed a tiny hat and lavender half veil from Mary Lib, who had a collection of them. Tony, the nursemaid, and I boarded the train, Chepi occupying an upper berth, and Tony and I in the lower. When we arrived, my mother immediately expressed her opinion that it was terrible for this lovely young girl to "sell" herself to an old man, but I thought it was very glamorous, and was slightly envious of the life she would lead.

The first day I visited her, she showed me her engagement ring, a five carat diamond, which must have cinched the deal which convinced her to go ahead with the marriage. She took it off and handed it to little Tony who was intrigued by its sparkle, and who sat on the floor handling it, but I quickly relieved him of it, frightened he might misplace it. As a wedding gift I had brought her an Emily Post Book of Etiquette, believing it would be very handy in her new life, where she would have to entertain many wealthy guests from the social and political world.

The day of the wedding rolled around, and I attended the church ceremony with my mother. Tere looked beautiful and virginal, and the old groom look like a silver fox. From there we separated, as mother had another engagement, and I went on with Tere's family to the wedding banquet, where I was seated with the bride's sister, the son of ex-President Miguel Alemán, a well-known society girl whom I knew slightly, and four important members of the government. President Lopez Mateos sat at a nearby table with the bride and groom and family members. I was on cloud nine, drinking champagne and munching on finest caviar. The dinner was exquisite, and my table companions all paid me exceptional attention, being from out of town. I was feeling very glamorous in my lavender outfit, with my hair newly lightened to a platinum blonde, and later, when I ran into two fellow students from high school, they were amazed at how changed I looked since graduation. The dinner went on forever, with more champagne, followed by coffee and cognac, until it came time for the bride and groom to leave. They disappeared, and many of the group decided to meet them at the airport where they would be taking their flight to Paris. We crowded into cars and drove through the newly constructed " viaductos", a series of tunnels which carried us directly to the airport. We had two hours to wait for their departure, so in the meanwhile had umpteen cups of coffee. The brother of the bridegroom, only slightly younger than him, kept pleading with me to meet him the next day for coffee. I had forgotten how persistent Mexico City men can be when they set their sights on a woman, and although I kept reminding him I was married, and not open for coffee dates or any other type of meeting, he was stubborn. At the end, seeing my resistance, he gave up and invited me instead to a welcome home party for Tere and her husband when they returned from Europe, even promising to send his private plane for me and my husband.

At last the bride and groom arrived and boarded their plane midst mariachi music and loud goodbyes, and we were finally ready to go home at midnight. Needless to say I felt terrible next morning. My mother reminded me we were invited to lunch at my brother Bill's home. We went, but I must have looked like something the cat dragged in, circles under my eyes and still feeling altered from so much coffee and champagne. Bill took one look at me, heard about the wedding, and informed me that what I needed to perk me up was one solitary beer. I drank it under duress, and actually felt much better. A couple of days later we took the train home, and Frank and all our friends wanted to know about the big wedding. It had been in all the newspapers, and my picture had come out front and center standing by the bride and groom and his brother. Frank was not pleased. The sad part was that when the couple returned from Europe ahead of time, the bride went to her own home and starting filing for divorce. She told me later that he had taken his "man friend" with him, and was expecting a little "menage a trois" the second week in Paris. She was not game, and they ended by breaking up and returning to Mexico.

Back home, early on a Sunday morning, I was awakened by a wail in the distance. Finally I made out the words "Mammy, Mammy". I still did not connect them with Tony, thinking it was someone else's child wailing in the distance. Suddenly I bolted out of bed and looked into Tony's room where I saw his empty bed. I dashed to the front door, found it open, and looked across the street, where I could see a little head bobbing up from a hole in the sidewalk. I rushed across, and sure enough, the hole was full of water and my child was in it up to his neck, leaves all over his head, his tricycle wedging him inside. I yanked the tricycle out, pulled my son to safety and crossed to our front gate where I began to call Frank as loud as I could. He came out, and both of us hugged Tony, who was crying inconsolably. Later we crossed over and examined the hole. It had been made to unstop a gutter, and not covered over, now being a certain danger to anyone who passed by. It had rained the night before and filled the hole with water and leaves. Tony had risen before us, crept to the front door, unlocked it and grabbed his tricycle to ride across the street, where he peered into the hole and lost his balance. All this while we were sleeping soundly. After that, we put in a crossbar higher than he could reach, although I don't think he would ever have tried that trick again!

Tony had started to go to playschool when he was three years old. I rememer the first day I took him to Miss Marta's house where she had a small group of children who all lived in nearby houses. She was a darling young girl who had just received her certificate as a teacher, and loved little children. Tony started bawling as soon as he realized I was leaving, and clung to my legs in desperation. I was ready to take him home again, until Marta coaxed him away and suggested I leave, assuring me he would calm down better without me. I didn't really believe her, but left, and hid outside the front door. Ten minutes later I went back to peek in, and to my surprise, Tony was already sitting with another little boy building a house of blocks, perfectly calm and satisfied. From then on, he went happily to play school five days a week.

About that time I wrote a poem for Tony:

"Though you are yet a child, my son, You'll make discoveries day by day. You'll find them not by my advice, But learn of them in your own way. You'll feel the bruises on your limbs, From falls, when learning how to walk; you'll know the joy of highest praise, When finally you start to talk. You'll fall to depths with each defeat, And rise again when once you win. You'll have to learn of Love and Hate, And words like Honesty and Sin. And then one day, a girlish form will make you see as lovers can… A sweet full mouth, a creamy leg, And you'll discover you're a man."

There was a new couple in town. He was a tall, very handsome man, George McKay, who was the new Superintendent at the Light and Power Company; Jane was a tall stunning brunette who used to come visit him from Mexico City, always bringing with her an older woman friend as a chaperone. Both Jane and George had been previously divorced, met in Mexico City, and after a few of these visits, decided to marry. We were very happy for them, and both were a glamorous addition to our group. She decided she would like to build a house, and like everything else she did, when finished, it was out of the ordinary, tastefully done, and rather exotic. The kitchen was round, and the whole house was floored in black tile. She hung black velvet drapes to frame the large picture windows in the living room-bar and her furniture was all in black, white and scarlet. Very dramatic.

Then the parties began. Jane loved to throw parties, and her first was a "Hangover Party" held on January lst, 1960, supposedly to get over the festivities of New Year's eve, which we usually celebrated at the downtown Casino. She met us at her front door with a small glass of a concoction prepared to "make you feel better". (I recalled my brother Bill making me drink a beer after the wedding in Mexico City.) This one had an absinthe base, which we tasted again when we visited New Orleans years later. Her table was set buffet style, with comfort food: a large tureen of "Fabada" , which is a Spanish recipe for a soupy dish of lima beans cooked with ham hock, pieces of ham, chorizo, tomatoes, onions, and garlic. She had small bowls for her guests to serve themselves, and hot buttered French bread in baskets. Delicious, and just the thing one felt like having after a night of mixed drinks. Needless to say, drinks were served, and when we left, everyone felt they would need another hangover party the next day!

That same year, Frank bought a new car, an English Vauxhall. It was a small, compact, pretty little car in navy blue, and we loved it. We had already started construction on our new home, about three blocks away from our rented house. We had chosen a popular young architect who had recently built the Gilman's and the Barnett's homes, both close friends of ours, whose houses we admired. I had seen pictures of what I wanted in an American magazine, and sent for the plans, which we handed over to Arquitecto José Tomás Ocampo. Of course the difference in the type of construction would present a problem because the American house was built of wood, and would need adaptation to the Mexican type of construction, which would be with bricks and cement. Aside from that, everything went well.

Almost every year I went to visit my mother in Mexico City, sometimes with Tony, sometimes alone, for a few days. At first I used the train, but later on I used to fly, taking a cab over to Mother's apartment. Most cabs in Mexico City are an experience in themselves, the front windshield usually decorated around the edges, and a virgin or religious ornament hanging from the rear-view mirror. The chauffeurs are very talkative, in their typical singsong lilt, and will comment on the weather, the political situation, and the economy in general. By the time I arrived at my mother's apartment, I knew a lot about what had been going on in the city. She and I would spend our days talking and going out to lunch every day, trying all the new restaurants, as well as the old ones we had previously frequented. Sometimes, outside of my mother's apartment, we could hear the "cilindrero" (organ grinder) playing. I have always loved that melancholy music, although their repertoire is rather limited. Once, when I was growing up, I paid one of them to play "La Palma" for me 14 times, but after about five repetitions, the neighbors came out on the street and told him to play something else, for heavens' sakes. During these visits to Mexico City, I got to see many old friends of mine as well as my mother's. In the evenings we would attend the theatre, for Mexico City always had a wonderful selection of plays, many of them translations from plays on Broadway. I would then return to Torreón, refreshed and eager to tell Frank of all the novelties in the beautiful city where I had grown up. But before I left, my mother and I would always walk to the corner Panadería

Elizondo, a wonderful bread shop, where my mother would treat me to a bag of good Mexican "pandulce" sweet breads to take back home, for they have never made pandulce in Torreón like in Mexico City. The selection was enormous, starting with Alamares, my favorite crisp, light, figure eights with big pieces of sugar on top; Conchas, in the shape of a puffy seashell; Puerquitos, little gingerbread pigs; Pambazos, puffy rolls covered in powdered sugar: (when a lady has too much powdery makeup on, she is snidely called a "Pambazo face"!); Bolas de Berlin, ball-shaped doughnuts with cream inside; Semitas, plain dark floured buns; and last but not least, the prize of them all, the Campechanas, a multilayered fragile pastry with melted sugar on top, hard to pick up, and impossible to take in a bag with the rest. These we'd eat as soon as we got home! I would descend from the plane in Torreón with my treasured bag of pandulce, and Frank and Tony and I would have some of them for merienda that night with hot chocolate.

The Gilmans had once invited us to go with them to spend the day at Rincón del Montero, a simple resort hotel in the nearby old town of Parras, 150 kilometers west of Saltillo, the capital of the state of Coahuila. They had two daughters, about 12 and 10 years of age, who loved to amuse our little Tony. We set out, going east, about 9 A. M., and by 11 we were leaving the highway to Saltillo, and driving up the road to Parras de la Fuente, its complete name. Parras is known as the "Oasis of Coahuila" because of its many springs and cooler weather. Founded in 1598 it is one of the most colorful and typical towns in the area. It has an old aqueduct, an important winery, beautiful plaza, an antique church, and a quaint modest chapel built in 1868 on top of a hill. One turns off before arriving in town, to reach El Rincón del Montero, our destination, a motel which at the time had about eight rustic cabins around a main building which housed the kitchen, dining room and bar. A long porch ran along the length on one side, under high arches, overlooking a small swimming pool. Huge Mexican wooden armchairs with leather seats sat on the porch. Included was a little 7-hole golf course, very untrimmed, and very hard to play because of the streams that crossed it and the clumps of dense vegetation. When we arrived, we sat on the porch to rest while the two girls took Tony by the hand and went to run up and down a grassy hill on the side of the pool. We left them, and the four of us went and played a disastrous game of golf. When we got back, the kids were playing on the porch, and we all went into the glassed-in dining room and had a home cooked lunch, followed by a slow tour around town before driving back to Torreón. It was a lovely relaxing day. The Rincón del Montero has since built a nice hotel, lengthened the golf course into nine holes, and now has a large colony of summer houses built around it, belonging to residents of Torreón and Saltillo, the capital of the state of Coahuila.

The Brown family in London. My father, Fred Brown is the boy at the back, 1896

My grandmother on my mother's side,
The Hon. Margaret Rowena Richards about 1889

My grandfather on my mother's side, Thomas Ford as a young man, 1882

London 1937, my mother, brothers:
Bill, Bob, and Ted in gray suit, and me in front of our home

My glamorous sister, Vicki, London, 1937

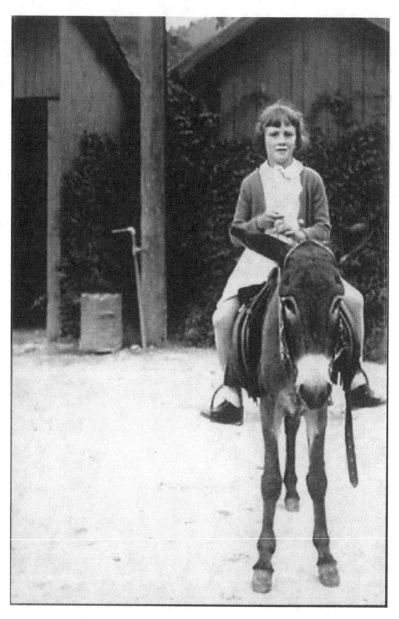

Angangueo, Michoacán, Mexico, me with "Huesos" my donkey – 1939

Angangueo, me with my beloved Teddy Bears

Mexico City, Paseo de la Reforma, Mom and Dad in 1945

Mother in South Africa with Fred, my eldest brother, about 1968

Dick, my second brother, about 1946

Bob, my fourth brother, Mexico City, about 1950

Myself, modeling in Mexico City, 1951

Sweethearts in 1951, Frankie and Peggy Brown Balderrama

Married, in Campeche, 1953

Mother, and my brother Bill in Acapulco, about 1965

Frank, Peg and Tony, with little Dukey, about 1965

Below Windsor Castle in England, Tony, Peg, Frank, 1981

Peg, Dan Tolbert, Vicki, Bill their son, and wife Chris, Denver, 1989

Frank and I on St. Thomas Island, Caribbean cruise, 1997

Frank's parents, Francisco and Rafaela Balderrama,
Golden Wedding Anniversary

My third brother, Ted, and I in San Mateo, California, 1994

Frank, as a Lt. Colonel, 1978

My mother in her apartment in Torreon, about 1978

Our son, Tony, on our back porch, Torreon, 2008

Tony, Melanie, Anthony, Sophia, and Allegra, 2006

OUR NEW HOUSE

Our new house was finished in June 1960. We had been visiting the construction almost every day for months, from watching the rooms outlined with white lime, the pouring of cement for the base on which the bricks would stand, and finally the network of metal cables that would support the roof. Houses throughout Mexico are not built of wood, but are constructed of cement and bricks, including the roof. The albañiles, or masons, always keep a loud radio going the whole time they are working, accompanying it by singing themselves. They are a merry lot, despite the fact that they are all dirt poor, but they make the best of it, and are helpful to each other. Each worker brings his own food with him, usually consisting of beans spread on a French bread loaf, which might have added sardines, ham, or cheese. There is usually a picture of the Virgin attached to one of the pillars, and each man blesses himself before starting in the morning, thus ensuring his safety throughout the day. Once a year, there is a "Builders' Day", Día del Albañil, which they celebrate with permission from the architect, who supplies them with a bottle of Tequila. They hang ornamented tissue paper, attached to strings, wall to wall, and one can hear the festivities going on when approaching the construction: a lot of singing and joking and passing around the bottle. In the evenings, they all trudge home, be it as it may, or continue at the local cantina with their drinking, spending all their weekly pay, much to the distress of their families.

We were thrilled with the result. Arquitecto José Thomas Ocampo had miraculously roughly kept within the estimate and used his imagination to enhance certain areas of the house beyond our imagination. The large living room, facing the back garden, was the focal point as one came into the hallway at the front door. To the left, was the dining area, followed by a separate ample kitchen and pantry. Two steps down into the living room, to the right, was the den. Another step down were a hall and three bedrooms and guest bathroom. The master bedroom faced the back garden, and had a lovely long bathroom with white formica counter and cabinets. The closets were adequate for our needs in those days before I accumulated my vast wardrobe of today, which I constantly have to weed out. We have since made adjustments. Tony's bedroom, guestroom and bathroom were to the right of our bedroom. There was a maid's room and bathroom above the kitchen with an interior narrow stairway.

We moved in that month. Tony was 5 years old, one reason for which he adores the house to this day, and begs us to never sell it. All his pleasant childhood memories start within this house, and although he has since married and has three children, they come every year from Los Angeles, and occupy Tony's room, still with the same posters he stuck up when he was a teenager. Not that we want to sell right now. Frank says they'll have to carry him out feet first. I adore my house, but am more open-minded about moving out when I am no longer able to run it the way I do now.

Then came the furnishing. At first, we used what we had from the other house, but gradually, during the first year, we were able to have the architect, who was also an interior decorator, design and make furniture. He made us a long mahogany sideboard that divided the dining room from the living room, a long sofa on the other side of it, two lovely Swedish design armchairs, and a huge coffee table. He had totally unique ideas, and was a perfectionist, so we approved most of his designs and added some of our own. Our old living room furniture was recovered and went into our den.

When we were to leave the rental house, Toña, my maid informed us she was going to get married, but would help to install us in our new home before she left. I was extremely grateful, as the house had a type of marbled flooring which needed daily mopping in our dusty climate, huge picture windows facing the garden which would need cleaning and waxing, as well as linen closets and shelves in the kitchen which needed lining before unloading our kitchen utensils and provisions. I was intimidated with the immensity of the project, and Toña took care of most of it herself with vim and vigor. I have never forgotton her. I even went to her church ceremony.

As luck would have it, and I must add that we have had incredible luck in most of our endeavors over the years, the owners of the department store, El Puerto de Liverpool, one of the finest in town, had received a visit from a woman who had married one of their employees and been abandoned with a little girl. She had gone to seek work with them, and Mrs. Volkhausen, not needing her at the time, asked her if she would accept a job as a maid for a small family she knew. Lydia was willing, and came to our door highly recommended. From the very beginning, we realized that this was a woman of higher class and education than the usual maid, and were delighted to have her work for us, even though it entailed having her young daughter live here too. The girl was about thirteen, and able to go to her nearby school alone on the bus. They would both occupy the ample maids' room and bath above the kitchen. As it turned out, Lydia was the best thing that could have happened to us as far as maids were concerned, because not only was she capable enough for the housework, but suggested that she'd like to cook for us too. And she turned out to be a good cook. Added to this, she adored little Tony, and would amuse him in the afternoons after her work was over. One day when we had both gone out briefly, we returned to find her on her hands and knees, Tony dressed as a cowboy on her back, laughing and riding her as he patted her backside to make "the horsey go faster". When we told her she need not go to such great lengths, she just laughed and said she enjoyed amusing him. Lydia used to make the best little meringues whenever she had leftover eggwhites from having made a cake or a flan, (custard) and would serve them to us cut open with a dollop of icecream inside.

Her daughter, Mona, was a prissy little girl, who used to wear a lot of makeup, making her look like a 16 year old. She told her mother she'd like to take guitar lessons, and Lydia acceded, asking us for permission to have the teacher come to give her lessons in their room. It was fine by us, and the old professor would slowly climb the steep steps to the room every week, after courteously asking our permission. Gradually we heard the notes become tunes, and after a few months we rather looked forward to hearing her play her repertoire.

All this time Frank had been consulting at his office from 9 A.M. to 1 P.M., coming home for our main meal, having a couple of hours' rest, like the great majority in Mexico, and returning to work until 7 or 8 P.M. when he had a lot of patients, which he usually did. We were financially safe, and enjoying life. His parents came to visit us and see our new house, and we proudly showed them around. They were here for a couple of weeks, during which time Frank and his father fell into a routine of going off together in the morning after breakfast, Mr. Balderrama sitting in the waiting room reading the newspaper while his son consulted patients. At one o'clock they would leave together for a well known "cantina", where they would have a mid-day drink, such as a little tequila and a "botana" (tiny taquitos or chips) always served with drinks in every cantina. They would come home after that for our noon meal. In the afternoons Frank's mom and dad would stay home, and I'd usually ride them and Tony downtown to the shops for her to buy something, or take the three of them to the nearby town of Lerdo for icecream in the plaza, a favorite of the residents of Torreón and Gomez Palacio. I had become very fond of Mrs. Balderrama, whose name was Rafaela, but whom I always called "Mamá". His dad was serious and gruff, and I always had the impression that he thought I was a bit of a butterfly, flitting around, with no real housework or cooking to do, and only taking care of Tony as my main reason for living. However, he expressed his warmth toward me occasionally, and I felt he liked me.

My brother Bob, and his wife Lyn, were now living in

Monterrey, east of Torreon, about 4 hours away. They were still childless although they had been married for about a dozen years. They decided to adopt a baby, and were offered a newly born at the hospital, daughter of a poor woman who had disappeared without the baby. Soon after, they visited us with little Susan Jane Brown, still in arms, doting over her little brown face, black hair and huge black eyes. We oohed and aahed, and thought she was adorable. Years later, Lyn told me that the best thing they had done during all their years of marriage was to adopt little Susy. She is now a stunning young woman who surprises people when she speaks with a very British accent like her parents, despite her dark coloring.

That year the Organization of American States offered a scholarship to professors of gynecology and general surgery for three months at UCLA in Los Angeles. Frank applied and was accepted, so, shortly after we moved into our new house, he left for L. A. to take the course. However, in December, Tony and I joined him there at his parents' home to spend Christmas and New Year's and return home together. It was an unexpected and marvellous opportunity for Frank to spend those three months with his parents while practicing medicine. We enjoyed one of our only Christmases together with his family.

ANOTHER ACCIDENT

In October of 1961 I went to Mexico City to visit my mother. Vic, my sister, went also from San Francisco, and the three of us made the rounds of restaurants and theatres and contacted old friends. The three of us were out for coffee at a new restaurant one afternoon where there was a fortune teller who came from table to table. Mother's Spanish friend, Maruja, who had suggested the restaurant, mentioned that this woman had told her her fortune some weeks before, and everything had been true. She convinced me to have the woman look at my coffee grinds after swishing out the coffee. The woman was a well-dressed lady, not the typical gypsy type, and after looking at my cup for a while she said: "You are well-off financially at present, but one day you will have all the money you desire. (I'm still waiting!). I see you living by water, perhaps a lake, perhaps a pool. Someone very close to you is going to have a bad accident though, and it will happen soon." Well, we hadn't yet built our large swimming pool, so I thought she was mistaken, and as for the accident, I believed she was referring to Frank's past accident. My mother and I left the restaurant, and took a cab out to the airport to pick up Frank and Tony who were coming in on the evening plane. When they got off and started to walk across the tarmac, I saw Tony limping, with a bandage on his knee, and Frank with a big patch on his forehead. I rushed toward them, and Frank said, "Don't be frightened, but we had a little car accident this morning." It turned out that he had Tony in the back seat when another car ran into them and totaled our fairly new Vauxhall. Tony flew over the front seat and hurt his leg and Frank hit his head on the windshield. I was shaken because of what the fortune teller had told me, but later considered it a tremendous coincidence. We were grateful the consequences had not been worse.

THE DIAGNOSTIC CLINIC

In 1963, Frank and seventeen other doctors inaugurated the new Clinica de Diagnóstico in Torreón. Frank and three other doctors had travelled to Houston, Texas, New Orleans and LaFayette, Louisiana, to interview the directors of medical clinics there, and begin their own clinic in Torreón, based upon what they had learned in the U. S. It was connected to the Sanatorio Español, the main hospital in town, and when they finally inaugurated it, Frank was named its first President. Thomas Ocampo, our architect, had designed the furniture for his new office, which he started occupying right away. This was the building where Frank would consult until they decided to build a separate building later on. Frank suggested we give a cocktail party to introduce each of the couples to each other. About ten couples came, and I had made all sorts of hors d'oevres, tiny sandwiches (not carrot this time!) and dips, and crackers with assorted cheeses. We had hired a waiter, who came out with trays of white wine or Scotch and Sodas, which the ladies refused, asking instead for a coke or refreshment. Of course, all the doctors took one or the other, but I realized that ladies here did not drink in public. Not ladylike. Of course, it was a rather stiff reunion, although the doctors seemed to really enjoy themselves, and said it was a wonderful idea of ours.

A few years later, when we all knew each other better, and we had recently built our pool and covered porch at back, we invited the same crowd over for noon drinks and appetizers. But this time, I made Bloody Marys for the ladies. They all accepted, thinking it was plain tomato juice, and after the first hour or so, the noonday heat got to them, and suddenly one of the ladies took a running leap into the pool, fully dressed, pearls and jewelry and all, followed by three others. Two more asked me for bathing suits, and soon we were all swimming together. The men had been swimming since they arrived, but the ladies had sat primly, baking, despite my urging them to change and take a dip. At a recent homage forty years later for the doctors who had founded the first Diagnostic Clinic in Torreon, everyone, now all great friends, remembered the fun we had all had at that gathering.

One summer we three flew to Puerto Vallarta on the Pacific ocean coast in the state of Jalisco for a week's holiday. At the time it had received a lot of publicity, because Liz Taylor and Richard Burton had vacationed there. However, the first day when we went to La Playa de los Muertos, Beach of the Dead (I have no idea why they named it so) which was recommended as the place to go, we saw two drunken American women tourists flirting with the beach boys, and the sand looked frankly dirty. I was suffering with a bout of Malta Fever, which never kills you, but makes you feel lethargic all day, so perhaps that is why I didn't really enjoy this trip, even though we took a boat out to the island of Mismaloya one day where Burton and Liz were supposed to have a house. Mostly we swam in the hotel pool, and in the evenings we would adjourn to the hotel restaurant where they had music, and Frank and I would dance a piece or two while Tony watched us, delighted and giggling.

We had become very close to a couple named Withington who had moved into a house in front of ours, and we started to see them more often. Jo and David had met in Hawaii, where she, who was from Washington state, was working as a secretary with a foreign firm. He had been born in Hawaii, the son of a physician and his wife, both of English descent. They married and lived there for a few years before he was offered a good position with John Deere, an agricultural company, which transferred him to various parts of the United States, and finally to Torreón. They had two children, Connie the eldest, about 10, and Toddy, whose name was really Philip, about a year older than Tony, both of them tow heads. Jo was tall and Nordic looking, about 5 years older than I, unpretentious but very well educated and well read. I feel I learned a lot from her during the time she lived here, as I did from some of the other ladies in our group. She used to make a wonderful steak and kidney pie, substituting chicken livers for kidneys, thank goodness, and on several occasions, after a late-ending party, she invited everyone over for impromptu scrambled eggs, which she would make in a double boiler. She and I played golf together about three times a week, although she was a much better golfer than I. Jo's little boy became friends with Tony, and whenever I did errands in the afternoon, I always took Tony with me, Toddy tagging along too. Sometimes Connie would come with us. In those days I used to go to the Torreón post office very often because I was always writing letters to my mother and to my sister, Vic. The kids would be by my side, and the girl who sold me stamps asked one day if the little brown-haired boy was mine too. She had assumed, wrongly, the two tow heads were mine. I cleared it up and informed her that the little brown-

185

haired one was the only one who was mine! Many people who did not know me well, believed for years that I had three kids.

Whenever a circus came to town, and various ones came about three times a year, Jo and I would take our kids to see them and have just about as much fun watching the show as the kids did. Most were pretty scruffy acts, the animals not looking very well fed, and the costumes pieced together rather pathetically. However, we enjoyed the humorous exchange between the clowns and the public, and it made for a fun afternoon.

Unfortunately a few years later the Withingtons moved back to the States, and I missed her terribly. We kept up our correspondence for Christmas and birthdays, and years later, she and David and the family came to visit us when Connie was newly married.

Every year, in March, when it became Tony's birthday, I would give him a party in our back garden. He would invite his classmates from the American School, as well as friends who lived nearby our home, and I would hire a clown to amuse them after playing games like pinning the donkey's tail, and hitting the piñata. They were served slices of either my homemade chocolate or lemon cakes with icecream, but I noticed that the ones who ended up getting lemon cake felt shortchanged. From then on I'd always make two chocolate cakes. Sometimes as many as fifteen kids would show up, in those days wearing cute suits, some with bow ties. My sister-in-law in California, looking at the photos I took, commented that they looked like a Kennedy birthday party, because the kids were so elegantly dressed, not casual, like in California.

Around this time, many movie companies visited Torreón for filming with our rustic desert and mountain scenery as a background. They would check into downtown hotels, drive out to the different sites, and on weekends use our local country club for swimming. One year we heard that James Garner and Robert Ryan were filming a western movie near here. Tony was about nine, so another lady and I drove out with our kids to a set in the middle of nowhere and watched the filming. James Garner was at his peak of virility and good looks, and I admit I was star-struck. Tony watched me closely as I sat on a low wall talking to him along with others, only to tell his Dad later that I had been showing off my legs and flirting with the actor! I could have strangled him! Garner later played golf with my husband, and then we all sat a long table at the club having beers afterwards. He was most courteous. Another time Edmund O'brien was here filming a western, The Wild Bunch, with William Holden in 1968. I happened to meet O'Brien and invited him and his wife over for a party which we were giving. They arrived, but to my dismay, they brought their little seven year old son with them. This is a no-no in Mexico when one is invited to a night party. Well, I left the little boy to play with Tony in his room, and we all went back in the garden for the party and the food. But the child, his name was Brandon, came out to join us, and his father, who obviously doted on the child, encouraged him to sing for us The Impossible Dream. To this day, we will always remember that tiny boy, all dressed up in a suit and bow tie, in front of all the adults, singing to the top of his little lungs that difficult song, and to his credit, he did a fine job. We all clapped wholeheartedly. I heard a few years ago that he was writing a biography of his father, a magnificent actor. We shall always remember him in the film, The Barefoot Contessa, with Ava Gardner, where he had received the Best Supporting Actor award for his role.

Another year, 1972, we went to see the great William Holden act on the set in the movie, The Revengers. I think that is when Tony decided he wanted to work in the film industry in some category. I have a photo of him sitting in William Holden's director-chair, looking very smug. We were invited onto the set by one of the Producers and were sitting at the luncheon table when Mr. Holden asked someone who we were and came to sit with us. I was flattered. He sat by me, and we carried on a nice conversation, watched carefully by Tony and my mother who had come along. I asked him about "Sunset Boulevard" that he had filmed in 1950 with Gloria Swanson, one of our favorite alltime movies, and he commented that this was the first film which had afforded him the opportunity to work with big names in the industry. He was not young anymore, but still very handsome. Frank had visited him medically at the hotel a few days before, so that broke the ice between us.

As far as actors are concerned, we had a lot of contact with them over the years. Once, Frank was flown by helicopter to some nearby caves to take care of a cut on Ernest Borgnine's hand, and another time he attended to Glenn Ford at his hotel, who graciously gave him a lovely necktie. Another time, at our country club, Burt Lancaster was playing golf, and was joined for lunch by Telly Savalas. Tony our son, and Tina Barboglio, Fran's daughter, went to their table to ask them for their autographs. Burt, without looking up, said "Can't you see we're eating?!" and as the kids backed away, Telly graciously said, "Wait a minute, kids I'll give you mine." Twenty years later, Tony, now a Director of Photography, filming a a commercial with Telly Savalas, went up to him on the first day and started to recount this story, but before the end, Telly said, "And I sure hope I gave you my autograph, kid, and that you aren't thinking of punching me in the nose now!"

In 1966, we three drove to Houston, where we went to the new Astrodome for a football game, then flew out next day to Washington. After we visited all the monuments and tombs and points of interest, I called my childhood friend from Garside School, Shirley Camus, who was now married and living outside Washington, in Maryland. They came by for us so we could dine with them at their lovely home, and then drove us back to our downtown hotel. I have kept track of all my friends over the years, and exchange Christmas cards with them. Shirley and I had been avid readers of all the Nancy Drew detective books, and would buy each other the newest one at the American Bookstore in Mexico City for Christmas and birthdays. I kept my collection for years, but one day in a moment of madness, trying to rid myself of excess baggage, I donated them to the American School in Torreon. I'm so sorry I did not save them for my two little grandaughters, who are now good readers themselves.

From Washington we took a bus to New York, where we climbed the Statue of Liberty and coincided with the Queen Mary sailing below us out to sea. From there we went to Niagara Falls, and on to Chicago, where we visited Frank's youngest sister who was newly married and expecting their first child.

On all these trips, Tony was the perfect little traveler. We would look back in the car and he would be sitting with all his bears and animals he called his "fambly", which he would sneak into the car right before we left the house. The three of us often played the road game, long before divided highways, guessing and betting on brands of different cars coming toward us. On our yearly road trips to California we would always stop at Tony's favorite Jack-In-the-Box restaurants for hamburgers. Many times I would take over the back seat and Tony would ride in front with his father, wearing earphones to listen to his music, but always watching the road. Once, after stopping in Chihuahua for lunch, and Frank feeling drowsy, while rounding a curve, Tony spied an oncoming train before we did, and Frank was able to screech to a halt, only a few feet from the train. We always referred to this incident as, The Day You Saved Our Lives!

In 1968, eight years after we had built our house, we bought an adjacent lot, facing the back street, and built a lovely kidney-shaped pool and game room with bathroom. It increased the beauty of our garden, and we started to enjoy swimming every day in summer. Tony would invite his little friends over, and on weekends Frank and I would serve barbecued hamburgers to various groups of friends. At the time, we had a pup named Terry, and when the children would come over and leave their socks and shoes by the pool, Terry would swallow their socks. How he got them down we'll never know, but swallow them he did, and the next day he would excrete them on the lawn, looking faded and soggy. The children began to carefully put shoes and socks in the pool bathroom after that.

Many of the foreign group had been leaving, returning to the United States to retire, or being transferred, so we began to lose many friends. We had become close to many of them, but still had our original friends, the Botellos, and the Barboglios who had roots here in Mexico. Mary Lib Botello was the dearest woman I will ever hope to know. She would take the shirt off her own back and give it to you if necessary. She was the one, along with her husband, Rafael, who had given that cocktail party for us when we first arrived, and thus introduced us to all the foreign group, who in turn became Frank's patients. We saw them less now that we lived in Gomez Palacio, but we often talked on the phone, and I would swing by her house to chat whenever I went to Torreón, which was often. The Barboglios, Fran and Pete, whose cattle ranch was about two and a half hours from town, we only saw on weekends as he was mostly at the ranch, but she usually stayed home here in the same colony where we lived, and she and I got together sometimes for golf or Book Club. When Pete came into town, they would have marvellous dinner parties, and gradually started inviting some of the Mexican crowd who had business connections with Pete, so little by little, our dwindling circle grew larger.

When we arrived in Torreón, there was already a book club, started by long-time English-speaking residents. I was invited to join them once a month, at the Casino downtown, where the hostess and other ladies would carry boxes of books which had been gradually ordered from the U. S., or brought in by any of the existing members. We were about 15 or 20 at the time, and it was an enjoyable gathering, with everyone exchanging impressions and comments on books they had read. Thanks to this club, I was able to continue my hobby of reading, and every time I, or anyone else went to the U. S. we would go with a list of two or three books the members had voted on. Thus, our library grew, until someone suggested it remain in a member's house instead of being taken to the Casino, and everyone taking turns to keep the books for six months. This worked out satisfactorily, instead of lugging the boxes every month to the Casino. Our gatherings were more fun, with the addition of coffee or refreshments being served by the hostess. I always preferred biographies, so got to read about the lives of famous artists such as Rembrandt and Rodin, as well as famous personages in history. As more and more members left for the States, and local members shied away from having the books in their homes, I was landed with the collection because I had that back cabana by our pool. For years I had a once-monthly meeting, which I really enjoyed. However, as time went by, I noticed less and less members showing up, until one day I decided we should donate our collection to the Municipal Library downtown. As they had no room to keep our books in English, apart from their regular collection, we donated five metal bookshelves, and helped to arrange them in an alcove in one of the halls. There they sit today, but at times I'm sorry not to have them handy to look up some author or title which I would like to refer to.

LAS VEGAS, LOS ANGELES, SAN FRANCISCO

There was a very attractive Mexican widow, Bobby Riveroll, who had recently married a young American man a few years younger than her, Vernon Moore, when he arrived in Torreon in 1956 to work for Anderson Clayton. At first they only ran around with Bobby's friends, a strictly local high society crowd she had always been a part of, but the social events soon brought us together, at which time they gradually joined the foreign crowd. Bobby played golf with Fran and I, along with Jean Poché, whose husband, Jim, worked with Vernon at Anderson Clayton. Vernon was a party-goer, and a born leader. We and the Barboglios often got together at the Moore house for a drink, some music, because

Vernon loved to play records, and dinner at a popular restaurant where there was dance music, Los Sauces, (The Willows). Then one night, out of the blue, Vernon suggested that we three couples go to Las Vegas. All agreed, and the next week, the six of us and Tony drove to San Antonio, Texas, where we took a flight to Los Angeles, where we left Tony with his grandparents before proceeding to Las Vegas. Frank and I did not have credit cards in those days, so we took cash, which turned out to be the wrong thing to do. We started playing the slot machines at the airport, transferred to The Sands Hotel, checked our luggage, and immediately started gambling at the tables. Frank and I played Black Jack, first at the dollar tables and then at the five-dollar tables. I noticed that every time one of the leggy waitresses came by with small trays of Scotch and Soda, Frank would thank her warmly and take a free drink. We lost all notion of time, there being no wall clocks in the casinos, and were in the heat of the game about 3 A. M. when Frank took me aside and said "Give me the rest of the money you have. All mine is gone." Well, I had earlier given it all to him, and it had disappeared at the tables. We were suddenly penniless. And this was only the first night. We had planned on staying three nights before proceeding to Los Angeles for a couple of days to see the city, which Frank knew so well, leave Tony more time with his grandparents, and continue our trip by rental car up the California coast to San Francisco. Frank called his brother, Hank, in Los Angeles for a loan, and immediately he wired us some money to pay for the hotel. Embarassing, but you think it soured the rest of our stay in Las Vegas? No, we just didn't gamble any more. Mostly we tried all the restaurants, saw wonderful shows at night, and continued with our trip.

We spent two days in Los Angeles with Frank's parents and Tony, and left again for the road. Vernon had rented a large, roomy car, and so we drove up the beautiful California coast to San Simeon, and the Randolph Hearst Castle, which is on a hill overlooking the Pacific Ocean, halfway between Los Angeles and

San Francisco. It was built between 1919, and all the way up to 1947, because Mr. Hearst would tear down parts and rebuild them again more to his liking, always adding objects of art which he brought back from his worldwide travels. From there we continued to Carmel by the Sea, where we went out to the famous golf course, dined, and spent the night in a wonderful inn, before driving on to San Francisco. Frank and I stayed with Vic and her husband, Dan, and one night all of us went to the Fairmont hotel to see and hear Rosemary Cluny. She was splendid, one of our favorite alltime singers.

Courtesy of Vic's credit card, I purchased a beautiful beige mink stole at Saks Fifth Avenue the next day. This was in an era when we still did not stop to think of the poor little minks being slaughtered for their furs! (I never wear it any more!) We visited many of the famous tourist spots Frank and I had already seen, and handed in the car so as to fly back to Los Angeles to retrieve Tony before leaving for Torreon again. Of course when we arrived, Frank and I had many debts to repay!

NEW ORLEANS

Next year we three couples visited New Orleans for Mardi Gras. Tony would stay at home, and go to school, supervised by Lydia, our trusty wonderful maid. We planned to meet another two couples from Mexico City there, friends of Bobby, as well as a priest who had his parish in that city. At first, I thought the idea of having a priest join us during Mardi Gras festivities was a bad idea and would sort of curtail our partying. To my surprise, Father Pete met us on the first day at the famous restaurant, Antoine's, while preparing Martinis for us at the table. A big, florid complexioned man, with a winning smile, he had to be one of the most charming and handsome priests I had ever met, and by the time we left, we admired him as much as all his parishioners did. He was also a member of the Fire Department, and one afternoon while we were partying with him at his house, they called him urgently. He immediately donned his red fireman's helmet and took off, ready for duty, where many times he was forced to perform the unpleasant duty of giving last rites to burned victims.

When we arrived, we checked in at the downtown Monte Leone Hotel, and partyers were already in full swing, yelling and throwing streamers and making merry. In retrospect we seemed to be going from restaurant to restaurant for the three days we were in the city. I can't remember all the names except for Antoine's, one of my favorites, Brennan's for breakfast where I tasted the best bread pudding which topped my mother's recipe, The Old Plantation, where we all had freshly cut Mint Juleps, and many others, where we heard jazz and cajun music until the wee hours of the morning. One of our group had obtained invitations to the main Ball, for which our husbands had to rent tuxedos. We ladies had been warned to take long dresses, and Frank and I thought we'd be dancing the night away, but no, it took place in an auditorium, culminated by the crowning of the Queen. Of course there was the Mardi Gras parade of decorated floats, which all looked rather garish to me, in comparison to the famous Rose Bowl Parade in California, because one could see the trucks underneath, carrying the floats. However, it was an unforgettable trip, and we ended up by inviting Father Pete and two other couples to Torreon, even leaving them paid tickets. How splendid can you get!

THE FLOOD

In 1968 there was a very heavy rainy season in September. Usually we had sparse rains for a few days and then nothing for most of the year. This time it filled the dams, one which had been recently finished, and everyone was afraid it would not be able to hold the amount of water filling it. Our normally dry river bed was flooded, and one morning at 3 A. M. we heard a

desperate knock on our front door. When we opened, it was a
neighbor who was advising everyone on the street that the dam
might not hold, and our homes here in Gomez Palacio would be
flooded. We had my eight year old niece, Bob and Lyn's daughter,
staying with us, and of course our own twelve year old son, so
we hurriedly packed two suitcases and prepared to flee our home
over the bridge to nearby Torreón which is higher up. But not
before Frank called some soldiers from the Military Hospital to
come to raise our washing machine and dryer up onto boxes to
save the motors if the water came in. Not much else we could
save, so we closed the door to our home, and left, not knowing
whether we would ever be able to occupy it again. The soldiers
remained in our house and garden to guard it against looters. We
checked into a ten story hotel in Torreón and prepared to wait
for the outcome. Then we had a phone call from Alan and Jodie
Evans, an American couple who lived in back of us. They too had
evacuated their rented house and checked into a nearby hotel,
but in contrast to us, had little to lose should the waters come
into our homes, as they were only living temporarily in Mexico
while they had dealings in a mine. "Cheer up" Alan laughed on
the phone. "Let's go out and celebrate the 15th of September in
style at 'Los Sauces'. A couple of drinks should make us all feel
better!" Against our better judgment we agreed, and they came
by for us with their little son, Victor, left him with our two kids,
and off we went to celebrate what is known in Mexico as the
night of the 'Grito' (the Cry) to celebrate the Independence of
Mexico. Other families from our street were occupying the same
hotel that night, so we had no qualms about leaving our kids
together in our room. At the restaurant, Alan promptly ordered
four Martinis before we had a chance to think about it, and after
our second Martini, we were laughing and snacking and talking
as if nothing was wrong. They took us back to the hotel after
midnight, collected their little boy, and next day when we woke
up we felt a lot more resigned to our fate.

The Botellos, our dear friends, invited us to their house for lunch, and as we were finishing, Vernon Moore, (they also lived in Torreón) came by to ask us if we wanted to join him in his little plane to fly over Gomez Palacio to see if our house had been invaded by water. When Frank, Tony and I flew over our property we were amazed to see that the river water had surrounded all the surrounding houses, except the church on the corner and our house! We looked down on the soldiers standing by the pool in our garden, and waved, and they waved back. The new dam had held, and only a small amount of river water had invaded our area. We had been spared. It was just one of those lucky things that happen to you once in a lifetime. A few days later the waters receded back into the river and into the thirsty ground and we were able to go back home. When we saw, recently, the tragedy in New Orleans, we identified with the people living there, and again realized how tremendously lucky we had been in 1968.

Christmas rolled around. At Vernon's suggestion, each of the three husbands, Vernon, Pete and Frank gave each of the three wives a card with a note which promised a trip to Europe in 1969, exact plans to be made together. Of course, Bobby, Fran and I were thrilled to death, and I immediately started to take out maps and suggest a plan to the rest. Bobby insisted on having some relatives who had an agency in Tampico come here to arrange our trip for us. We all gave them suggestions, and the itinerary was finally completed for a six week grand tour. I insisted the trip include England, and I am so glad, because it gave us the opportunity to meet my niece, Mary, daughter of my brother Fred, who long ago had separated from her mother and gone to live in South Africa. She was my only blood relative in England, as my sister and brothers had long ago left for Mexico, the U.S.A. and Africa.

Frank's mother and father offered to stay here to run the house and take care of our son Tony while we were away. We were thankful to have them, as Tony adored them, and we could leave without any qualms. Both the Barboglios and the Moores had cattle ranches, and as the date for our trip rolled around, a serious problem developed, in that there were "paracaidistas" (illegal settlers) trying to take over terrain on people's ranches. They were afraid the law would not be able to evict them, and that they would lose part of their land. They decided they would have to cancel their trip. Plans were already made, so Frank and I decided to go to Europe alone.

Frank's parents arrived. I gave instructions to the maid and the gardener, and we readied ourselves for the trip the next morning to Monterrey, with the Evans, who graciously had offered to take us to catch our plane there. That night I had rollers in my hair, an old dress, and was throwing a load of sheets in the washing machine, when I heard the mariachis out in our garden. Our property's back garden gate looks on to the street facing the Evans' house, and at the sound of music, Frank and I looked out through the living room windows to see Mariachis leading a group of our friends into the garden. They had come the back way to serenade us goodbye before our trip. Tony and Victor were in on the prank, each with a flashlight on either roof, signalling each other about the right time to come in. Tony had opened the back gate, and a group of about twenty came in together. Frank and I rushed out into the garden, and noticed that everyone was holding a drink. They had all gathered at the Evans' home first, and from there to our garden. I admit I had tears in my eyes because I became emotional at knowing the trouble Jody and Alan must have taken to invite our friends, and furthermore to make a cold buffet for all of us at their house, where we went after the mariachis left. We were amused too that Tony and little Victor had been so secretive about their roles in the party. They both burst out laughing at Frank's and my expressions of bewilderment in the beginning.

We all adjourned to the Evans house, where Jody had made delicious fried chicken and potato salad, and hot French bread, and then we were instructed to go home early to finish preparing for our car trip next morning with them to Monterrey. We would take our plane from there to San Antonio, Texas, and from there to Houston and across the ocean to Amsterdam, where we were to change planes and continue to London, our first stop. So complicated in comparison to our later trips to Europe. It was 1969, and since then Torreón has built an international airport where we have various connections to Houston, Dallas, and Los Angeles. Tony and Victor came with us in the car, and before leaving the city, we had been instructed to stop on the way at Jane and Mac's house to have a little drink of Champagne and caviar before going out on the road. I thought it was a bad idea, but had to change my mind when we arrived at their house and found they had set up a tiny table out on the front sidewalk with glasses, and caviar on toast. We realized just how happy all our friends were that we were finally to experience our first trip to Europe, this being a particularly sweet gesture.

Since then, we have taken many trips overseas, but none have started out with such a bang as our first. In Monterrey we checked in at our favorite hotel, the Ancira, an elegant aristocratic hotel, dating from 1910. The checkered floor of the lobby where the main desk is, beside the winding marble staircase, give it an air of old refinement, and we knew it was the appropiate place from which to start our exciting journey. That night after asking for room service for the two children, we four walked across the Plaza to the famous Louisiana Restaurant, where we ordered an exquisite dinner and were impressed when the well-traveled Evans introduced to Liebfraumilch for the first time.

Our travel agents, an engaging couple, met us next morning for breakfast, and gave us last minute tips about restaurants and sights in the cities we would visit. I was a little nervous about the unknown adventures that might befall us, and expressed regret that they were not going with us. They assured us everything would come out perfectly, as it did.

The Evans left that morning for the return trip to Torreón after saying goodbye to us at the airport. We were to be gone for six weeks, and were teary-eyed when we said goodbye to Tony. The Evans had promised him and Victor a visit to Horsetail Falls and the García Caverns on the way back, so they were eager to get going.

EUROPE

In San Antonio, Texas, we changed planes and flew to Kennedy airport in New York. Our two days and nights there were filled with visits to the Metropolitan Museum of Art, the Guggenheim, the department stores, and walking around Central Park, where we ate at the well-known restaurant, Tavern on the Green. At night we took in a Broadway play, "The Man From the Mancha", and when the main actor sang The Impossible Dream at the end of the play, we had to remember that tiny little boy singing it on our porch the night Edmund O'Brien came over. Next morning we left Kennedy on KLM for Schiphol airport in Amsterdam, where we changed planes and flew to Heathrow airport in London. How to express my feelings when we first flew over the old continent, first France, and then the greenery of London in April? I wept. It had been thirty years since I had left with my mother, and had not known when, if ever, I would be back. Now, thanks to my darling husband, we were about to pace hallowed ground, and my emotions were spilling over.

Our plane was late, and our contact was not at the airport to meet us, so I called the phone number on our itinerary and a rough Spaniard's voice answered, telling me he had been at the airport earlier to meet us, but as we were late, now we'd have to take a cab on our own to the hotel. I was furious because of his attitude, but did as we were told, and arrived at the Park Lane Hotel in front of Green Park in good time. Lovely quiet hotel, with pure linen sheets on the beds, feather eiderdowns and pillows, and warm towels in the bathroom. Small details that were different from our stays at hotels in America. We went that afternoon to its very British tearoom, where, while sipping tea, the loud Spaniard burst in, yelling that we were supposed to have been in the lobby at that time for our city tour. How uncouth!

We were in London for five days, time to meet my niece Mary, daughter of my eldest brother Fred, her husband, Mike, and their toddler. We saw all the usual London sights, the Changing of the Guard, Buckingham Palace, The Tower, the Houses of Parliament and Big Ben, St. Paul's Cathedral and Westminster Abbey. We took a tour out to Eton and Cambridge one morning, and to Hampton Court another. I must add here that when we were arranging our trip together, the three couples had decided we would like our tourist guides in Europe to speak to us in Spanish, because Americans were not well-liked in France. Bad idea. In London, the guides on our private tours were all Spaniards who gave us the names of Castles and Kings with a Spanish accent. It took us a moment to figure out that " Enrique octavo" was Henry the VIII and that his castle, "Anton Kur" was Hampton Court. Luckily we went to Windsor Castle on our own. We were lucky to get tickets to "Fiddler On the Roof" as well as another very British political play, which left us totally in the dark, because we hardly understood one word they said, or the innuendos, despite the roaring crowd, not being familiar with British politics. We flew to Paris, and were there for another five days at Le Grand Hotel, which had an old cage elevator, reminiscent of the one at the hotel in Veracruz. Took a tour of the city, this time in English, thank God: the Louvre, Notre Dame, Sainte Chapelle, Versailles, Rodin's Museum, Les Invalides, and of course the Eiffel Tower. Next day we went out on our own, and dedicated time to each of the points of interest. Then, who should we run into, but our architect, José Tomás Ocampo, on the Champs Elysees, and oh, what a joy to see someone from our hometown. He was making the trip with his mother, who turned out to be a really dear lady. Together we took in the night sights, The Moulin Rouge, Lido, and the third night, being tired of bare-breasted girls, went to the Opera House to hear Faust. After dinner at a sophisticated restaurant José Tomás suggested, we four walked back to our hotels along the River Seine. What an enjoyable visit.

We flew to Madrid, and found it cold and rainy, but still took in the sights, the Prado Museum, the Royal Palace, and the wonderful Retiro Park, made more beautiful by our lovely old Spanish guide, a pretty lady about 70 years old whose Spanish diction was soft and beautiful. We had pictures taken at the Puerta del Sol, on La Gran Vía avenue, and in front of the beautiful statues and fountains downtown. We took a tour out to Toledo, home of the famous painter, El Greco, and another day to the magnificent monastery El Escorial, about 49 kilometers from Madrid, surrounded by the majestic Guadarrama mountains. The construction dates from the sixteenth century, built by King Phillip II as a Royal Pantheon as well as a palace for himself. Included was a tour of the monumental memorial, Valle de los Caídos, erected by the Spanish dictator, Francisco Franco, to honor those who fell during the Spanish civil war.

Went to a nightclub to see Flamenco dancing, and ate at a variety of restaurants, elegant ones or popular ones, where large families got together and ate huge meals. I was amazed at what Spanish children consumed!

In France, Nice was rainy on the first day, but then came a sunny one, when all the bikinis came out on the beach, right in front of our hotel on the famous Boulevard des Anglais. Rode over to the Monte Carlo Casino, but wouldn't you know that Frank had left his passport at the hotel in Nice and wasn't allowed to enter. (We finally entered on future trips).

Took a flight out to Zurich, after almost boarding the wrong plane in Nice. Could not understand the directions over the loud speaker at the airport, so walked out onto the tarmac and boarded the wrong plane, where a woman was vacuuming the carpet. She shooed us off, and they set us straight at the desk, but we felt like a couple of hayseeds! Our trip did not include seeing the city in Zurich, so we were met at the airport in a sleek limousine which had been calculated to take the original six people, and driven through the city on to Lucerne, where we had reservations at a beautiful peaceful lakeside hotel. The staff was typically suave and gracious throughout dinner, and later while we sipped our demi-tasses in the parlor, we listened to a pianist play Lizt and Chopin. This was living! Next morning, Mount Pilatus, covered in snow beckoned to us, so we took the funicular to the top. Had lunch on the Old Bridge restaurant, fondue for the first time. A lot of firsts on this voyage.

We had a private compartment on the train from Lucerne to Milan through the mountains. What a difference from Switzerland. Big, noisy, industrial Milan, but as we found out later, with its own personality. The imposing Gothic "Il Duomo" is the second largest Roman Catholic cathedral in the world, the cathedral in Sevilla being the largest. (Saint Peters is not a cathedral, it is a Basilica.) On the very peak of the highest tower, there stands a beautiful golden Madonna, "La Madonnina", shining in the sun. We visited La Scala Theatre, where one night we attended the lovely opera-ballet, "Romeo e Giulietta". Also, we were fascinated by the Galleria Vittorio Emanuele II, which has to be the most beautiful shopping mall in the world. Under a vaulted glass roof and hand-painted frescoes, the mall has cafés, restaurants, boutiques, and only recently, a luxury hotel. Unfortunately we missed seeing Leonardo's painting of The Last Supper at the old convent, Santa Maria de Grazzie, as it was closed for repairs. Our guide thought it necessary that we admire the statues in Milan's Monumentale cemetery, and led us from tomb to tomb, showing us extraordinarily exquisite sculptures, some in marble, some in bronze. Although we had really not wanted to visit the place, it was like being in a gorgeous museum, truly worth our while.

Lovely bus ride out of Milan through Lombardy wine country, to Veneto county, passing through Verona, where we visited Juliet's fabled balcony and heard the tale from the lady guide about her romance with Romeo. She actually had us believing that Shakespeare had written a true story about the lovers. We arrived in Venice at dusk and were whisked to our hotel by water taxi, right to the front steps, a few paces from St. Mark's Square. Although we had seen many photos of Venice, it still has tremendous impact when viewed for the first time, truly a dream world, and perhaps a little nightmarish, some would say, with rot and evil odors hitting your nostrils at first, but in time fading away as you become accustomed. Huge stone steps of the churches disappear below water level, and dark buildings rise from the depths into frightening shadow shapes. Plus this, there are always the groans and gurgles from the gondoliers as they round corners of the canals, warning of their imminent arrival to avoid crashes. No cars are allowed, and one must walk on the narrow sidewalks. or ride in the gondolas or water taxis. At night, residents close their shutters air-tight, so not a ray of interior light comes forth, making it look like a haunted city. However, churches and palaces are illuminated, giving your ride on the canals an out-of-this-world feeling.

Despite all this, next morning Venice redeemed itself in the brillian sunlight over St. Mark's Square, with so many pigeons around our feet that one has to be careful not to step on them. The Palazzo Ducale, or Doge's Palace, lay on one side, a long limestone and pink marble building, softened by the white porticos below, and the Byzantine-styled San Marco Basilica at the end, with its gilded mosaics and four gilded horses above the entrance. The inside was no less imposing. We visited the Bridge of Sighs, ate at various small restaurants overlooking the canals, and in the evenings sat in the Plazza listening to the orchestra play, while sipping Camparis or Cinzano. One morning, we took a tour over to the island of Murano where a dead-ringer for Rossano Brazzi showed us around the factory. I admit I paid more attention to the man than to the lovely crystalware and blown glass he was showing us. For that matter, the temptations in Venice are tremendous: artwork, cameos, mosaic jewelry, leather goods, silks, etc. A husband's nightmare. We ended up buying six crystal, etched snifters, to be delivered in Mexico, even though we never drink cognac!

The busride to Florence showed us countryside just as lovely as the one from Milan, passing by Bologna, where we had lunch. Bologna, a big bustling city, is known for the best food in Italy, or so we were told, where we tasted a white Lasagna which has never been equaled in my humble opinion. Anyone who has ever been to Florence will agree that this is the city that cannot be missed. It is truly the heart of Italy. The art is breathtaking, marble statues and fountains everywhere. We started by checking out the famous doors to the Baptistry by Ghiberti, going on to the Pitti Palace, the Uffizi Museum and the Accademia, where we admired Michelango's David and other works. I personally prefer looking upon his great massive Moses, in Rome's St. Peter's in Chains, but then I'm getting ahead of myself. Our visit would not have been complete without a walk over the Ponte Veccio bridge where gold jewelry sparkles and commands your attention, as do the vendors. Florence definitely needs more time. Too many treasures to be seen in a four day stay.

We left for Rome, driving through Tuscany, eleventh century castles along the way, some still inhabited and sporting T. V. antennas, stopping at Perugia for lunch and in the afternoon at St. Francis Assisi, where a darling old monk in the church proudly pointed out that Giotto and his followers had painted the ceilings. We asked him if we could take his photo, and smilingly he answered yes, unless it was for magazine publicity!

Upon arriving in Rome, after checking into our hotel, we made our way to the Via Venetto to sip a Grand Marnier and watch the evening activity swinging by, a real style show. Next morning, St. Peter's, where, being Wednesday, the Pope was giving an audience. We wandered around, mostly admiring the statue of La Pietá, totally unprotected in those days before a madman's attempt to mutilate her. Suddenly we turned, and saw a wizened old Pope Paul VI being carried out on a throne, high above the heads of the crowd. We were very lucky to see him from up close and I was able to snap a picture. Other days we saw all the famous sights: the Vatican Museum, Sistine Chapel, Fountain of Trevi, Piazza Navone, where we ate lunch, the Pantheon, and St. Peter's in Chains, where we came upon Moses, with his veined, muscled arms and great legs, making David look like the slim young boy that he was. We wandered around the Roman Forum, tried many restaurants where we always included pastas in our order, spaghetti, lasagna, ravioli, with gorgonzola or parmesano cheeses, red wines, white wines, rum cakes, and a variety of delicious foods. Good thing we walked miles every day. I asked myself, are there any bad cooks in Italy? We found none.

We flew to Athens on Olympic Airlines, with a meal fit for kings, and excellent service. Our hotel was the Grande Bretagne facing the House of Parliament on Constitution Square or Syntagma Plaka. It was a former palace, and our rooms were gorgeous, with a breathtaking view of the city and the Acropolis. We tipped our hats to our travel hosts who really knew how to pick hotels for this, our first trip. Next morning we trudged up to the Parthenon and were struck by its immensity and timeless beauty. Other points of interest were a Byzantine Church, the National Museum, (I believe the Elgin Marbles taken from Greece to the British Museum are more extensive than the ones in Athens, and I personally believe they should be returned!) Omonia Square, the central market, a spectacle of Sound and Light, and some typical nightclubs with Greek folk- dancing. Then we took a ride out to the port of Piraeus, and from there a boat to the islands of Hydra and Aegina. It was sunny on both islands, and we had time for swimming and lunching and a visit to the Temple of Athena. Sailing on the Adriatic, the wind blowing my hair, I felt for a moment what Jackie Onassis must have felt when she and Ari sailed the same sea. We found that neither he nor Jackie were liked in Greece. They admired her when she was a Kennedy, but felt she degraded herself by marrying Onassis. Opinion was that he did nothing for his country, despite his millions. He could have done so much, for it was noticeably poor in those days.

We wound up our trip in beautiful Amsterdam and found it has more canals than Venice, but unlike that city, traffic is allowed here and one can walk on the ample sidewalks and bridges. We visited the Rijkmuseum and finally saw the famous Night Watch. I had recently read a marvellous book about Rembrandt's life, so was interested in what his first wife Saskia looked like. I tactlessly had commented to a young German girl who lived in Torreon that I imagined she looked just like what I imagined Saskia to look like. She was horrified, and said in her German accent: " But haf you nefer seen Da Night Watch? She wass very homely leettle woman!" Sorry. But she was right. We loved the museums, and when I gazed upon Van Gogh's paintings for the first time, I realized one has to see the originals with their thick brush strokes to appreciate his work. Little by little, visiting the various museums, I was developing a passionate love of art which has endured and grown over the years. We saw Anne Frank's house, and of course could not bypass the diamond factory, where we purchased two small diamonds for earrings. Our trip included a tour to Volendam, a quaint Dutch village with many windmills, driven and guided by a distinguished older guide who was a look-alike to President DeGaulle, and who lectured us about the constant fight of the Dutch against the sea. He showed us paintings by Ruisdael, and called our attention to the beautiful clouds in his landscapes, little tips we have never forgotten. I must add that my husband has to be the best travel companion I could ever want to have. His aesthetic senses have developed over the years, and when he realized that art is so important to me, he went along with it, until he too enjoys visits to museums and galleries as much as I. In fact we are very responsive to each other's ideas on every trip we have ever made together. Other couples should be so lucky! Selfishly, on the other hand, I have never been able to whip up any enthusiasm for watching baseball and football with him on T. V. In fact I'm jealous of the fact that he dedicates so much time to watching the Yankees every night during the baseball season and gets so upset if they don't win. I feel like telling him: IT'S JUST A GAME! But that would certainly not be the wise thing to say!

Our trip back to Houston was long and tiring, and we had to spend a night at the airport hotel to take our flight to Monterrey, next morning. We called home, eager to talk to our little boy and Frank's mother and father. In Monterrey we were lucky to arrive in time to connect for a flight to Torreon, where Frank's parents met us at the airport. Tony arrived home for lunch, and we were so thrilled to see him at last and recount some of our adventures. What a delightful end to a wonderful trip. We had sent them postcards from each city, most of which had been received already, so they had followed our travels throughout. When I asked Frank's mother how our cook had behaved with them while we were away, she laughed and replied that they had been served breaded veal cutlets and Mexican rice almost every day, because that is what Tony had ordered. They spoiled him rotten while we were gone, but how lovely that they were there for us. We could never have taken that trip without having them and we will be forever grateful

OUR INVESTMENTS.

Although we were doing very well financially, due to the large amount of consultations Frank was giving at the clinic, and the many operations and deliveries he was having every month, we had not done well with our investments. I already mentioned about the mine when we first arrived in Torreón. But when Frank went to inspect it for the first time, he was disappointed to see it was only a hole in the ground, and did not have an upright entrance like one sees in the movies. However, it had produced a small amount of silver, and the other doctor who knew more about mining, had faith they would find more veins. So they sat back and waited. Needless to say, it never produced anything, and the money, although a very small amount, was lost. Then there was the drugstore investment with three other doctors, but my husband was too busy by this time to check up on it every day the way the others did, and after a while, not seeing any profits, he sold out his share to the other three at a loss. By this time, one could see the trend of wanting to put his savings into a profitable investment instead of letting it lag in a bank, so in the seventies, when he was at the peak of his earnings, he and four doctors from the Diagnostic Clinic decided they would start a chicken farm. This area and climate are good for raising chickens, and there were already several businessmen who had made a large amount of money in the same line. They bought some land about three quarters of an hour away from Gomez Palacio, and each invested a rather large sum of money for the construction of the coops and other necessities. One of the doctors was supposed to take care of the finances, already having experience on his own farm, and the other three were supposed to occasionally check up on the books. Well, things went beautifully, so much so that someone suggested also having pigs on the farm, so pig pens were built and we got to watch the sows with their little piggies when we visited the farm on weekends. The feed for both the chickens and the pigs was all bought from Anderson Clayton, so to cut costs, the owners decided to make part of the feed themselves at one of the doctor's ranches. From there they decided that they would start their own packing plant to sell chicken and pork to the public. And this is where it all went wrong. It turned out that the employees and manager of the packing plant betrayed the owners, selling the product on the side. To make a long story short, the whole business went under, and the doctors ended up by owing Anderson Clayton and the banks a lot of money. At one time, the five wives were afraid we would lose our homes, because every week we had to sign reams of I.O.U.s, until one day we decided we wouldn't sign any more. But we were forced to, because money and properties were in both our husbands' and our names in each case. It could have been a most profitable venture had the group's vision not been so greedy and remained with the original chicken farm, of which there are many here today, all profitable. Luckily, Frank continued to have success in his career, and soon we were back to normal financially.

TRIP TO SILAO, GUANAJUATO

On one of my yearly trips to see my mother in Mexico City, I noticed she was getting very absent minded. She had recently retired from teaching English at the British Institute, and was only giving private classes at her apartment. My brother Bob, and his wife Lyn, and Susan, their little girl, were living across the street from my mother's apartment, and they would look in on her almost daily, but it seemed to me she was not receiving the care and attention that an eighty-year old woman should receive. I talked with Frank when I returned from my trip, and we both decided we should move her to Torreón so we could take care of her when she needed it. She was receiving financial help from my sister, my five brothers, and me, so, added to the money she received from her classes she was fairly stable economically. We talked with her, and she agreed that she would come. At the time, she still had an active social life among friends she had known for years. Often she would invite a small group to her apartment for a glass of wine and a light supper, and they would compare notes about books they had read or poetry they had written, until late at night. Other times, she and her lady friends would meet for breakfast or tea at Sanborns. She also had some old male friends who still found her charming and attractive, and would either meet her for coffee, or invite her for dinner in the evenings. In short, although what we were offering her was stability and tender loving care, we realized that she would miss her friends and her social life. With no help from me, she packed up her belongings and shipped her furniture to Torreón, where we had found her a lovely little apartment near town like she had wanted, so that she could walk to the different shops without having to ask me for a ride. Always having been completely independent, it was hard for her to rely upon anyone else. The day finally came when she sent us her dog, a large brown French Poodle with a long pedigree, who was to live in our garden while she occupied her apartment. Her furniture arrived, followed by her, looking radiant and excited about her new adventure. She stayed with us while I helped arrange her belongings, aided by two stalwart soldiers Frank requested, and when we were finished with details such as new curtains and rugs, she finally moved in. I put double locks on all her doors, and was confident she was going to be safe. It didn't take her long to make friends with the old couple who owned the building, who lived downstairs, and who would often invite her to have a little drink with them in the afternoons. I would stop by to see her when doing my many errands in Torreón, and she always came to us for weekends, at which times she occupied the guest room. She seemed to be very happy with her new life, an incredible triumph for a woman of her age moving from long-time surroundings. But one of my friends told me that she had said, "In Mexico City, I was known to everyone as Louise Brown, but here I'm just 'Peggy's mother!" Finally, she decided to give English classes to some of our friends' mothers and relatives. This brought her in contact with acquaintances of her own making.

One day while reminiscing about her youth, my mother expressed the desire to one day go back to visit Silao, in the state of Guanajuato, where she had spent some time with her parents when they owned a small farm there. I told her I would accompany her, and that we two could travel there for a few days if she so wished. Frank suggested we go by train, as in those days the trains were still comfortable and, on the most part, ran on schedule. We planned our five-day trip and proceeded to take the train to Silao, a small city in the west central part of the state. When the conductor came around and asked us where we were getting off, we told him Silao. He looked surprised, and informed us that the train would not be arriving there before dark, and that it was recommendable that we disembark instead in Leon, a previous stop, as in Silao he doubted we would find good lodgings. He suggested taking a taxi next day from there to Silao, as it was only about fifteen minutes away by road. We were grateful for his advice, and disembarked in Leon, where sure enough we found a suitable hotel in town. Next morning we walked around the lovely little plaza and admired the trees' folliage, which was trimmed in a unique mushroom cut. As luck would have it, we found a gaily decorated little restaurant right off the square, with chairs and tables painted in various colors and covered with pretty cloths, where we had breakfast. We hired a taxi with an amiable old driver, who said he'd be happy to drive us to Silao, and suggested waiting for us while we visited it. He could then drive us to Guanajuato, the capital. So off we went, and arrived at the main plaza of Silao, the very place my mother had wanted to visit, for it was here that her parents had owned an old house seventy years before. The old driver was happy to wait for us, keeping our small bags in the car. My mother and I both, having lived so many years in Mexico, considered ourselves good judges of character, and knew the old man would wait for us as promised, and not drive off with our bags.

Silao is an agricultural area, where a few miles away, lies the famous "Cerro del Cubilete" hill, on which stands a twenty-meter high monument of Christ the King, representing the unity of the Mexican people in the Catholic Faith. We walked around the plaza, my mother excitedly pointing out the balcony of her bedroom in the old house which was still standing, albeit now occupied below by a cheap taco stand with a coke sign partially obstructing the view. We sat on a bench to take a picture of it, although I knew she was disappointed at the sight of a house that had once been beautiful in memory, and now was converted into an ugly commercial property. There, facing her old house she began to relate the story I had heard many times during my lifetime, of how, when she was fourteen, she hade been in love with a local boy named Raúl. He was fifteen years old, the son of a wealthy rancher, and they had met in the park during those evening walks that girls and boys take around the central plaza throughout the provinces. The girls she was with were older than she, only reason her strict parents had allowed her to walk unchaperoned. According to my mother, it had been love at first sight when they had seen each other in the Plaza, and Raúl had finally convinced her to break away from her friends and sit with him on a bench to talk. And so commenced a romance of sorts, first, just talking to each other, and finally building up to holding hands briefly. It was an innocent romance, until one day he blurted out that he'd like to marry her, and suggested they run away together. She was breath-taken, but the second time he suggested it, she actually thought seriously about it, and asked him how they could do it. At which time he unfolded his ill-thought-out plan of coming to her balcony a certain night, on a white horse, and throwing her a rope so that she could climb down onto the horse, and together they could gallop off together. They would take the night train to Mexico City, where his parents had a large house, empty while they were at the ranch, and where he and she could remain until he found another place to live. He had his allowance to keep them going for a while, or so he said. It all sounded feasable.

The planned night came, and at midnight Raúl and his horse rode beneath her balcony, and waited. Little Lucy opened the window, and as she started to climb over the balustrade, her mother and father broke into her room and dragged her back inside. They looked out, saw the boy on his white steed, and told him never to come back or they would talk to his parents. Hysterical now, their daughter told them that they were in love, and would try it again until they succeeded. Needless to say, she was not allowed out in the plaza any more, and shortly after was sent away to boarding school. End of romance. But over the years, in the Mexico City papers, Lucy had followed Raúl's life, for he became a prominent wealthy banker, often mentioned in business and social circles. Although my mother had gone on to love and marry my father and bear him seven children, she never forgot her very first romance.

My mother was re-telling me this story that morning, while sitting beneath her balcony, when suddenly we heard the church bells ringing. "I imagine it must be a special eleven o'clock mass", she commented. Then, listening to the slow, solemn bongs, she added, "It sounds like a funeral mass at this hour." She got up to ask an old man selling Mexico City newspapers if he knew who the mass was for. He handed her a newspaper. Across the front page, a headline, "Hoy Murió Don Raúl Bailleres, Conocido Banquero", Today Don Raúl Bailleres Died, A Prominent Banker. I thought my mother would faint. She walked unsteadily toward the bench and sat down heavily. How could it be that we had come to this very spot where they had courted so many years ago, on the very day that he had died. The old newspaper vendor told us that Don Raúl had not lived here for years, but had always financially supported Silao's church over time, reason they were dedicating a special mass to him although he lived in Mexico City. Truly, at times, life can be stranger than fiction. I gave the old man a few coins, and we attended the Mass. Our cab was waiting for us, and we continued our travels toward Guanajuato and San Miguel de Alllende, but everything we saw and admired in the following days in those picturesque cities, was overshadowed by the earlier happening in Silao. Still, it was a memorable and most unforgettable trip. We came home with a good supply of Cajeta (a delicious burnt sugary milk) typical of Celaya, in the same state, and Charamuscas, a crisp toffee in a short rope form. This last one I had not tasted since I was a child and it brought back memories of what Roberto and I used to buy in the local cinema to munch during the movie.

LOSS OF A FRIEND

In September of 1971, our friend Vernon, forever the fun-seeker, suggested going to Las Vegas again. Everyone was game, and the plan was for the same three couples to leave the next week and remain in Vegas for a few days. Vernon and Bobby owned a large cattle ranch a day's drive away from here, so Vernon had bought himself a small plane for transportation to and from the ranch. This was the plane we had flown in with him over our house during the flood. The day before we were to leave, anxious to get home from the ranch to meet us for the upcoming trip, he decided to fly return, despite bad weather and his pilot's recommendation that they not risk it that morning. But Vernon, always eager to be on the move, insisted they take off in heavy rain. We got the call a few hours later from Bobby's secretary. His plane had flown into a mountain and gone down, both occupants killed. None of us could believe the terrible news.

One of the saddest days in our young lives was when we buried Vernon at the Torreón cemetery. His elderly mother and father had come in from their home in Cuernavaca, as well as his twin sister from Washington state. His elder sister from Dallas also arrived for the funeral. Bobby was left with three little girls from her marriage to Vernon, and two boys from her previous marriage. It was a sad group at graveside. Furthermore, it took us months to halfway get over his death. When one so high-spirited and energetic passes on, his absence is deeply felt, and for a long time none of us could hear any record that he used to play during those long evenings we had all spent in their den, without breaking up. His death put a great damper on our lives, and only time helped to assuage our feelings and raise our spirits. Gradually we and the Barboglios branched out and connected with other couples, but it was never the same.

That Christmas Frank and I decided we would spend the week with Tony in Acapulco. We drove by Cuernavaca, and there visited Vernon Moore's parents at their beautiful home in that paradisiacal city before driving on to Acapulco. I remember that I had suggested to Frank to not exchange presents that year, so had bought nothing for him or for Tony. I have never really been in accord with gift exchange on any pre-ordained day, so thought it was a good idea. That day on the beach though, Frank brought out two little packages, one for Tony and one for me. I was really surprised to find a lovely set of gold earrings and ring for me, and a beautiful camera for Tony. Talk about feeling little! I was truly ashamed of my thoughtlessness.

In January of 1973 Johns Hopkins hospital offered a week long symposium in Family Planning for professors of gynecology and obstetrics all over Latin America, all expenses paid. Frank and another doctor who taught at the Medical University here applied and were granted the stay. They left for Baltimore, Maryland for the symposium, and while there, Frank took advantage and crossed the Chesapeake Bay to Chestertown, Maryland, to visit Washington College, where we were thinking of signing Tony up for entrance in September. What he saw, he liked, and so it was that our son was enrolled in that prestigious college.

Tony graduated from the American High School that June, and we three took off for Los Angeles to attend Frank's parents' fiftieth wedding anniversary with them and all the family. It was a beautiful and special occasion, starting first with a church ceremony where they took their marriage vows again, followed by a magnificent luncheon at a nearby popular restaurant in Capistrano, where they now lived, named El Adobe, and where President Richard Nixon used to often eat and entertain. Both of Frank's parents were in good physical health and looked radiant on that day, surrounded by all their family.

That same year, two years after Vernon died, Bobby said she'd like to intern one of her daughters in school in Switzerland. The girl was having an unsatisfactory relationship with a local boy, and Bobby wanted to get her away from Torreón for a year to break it up. She was planning on taking her daughter alone in September, but after discussing it one evening at her house, Fran

Barboglio and I said we'd like to accompany her. Then another friend of Bobby's, Doris Garza said she'd go along too, and Fran's daughter wanted in also. So eventually the trip was planned for the six of us. Pete and Frank were amenable with the whole plan, and said they would meet us three weeks into our trip, in Rome, to continue travelling together.

Our son, Tony, was now 17, and had just left for Washington College in Maryland. My mother and I had driven with him to San Antonio to take his flight to Baltimore, and when we saw him board, I was so happy she was alongside me, as I was ready to break down. This would be the longest time he'd be away from us, and we knew it would be the beginning of broken ties and his establishing his independence. I was depressed when we drove home, one reason I jumped at the chance to go to Europe to forget my woes.

SECOND TRIP TO EUROPE

This time we decided on a local travel agent to arrange our trip. The plans were as follows: We six would fly to Amsterdam, make connections to fly to Zurich, spend 3 days there, and from there to Berne the capital. This, we understood, was near Frieburg, where Bobby Sue's school was located. Once we had left her at school we would entrain to Paris, fly to Madrid, and take another train to Barcelona, where we would rent a car to drive along the coast to Nice, fly to Rome, meet with our husbands, and continue to Florence and Venice. As if that wasn't enough, we would still go on to Munich and Frankfurt where we would rent a station wagon and drive on to Amsterdam. End of trip, but in retrospect the whole itinerary looks daunting. Too many cities squeezed into six weeks.

The trip started out with a bang. The night we left for Mexico City to take our plane to Zurich, all our families were at the airport, plus a group of gay Mariachis to send us off. It was another memorable start to a European vacation. What we did not count on was broken-hearted little Bobby Sue crying all the way to Switzerland. I remember her long hair hanging over the seat as her mother held her head in her lap, sobbing deeply. She ate not a bite, hardly slept, and by the time we arrived at our hotel in Zurich looked like a little ghost. Bobby prevailed though, and after three days, (including a side train-trip to see our friends the Hubers, now living in Winterthur, an experience in itself!) we took the train to Berne. Bobby Sue cheered up a bit at the exquisite Hotel Schweizerhof and we spent a fun packed day before we boarded another train to take her to school in nearby Freiburg. But arriving at the school, none of us had expected to find such a drab atmosphere. The Directrice welcomed us formally and showed us the classrooms, then led us down long dark halls to where the pupils slept, large dorms for eight girls, beds separated by curtains, each with a bedside table holding a washbasin and a pitcher of water. I noticed chamber pots under the beds. When Bobby asked where her daughter would shower every morning, the Directrice looked surprised, answering, "No, Madame, the girls only bathe once a week. Every day they merely wash face and hands and teeth in their individual washbowl." She then showed us the large bathroom four doors away. We looked at Bobby Sue. She stood stiffly by her mother's side with a resigned expression, but I suspect she was already all cried out, for she uttered not a sound.

We left Bobby talking to the Directrice, and went toward the doorway to wait for her while she took up the financial details in the office. Then we kissed Bobby Sue and left, turning at the big gate to see the forlorn little girl standing by the nun at the entrance, sadly waving goodbye.

We boarded the waiting cab, and went to the train station, not before I grandly told him "A la guerre, s'il vous plais." He immediately corrected me, saying, "Non madame, a la gare, pas la guerre." No, madame, to the station, not the war." So much for my French.

217

We stayed another two days in the beautiful city of Berne, going down every evening to dine in the elegant hotel restaurant where, it turned out, all the Members of Parliament were dining while in session. The last night we changed from slacks and raincoats into fine wool dresses and heels, and actually got complimentary looks from the members, where as the previous nights in our unflattering travel outfits and flat shoes, we had been totally ignored.

We took a train to Paris, with instructions from our guide not to get off until we arrived at the Gare du Nord. However, I entailed a long conversation with the conductor in the hallway, only grasping half of it, as I was barely beginning with my French classes, and misunderstanding that we were to get off halfway to Paris and change trains. I ran into our compartment and told my friends to start grabbing their suitcases and be ready to get off the train at the next stop. At the station we all started to put our suitcases through the window, where stevedores relieved us of them, and when we were all standing on the platform, they asked us what train we were waiting for. I told them, the train to Paris, to which they frantically started to load our suitcases back on the train, informing us loudly "C'est ca le tren a Paris!" THIS is the train to Paris! We reborded, and of course my friends kidded me about my French the rest of the way.

In Paris, three of us headed for the Louvre the first day, Fran and Jan her daughter going shopping. Bobby, Doris and I went through the art galleries thoroughly, and Bobby kidded me that evening that every time she looked over at me, I was standing in front of some painting with my mouth open in awe while I listened to the description from the recorder hanging around my neck. My love affair with art had begun on our previous trip to Europe.

One night we went to the Pigalle district to a nightclub to see a transvestite show, not a particularly smart thing for five women alone to do. We stumbled out of there about one in the morning and I insisted we walk, as I knew the way back to the hotel. There is a saying in Spanish that God takes care of fools and drunkards, and although we were the former, and not the latter, He took care of us that night until, after many wrong turns, we finally found our hotel. When I related this story later to a French friend, she was horrified and told me we were lucky not to be robbed.

We flew to Madrid early one morning, expecting a gourmet breakfast because we were on Air France. All we got was a dry croissant and strong coffee. As I had been there before, I acted like the well-travelled sophisticate, and led my friends through the Prado Museum, and on to popular restaurants which they would not have found without me. We also tried many "tavernas" where we found all sorts of seafood delicacies to taste with our red wine. A photographer took a picture of the five of us sitting by a huge barrel of wine with a tap, from which we served ourselves amply. I suggested we send the photo back home to be published in our local newspaper, where travelers often sent back their photos from all over the world. I was met with laughter, as they reminded me that ladies on trips to Europe usually sent back pictures standing in front of one of the famous churches, certainly not sitting in bars with a barrel of wine.

While in Madrid my friends wanted to see a bullfight one day after lunch. I told them to go ahead. I preferred to stay in the restaurant and ask for a nice desert and coffee. I wasn't about to see a poor bull butchered in the ring. In Mexico City when Frank and I were sweethearts, I had gone to bullfights with him, because he enjoyed watching the bullfighters piroutte and show off with the cape. He knew the specific routines which should be performed, and when they were executed well, he and everyone else would get up and say "Olé" with vigor. But I was always horrified when the Toreros stabbed the bull with their decorated banderillas, a form of javelin, followed by the hateful "picadores" on their horses, who would dig their spear-ended poles into the top of its spine. Sometimes, the enfuriated bull fought back and gored the horse's belly, making a bloody show even more gory. At the end, after attracting the bull with a bright red cape, or

219

"maleta", the grand finale would arrive, with the sword, which had to be thrust at a certain angle near the spinal column, to run straight into the lung or heart, clearly a difficult thing to do, for few bullfighters were able to execute it right. After standing there dazed, bleeding through its nose and sides, the bull would sometimes have to receive a "coup de grace" from a dagger in the back of its neck, before it finally fell over dead. I did learn to appreciate the turns and daring feats of the bullfighters with their use of, first, the wide flourishing purple cape, and then the maleta, the red cloth used for the kill. But how much sportsmanlike it would be if the bulls were not tortured with the banderillas and speared poles, and the bullfighters would only tempt and tease him, practicing the art of "tauromaquia" which this is called. They could even be allowed to file down the horns to avoid a fatality. I feel that it is really sick to watch a beautiful animal, such as a bull is at the beginning of the fight, gradually be drained of its energy and blood before the end. So much for bullfighting.

We took a silver-colored train, El Talgo, from Madrid to Barcelona. Lunch was served at each seat, and I was enchanted with the best potato salad I've ever eaten. It tasted largely of olive oil, and the waiter told me it was because the mayonaise was made with olive oil. I have since tried to copy it on the few times I make my own mayonaise.Barcelona is my favorite Spanish city, the capital of Catalunia, with its own unique culture and personality. It is located in the northeastern part, facing the Mediterranean, and is the port from which Columbus sailed to America in 1492. It has a wonderful central avenue called Las Ramblas, where everyone strolls and or sits to have refreshments while watching the passerbys. There is an atmosphere of gaiety everywhere, and people live into the night, eating and drinking wine until the wee hours of the morning. One sees old men in the plazas playing dominos or chess, and many buildings on the crooked streets are constant reminders of the great architect, Gaudi, with typical tile decorations and curvy balconies. His Sagrada Familia church is so distinctive it defies description, as is his Parque Güell, park,where giant palm trees carved out of cement welcome you, and weird fountains and sculptures are scattered throughout. We tried the famous "tapas" in the taverns, French bread covered with a myriad of toppings, tomato, cheeses of all types, sardines, anchovies and what have you, which, accompanied by a good Sangría (a mixture of red wine and lemonade) usually made up our supper.

We rented a car. We had requested from Mexico a station wagon, having in mind the type found in the States during the seventies, to carry five women and five huge suitcases for our trip up along the coast to Nice. What they gave us was a small "Seat", a cousin of the Italian Fiat, and just as small. We insisted that it would not carry us and our luggage, but the agency man equally insisted that it would. (He obviously had not seen the size of our suitcases.) We took off early one morning, and about two hours out of Barcelona, heard a distinctive crack, and wobbled to a stop at the edge of a beach. We found a phone at a stall a few meters away, and were able to call the agency. They sounded mystified, but said they would send us another vehicle. Meanwhile we sat on the sand and looked at the ocean, eventually ordering from the boy at the stall some French bread and salami, plus a pitcher of sangría. The new car arrived, and the agents, after inspecting ours underneath, found that the axle had cracked slightly. They limped away, and we took over the newer car, only slightly bigger.

We took turns driving, and stopped along the way for the night in Narbonne, a small hotel where they were amazed at the size of our suitcases, in comparison to the way Europeans travel with one small suitcase. Ours were ridiculous in comparison. That night we walked down the middle of the dark street looking for a restaurant. Cars whizzed by, and whistled at us as they passed. Later the lady at the hotel informed us that only prostitutes walked the streets at night. Glad we weren't approached! Next day we drove through Marseille, and had lunch there at an open air café. The city looked interesting, and I wish we could have stayed longer, but we had to arrive in Nice because we had a flight to catch in two days to meet our husbands in Rome. We drove through beautiful countryside and vineyards laying in the sun, the ocean to our right. I was the chauffeur that day, and Bobby wanted to get off and cut some grapes, but I warned her that it was against the law, and they might arrest us, so we drove on and she never forgave me.

The first night we were in Nice we decided on going to the Casino in Monte Carlo. Fearless we were, and I would never attempt it anymore at night. With instructions which I did not understand clearly, (for a change) we set out, and when I came to some arrows pointing to "haute" and "bas" I decided on the former, and launched into a frightening drive over a narrow cement road with hairpin turns. We finally arrived, shaking, at the steps of the Casino, and when I commented about the road to the doorman, he looked amused, and told me we had taken the high road, built in Napoleon's time, when we should have chosen the modern lower one. The difference between "haute" and "bas"! We had worn our finery, long dresses, jewelry, high heels, expecting to find the crowd well dressed, but were surprised to find the women mostly in raincoats and slacks. Luckily we did not try our luck at the tables, only at the machines, and even those were hard for us to understand.

We flew to Rome, Fran and I eager to see our husbands. When we arrived, we hired two cabs, one for me with all the heavy suitcases, and the other four ladies with only their hand luggage. The cab driver and I chatted merrily all the way, he in Italian, I in Spanish, but we found we could understand each other. As we drew up in front of our hotel, Frank and Pete were standing there, and I jumped out of the cab to embrace my husband. Frank asked the cab driver how much I owed him, and hit the roof with the man's response. He thought it way too much, and that he was being taken. Pete closed in, and there ensued a heavy argument with the driver, who all but got out of the cab for a fist fight. I threw up my hands and went into the hotel. We had had such a pleasant trip up to this point, the other ladies and I, no fights with waiters, or drivers, or anyone, and now, with our men along, the prospect looked grim.

We did the rounds of Rome, enjoying the food as usual, and the rest of our stay ensued peacefully. The last day we took a trip to Naples to see the Blue Grotto. We had been warned about the city having had a bout with yellow fever, and had all been vaccinated in Mexico. However, the bus did not stop there, but carried us right to the wharf to our boat where two men would row us to the Grotto. With us, two tourists came, one a young handsome American who immediately started a conversation with me when he saw I was having trouble loading my camera. I remember the boat man pointing to an overlooking hill and telling us that Esther Williams had a house there. Jan, the Barboglio daughter, who must have been only about 23, looked at him and asked "Who is Esther Williams?" We all had to laugh. When we entered the cave we marvelled at the transparent pale blue water which looked like it had underwater lighting. Then we went to Anacapri for lunch and from there to Sorrento, the American being very solicitous with me, helping me in and out of the boat and the bus. Frank was clearly annoyed and we rode back in silence to Rome. Next day he was back to normal.

We took a bus, stopping at Assissi, Siena, and Florence, the cultural heart of Italy. No matter how many times one goes to Florence, there is so much to see, just the museums alone, the Academy, the Uffizi, the Pitti Palace, the Duomo, the various churches. But I was beginning with a bad cold, and actually missed the best dinner of all at a highly recommended restaurant. Frank took a city tour next day with Bobby and Doris, and found a young woman who was trying to start a flirtation, unaware of my two friends who were watching her. When they got back they were dying to report to me, but Frank just laughed it off.

In Venice, I stayed in bed one evening, and Fran, also with a cold, did the same in their room, so Pete, Frank, and Jan went out into the night, and later told us they had had a ball, each taking turns dancing with Jan. I really believe that was the highlight of the trip for the three of them!

The bus ride to Milan was uneventful, except for stopping in Padova at the Chapel of Scrovegni to see Giotto's beautiful 14th century paintings which we had missed on our previous trip. It was worth every minute, and I bought several postcards with reproductions of each figure, but unfortunately I mailed most of them when we arrived in Milan. I wish I had kept the collection for myself. Our hotel in Milan turned out to be dreadful, hallways with linoleum flooring and a bare lightbulb hanging above. However, it was located well, near the Duomo and the Galleria Vittorio Emmanuelle II. I guess you can't win every time. Next day we had a lovely old lady guide who took us through the Scala Theatre, while relating the story of the life and death of Enrico Caruso, and how when he was dying from a ruptured appendix he cried out to his wife, "I don't want to die, I don't want to leave you!" She was clearly emotionally involved with the story of this great tenor, and had us ladies on the verge of tears ourselves. Outside, we all bought postcards of Caruso, and begged her to have a glass of Cinzano with us at the Galleria. She turned out to be very interesting, giving us pointers about her city.

We took a train through the Brenner Pass to Innsbruck in the Austrian Alps, and were stunned with the beauty of the ride and the city when we arrived. I went to have my hair done, and the young male British hairdresser told me my hairdo was old fashioned and that he would like to give me one that any man would like to run his fingers through. I think he must have had himself in mind, for as I was leaving he asked me whether I was travelling alone so we could go out that night together. Opportunity missed!

We entrained from there to Munich, one of the highlights of our trip. We stood in Marienplatz square to watch the famous clock, and Frank and I danced to the gay music of an Austrian band on a nearby stage. Spent long hours at the Alte Pinakothek museum swept up by the works of Dürer and Altdorfer, where I had to be literally pulled away from the former's self portrait, and the latter's Battle of Issus. Connie, the Withingtons' daughter, all grown up now, was working at the American Embassy, so we phoned her to come over to have dinner with us at the hotel. How time had passed since she and her little brother, Tod, used to trail around with Tony and me on our errands in Torreón.

Poor Frankfurt. We didn't really give it much of a chance. I think we were tired of travelling by this time, and only paid half attention to our guide. Anyway, we rented a large van and started out to Cologne, along the river Rhine, but at a town called Rudesheim, our van had engine trouble, (apparently, European vehicles did not like us!) and the mechanic at the garage where we stopped, suggested we spend the night at the hotel next door while he fixed the van. We checked into the darling little hotel and went down to the restaurant, where a band was playing dance music and everyone was dancing. Later we found out we could not have found a nicer place to break down, as Rudesheim is known as romantic holiday town It didn't take long before we too were drinking and dancing.

Our van fixed, we proceeded towards Cologne, spending the night in Bonn, and arriving at our destination, where immediately we told Pete to drive us to the famous Cathedral. He drove along, and finally stopped at a church, but cries of dismay were uttered by the ladies telling him that this was not the Cathedral, to which he replied, "At this point one church is going to look like another to me!" Needless to say, we finally made it to the imposing Cathedral, and it was every bit as worthy as we had expected. I remember seeing a triptych there, depicting the figure of the pregnant virgin, which I had never seen in any other painting. Just one of those details which remain in my memory.

On to Amsterdam, our last stop, where Frank and I had been in 1969. Like us, our friends were impressed at the amount of canals, and the beauty of the city. Of course, one night we went to the famous street where all the prostitutes parade their half-naked figures through big windows, and stopped at a nightclub with a bawdy show. Halfway through, we left. It was even bawdier than we could have possibly imagined.

I called a friend who had worked with me at Retail Credit Credit company, and who was now married to a Dutchman and living in Amsterdam. She and her husband came by the hotel, and we four went out to a couple of bars before going to dinner. Talking to her, I was envious of the fact that every weekend they would take advantage to travel to nearby cities for a visit. Sounded so continental to me.

The end of our trip was now upon us. But before we left we heard on the news that Russia had sent troops to, was it Yugoslavia? Or was it Afghanistan? Bobby immediately assumed there might be a war coming up, deciding that she did not want to leave Bobby Sue in Europe with that scenario. We personally thought she had had second thoughts about leaving her daughter at that depressing school, and wanted to bring her home. But she insisted, and called her daughter's school, saying that "due to a probable war", she wanted her daughter to meet us in Amsterdam and return home. The poor nuns flew into a panic and said they had heard nothing about a war, but that they would pack up her daughter and send her to us right away. Bobby Sue arrived, looking calm, and somewhat heavier and happier than when we had left her. She told us she had eaten a lot of rabbit stew while in school, and mostly oatmeal for breakfast. Anyway, nothing came of the supposed war scare, as we had surmised all along, and we were ready to leave Europe.

When we arrived in Mexico City, the first thing we did at the airport before changing planes for Torreon, was to order good Mexican breakfasts, huevos rancheros, frijoles, and chilaquiles, with big glasses of fresh orange juice, which had been so expensive during our trip.

At home, I was so happy to see my mother, and find everything taken care of at the house by our maid and gardener. We called Tony at college and made plans for his coming home for Christmas. Needless to say, Bobby Sue took up with her old boyfriend again, and shortly after, they eloped and got married. The main reason for the trip to Europe was to avoid this, but sometimes one cannot change fate. Anyway, we all had a fine time.

On all our trips, I would write lengthy descriptive letters upon our return, to my mother when she lived in Mexico City, and to Vic, my sister in the U. S. Some of these letters were returned to me later by my mother to be included in my albums. Others were given to me when Vic passed away in 1997. These letters have been valuable to me when writing this memoir, as they are filled with details that photographs cannot show in my many albums. Mostly, to Tony, we flooded him with postcards from every city, and talked with him lengthily by phone upon our return. I truly believe that my mother, sister, and Dan, my brother-in-law, relived our experiences vicariously through my writings, and looked forward to our reunions here in summer or at Christmas to hear about our travels first hand.

Every year Vic and Dan would make it a point to come to visit us. When my mother moved to Torreón they had double reason to come, and those days have given me some of my happiest memories, when, all gathered by the pool, Dan, floating on an air mattress with a drink in his hand, would humorously say something to the effect of "I wonder what the poor people are doing today!" He and Frank played golf together on weekends and on Wednesday afternoons when Frank did not consult. Other days I accompanied him. Vic and my mother and I would have tea in the afternoons, or Vic and I would go on errands to the seamstress or tailor where Vic always had clothes to be adjusted, or to the jeweler, where she would have certain pieces mended or designed. Then when the men came home from golf, Dan would suggest around 6 P. M. "It's drinky time!" and we would have a drink and some tidbits before supper. They were such a delightfully attractive and dear couple that we looked forward eagerly to their annual visits. In the summer of '73, Vic's son, Billy, and his wife, Chris, and their tiny little daughter, Tara, came with them. Bill and Chris had married when they were nineteen years old, and Bill had graduated from the University of Wyoming with a B.S. degree in Civil Engineering. He was presently enlisted in the U.S. Air Force Academy in Colorado Springs, and brought his dress uniform at our request. We took many pictures of them and they were truly a handsome young couple.

While Tony was still in the American High School, he had started going with a pretty little Mexican girl named Veronica, who lived a few blocks away from us. They used to sit on the lawn in front of her house in the afternoons, and for a while I was afraid they might elope. But after he returned from college they stopped seeing each other, and he starting dating a lovely American girl, Debbie, daughter of some friends of ours here in Torreon. We started the tradition of going to Debbie's parents' home for dinner on Christmas Eve, which is the night one celebrates in Mexico, and then on the 25th, they would come over to celebrate at our home with the midday meal of turkey and trimmings. Here I should comment that at Mexican tables, before the turkey, families usually start with a codfish casserole cooked with tiny potatoes and capers in tomato sauce, followed by the turkey with a meat stuffing. In humbler homes, all this is substituted by home-made tamales. Anyway, we were pleased that these kids of ours were going together. Debbie chose a college near Tony's in the east, and they would get together for Thanksgiving over there. This went on for two years, until Tony decided he wanted to change his major from Political Science to Communication Arts at Loyola Marymount University in Los Angeles, at which time Debbie also changed to a college in California so they could continue seeing each other. We took it for granted that eventually they would get married.

MAZATLÁN

In the summer of 1974 when Tony was here from college, his three teen-aged cousins, daughters of Frank's two brothers and sister, came to visit us from Los Angeles. Debbie too was home visiting her parents, and Tony suggested that we all go Mazatlán, our nearest beach on the Pacific coast in the state of Sinaloa. It is called by the residents here, "Torreón Beach", because during Holy Week our city empties into that beachtown. To get there, one has to drive at least 3 hours to Durango city, and from there, another 8 hours to reach Mazatlán over the curviest, most dangerous mountain road I ever hope to travel. My friend, Fran Barboglio, wanted to go along, so she offered her huge station wagon to travel in. After all, there would be seven of us. Frank would remain here to attend to his practice, and Pete would remain at his ranch.

Tony drove all the way. He was, and is, an excellent driver, and when we arrived in Mazatlán we checked into a motel that had cabins right on the beach, Fran, Tony and I in one, and the four girls in another one. In the mornings we would wake up and go straight into the ocean. We had breakfast of sorts in the cabins, and lunch at the nearby restaurants. I found myself joining in the fun and games to such an extent that I felt just as young as the teenagers! I sunned a lot, despite my mother's previous warnings that I'd be sorry when I was seventy years old, but my argument was that I wouldn't care what my skin looked like at that old age. In the evenings, we'd go to the Hotel Playa for dinner and music on the verandah. The kids had a ball.

On the way back, after rounding a curve, we hit some oil on the road and skidded into the mountain, despite the fact that Tony was driving extra slowly. Thank God we didn't go over the cliff, as it is hundreds of meters down, and midst that tropical foliage we never would have been found. There was little damage to the station wagon, only a bent fender which Tony, and a kind, passing bus driver, helped to straighten, so we drove home, nervous all the way. The girls stayed on for another week, enjoying our pool along with Tony's friends who joined them, eager to meet the little Americanitas who were so young and pretty. It was a memorable summer for all.

In the summer of '76 my mother, Frank, Tony and I drove to Los Angeles. On these drives, and we made them every year, we'd leave the house at 4 A.M. and drive all the way to Tucson, Arizona, arriving about dark. Night in a motel, and on to L. A. the next morning, arriving at Frank's family's home about mid-afternoon. Their pretty house in San Juan Capistrano, where they had moved recently, had its back garden facing the freeway, and when we neared, we could see Frank's watchful father looking over the fence, waiting for us. He was such a dear man.

This time however, as we neared the U. S. Border, Frank instructed my mother to say she was an American, as she had not taken out her Visa at the British Consulate to go into the States. But when the Border Official looked into the car and I handed him my passport, and Frank showed him his Visa, he looked at my mother, sitting in the front seat, and said, "Are you a U. S. Citizen?". My mother proudly sat up and said, "Certainly not, I am an English subject." at which we all cringed while the officer said, "Well, in that case you'll have to turn around and go back to Juarez to take out a Visa." We could have gagged my mother, but Frank just nodded, went a few feet further on, made a fake half-turn, and when the officer was not looking, sped into the U. S. We looked in the rear view mirror, and he had paid no attention, so we proceeded with our trip. My mother was now an illegal in U. S. territory! In punishment, or so it seemed, we had a flat tire after Tucson, and stopped on the road to fix it. The wind was howling at about 60 miles an hour, and Frank found that our gardener had taken out his jack to change a tire on our other car, and not returned it to the trunk. Here we were, stranded in the middle of the highway with a flat tire and nothing to remove it with. I stood ahead of our car, asking for help, while almost being blown off the road, and sure enough, someone stopped almost immediately and rolled down their windows. I put my head inside their car and rattled on about our problem, asking if they had a jack they could lend us. They gave me a blank look. I could hardly hear their answer because of the heavy wind in my ears, but finally grasped that they didn't speak English. They were from Mexico and had only stopped because they saw our Mexican license plates and decided to help. It turned out that they knew Frank from the Clinic. Someone in their family was his patient. What a coincidence! They said they'd send us a towtruck from the next town, as their jack was only for a small car. After a stilted conversation and much hand shaking, they drove away, and sure enough, shortly after, the towtruck arrived. The driver said we should get into the cabin, as no one should ride in our car while it was being towed, but I knew my 86 year old mother could not get up his steps, so he allowed her to sit in the car all the way to the garage.

When we arrived in L. A., sure enough, Frank's dad was leaning on the back fence, looking down the freeway for us. Frank's mother always welcomed us with food we enjoyed, a freshly baked boysenberry pie, chile con queso for Frank, home-made cookies for Tony. The whole time we were visiting, she'd fuss around the kitchen, asking us each day what we'd like to eat. She was an excellent cook, not only with typical Mexican food, but American dishes also. After a couple of days, we put my mother on a flight to San Francisco, where Vic and Dan lived at the time, and when Vic found my mother was without her visa, she was furious with me and told me of the consequences if the border officials should discover it, but I hardly thought they would throw my aged mother in jail, and they didn't.

Before we left L. A., Frank and Tony went shopping for a second hand car for Tony. He needed it to go back and forth from his rental to the University. They came back, pleased as Punch with a three-year old Ford Maverick. Tony was going to keep it at his grandparents' home until he started school. Mission accomplished.

That same year, in November, I had a phone call from one of my mother's neighbors to come urgently. When I arrived, they had already called Frank, and he was kneeling by her outstretched body by the kitchen door. She had apparently had a small stroke and fainted. He called the hospital, and they came for her with a stretcher and carried her down the stairs. To make a long story short, next day she was back at our house, settled in our guest room and wondering what had happened. She had blanked out, but fortunately recovered her memory partially during the next few days. I called my sister and my brothers, and Bob came from Mexico City with Susan, his daughter, to spend a few days. Mother brightened up when she saw them. Then Vic and Dan arrived, Vic immediately taking charge, as she always did, and telling me what I should do. She brought Mom a memory book, and would sit and quiz her every day. They took over her apartment in the meanwhile, and this time stayed until Christmas came and went. We decided my mother could not go back to live in her own apartment, but should remain under our care here with us, which she did, resignedly. Finally she seemed to have accepted the situation, realizing her condition. She was still self-sufficient enough to bathe by herself, and to eat what was served to her. But she was bored, because she could not concentrate enough to read, so the only things she could do was to rifle through magazines, and watch television. Not a very interesting life after so many years of being so independent. Gradually, year after year, (and she was with us for the last six years of her life), her mind went blank, until she did not even know who I was. Frank did not think it was Alzheimers, but more a series of tiny strokes which gradually left her brain deadened.

In August, Bobby Moore invited four women friends and myself to her house in Mazatlán for a week of golfing and sunning. Her youngest daughter, Becky went with us, and invited a little girlfriend with her. We were five women and two girls, all packed into Bobby's big white station wagon. Again, those terrible curves all the way, but Bobby too was an excellent driver, and we were all chatting so much that we did not worry about going over a cliff. We chose rooms when we got there, and the girls slept on the living room couches. Every morning we would rise, breakfast and go to the golfcourse, where we would spend the rest of the morning. Tere, not being a golfer, would adjourn to the beach with the girls. We'd meet them there after golf, and swim and sun, eating seafood served to us by beachboys from nearby restaurants. One day the kids dared me to go up in one of the parachutes that we constantly saw being pulled by little motor boats. I was the youngest of the five women, so they picked me, and of course I felt I had to take the dare, although with misgivings, as I have a fear of heights. Anyway, two efficient young men strapped me into a halter, gave the boat the signal, and I was suddenly swept away, terrified, and gripping the bar before me with white knuckles. When I looked around, I saw I was higher than the hotels, and the little boat beneath me was miniscule. I could not conceive how I had done such a foolish thing, but could only grip tighter and be pulled along, absolutely frozen in space. When they finally brought me down and my feet hit the sand, the girls ran up to me, thrilled, and of course I grinned broadly and said it had been a marvellous experience.

Every spring, Bobby would invite us to drive with her to the States for a shopping tour. Fran, Doris, and myself would pile into her station wagon and we would drive to San Antonio, Texas, about ten hours from Torreón. We would go straight to the St.Anthony Hotel, check in and order room service, always the same: lamb chops, baked potato, and salad, which we would accompany with a glass of wine. Next day we were up early for breakfast and a trip to Joske's of Texas, a wonderful department store, where we would spend the morning, meeting for lunch, and continue to shop until almost dark. By the time we arrived at the hotel in the evening and had the doorman help us to unload our purchases, he had to make several trips, saying, "I'll bet Joske's was happy to see you ladies today!" We would have room service again,and the next day would be the same routine. The third day we would drive back to Mexico, scared at the border that we would have to pay duties on our purchases, which we usually did. But they were fun trips, and we all had a lot of clothes to wear that summer.

A year later Frank's father was diagnosed with prostate cancer and began radiation treatment. Unfortunately, the next year he had a stroke, and was completely bedridden. We were there with him when he passed away in 1977 in the hospital. Again, the whole family had gathered, and Frank's mother was devastated, as we all were, but she had lived such a close life with her husband for fifty odd years that we wondered how she was going to survive. Frank's eldest sister, Irma, moved her into a small apartment close to her and her family, where we visited her every year. She joined a senior citizen center, and took up cooking and yoga. She tried her best to live contentedly for the following six years, but in 1983 she began with a minor stomach ailment which progressed. One of the last times Frank talked with her, she told him she had no confidence in her doctor, and could he please come. He promised he would, and the next day he called to tell her that we were going to see her. But when Irma answered the phone she gave Frank the bad news that their mother had just passed away. My poor husband. It was what he least expected, and we were both stunned, but left immediately for L. A. Tony too was shaken that he had now lost both his beloved Balderrama grandparents

Rafaela Balderrama was buried besides her adored husband who had preceded her. I don't know how he managed it, but Frank said some words at graveside. She was a wonderful mother-in-law to me, tolerant and affectionate, and I had grown to love her dearly. To this day, whenever we go toLos Angeles, one of our first priorities is to visit Frank's parents' graves.

But back to 1978. That year, Tony graduated from Marymount Loyola University. Of course we were there, staying with Frank's mother in her little apartment. She attended the ceremony, along with Frank's sister Irma, her husband Fred, and their three kids,

Rita, Freddy, and Joseph, as well as Frank's brother and wife, Hank and Sally, and their children, Frankie, Larry, Vicky and Lisa. After the ceremony we all went to eat at Tony's favorite restaurant, The Warehouse, where he had previously obtained permission to shoot a film needed for graduation. He was treated that day like a young film director! After a few days in L. A. we left with Tony for Mexico so he could spend the summer months here with us before going back to L.A. to start looking for work in the film industry, an intimidating job, considering the enormity of the competition. Debbie too came to her parents' home and together they kept dating.

My mother had gone downhill gradually, and would rise in the middle of the night to wander through the house in the dark, terrifying me that she would fall down and break her bones. I prepared to lose her, and convinced myself that I would be relieved when it happened, as I preferred that to a disabled painful death. The night before she died I sat by her bed and told her that she was free to go, that her two main loves were gone, her beloved father and her husband. I informed her, although I had previously not done so, that her eldest son, Fred, had passed away a few years before in Africa, and now she should look forward to seeing them all again. She just laid there, her eyes watching my every move, and then she went to sleep. I went out into the garden and wept in the dark for a long time. I knew this was the end. I rose at dawn and went to her side and saw her countenance with a peaceful expression, and oddly enough, a drop of blood on the side of her lips. Her body was still warm when I kissed her and went to tell Frank, who came in and took her pulse. There was none. She was gone. It was a sad end for such an intelligent, charming woman who had enjoyed life so much, and a sad six years for us, her children, who had to watch her descend into oblivion

.I had promised my mother, ever since she came to live near us, that I would return her to Mexico City to bury her next to my father at the British Cemetery, so after her body was prepared here, we flew that night with her to the City after having had a Mass said for her at the church near our house. There she was taken to the funeral parlor, and we spent the night at a hotel. Next morning at graveside, my brother Bob, his wife Lyn, and their daughter Susan were there. Also one of my mother's oldest and best friends, Chavela, stood there to bid her goodbye. Dick lived in Florida, Ted in San Francisco, Bill in northern Mexico, Vic and Dan in El Paso, so they could not be present, nor did I think they needed to be. In life they had visited her as often as possible. I held up well until they lowered the coffin into the ground and then I went to pieces. I could not stop sobbing, and Lyn told me later that they thought I too would end up in the grave with my mother. From the cemetery we went to lunch at a nearby restaurant, and Bob made me chuckle when he woefully said with a long face, "Now we're orphans." I ordered her tombstone with the added words, "I shall return like rain", extracted from one of her loveliest poems. Bob insisted that that is why it had rained so much the night before.....

During this time Frank had gradually advanced up the ladder of military rank, starting with his graduation from the Medical Military college in 1952 as a Major. In 1972 he became a Lt. Colonel, and in 1978 a full Colonel. These promotions were obtained by going to the Secretariat of Defense in Mexico City where he would take written exams as well as physical tests at the Military Camp. When he returned he would describe to me how he had to climb walls, crawl on his stomach under barbed wire, and leap over large extensions of water, as well as prove his ability at the shooting range. The Mexican army, although largely a peace-time army, kept its doctors fit for any emergency such as floods and earthquakes, as well as any circumstance where army aid was required. Naturally the wages had increased with every promotion and were added to the money Frank received from his private practice.

I believe it was in the eighties when Frank and I started giving our traditional New Year's Eve parties. We would invite about

25 guests, and serve a table of appetizers and cold food, and at midnight Frank would ring a big brass bell and a waiter would bring out glasses of champagne. Everyone seemed to enjoy these parties, no less Tony, home from school, and his friends, who would make up a group out on the terrace with their own drinks and appetizers. We held these parties for about six years, until some of our friends starting dying off. Most of them were many years older than we, so it should have been expected, but it put a damper on our gatherings, for despite their ages, they were a merry lot, and contributed substantially to the life of the party. Instead, we started attending the formal New Years' Ball at the Casino in downtown Torreon, where at midnight the celebrators circled the dance floor giving abrazos to everyone else, even if we weren't close at other times. They were very gay parties, everyone dressed in tuxes and long gowns. I remember dancing "La Raspa" , a favorite of the crowd, where one jumps through certain parts of the music, and the Casino floor vibrating so much that I feared we would all plummet through to the salon below in one fell swoop

BEACH VACATIONS

About this time, we started going on beach vacations every year with three other couples, our old friends, the Barboglios, the Llorens, and the Fernandez's. Alberto Llorens was a Spaniard, as was Manolo Fernandez, and when they got to talking, perhaps arguing about soccer, one could swear they would come to blows, because like most Spaniards, they talked loudly and vehemently. However, they loved each other like brothers, both having escaped from Franco's Spain in the fifties. Their wives were lovely ladies, Maria Elena very subdued, and Sylvia very fiery and exotic looking, but we all got along merrily.

One of the first beaches we visited was Acapulco, the Hotel Princess, which we had all visited before, but which never loses its charm. We would sit in the evenings on that wide breezy terrace having a drink after a day at the golf course and the beach, to make time for our dinner engagement in the adjacent dining room. It was a pleasant week. The next year we decided on Las Hadas, in Manzanillo, a fairly new hotel at that time, of Moorish architecture, all white outside with white marble floors throughout. Very unique.To get there, we had to fly to Guadalajara, where we changed planes for Manzanillo, state of Colima, where the hotel is located. We loved the hotel, and the marvellous breakfasts included, like every beach hotel in Mexico: a vast array of fruits, eggs, bacon, cold meats, chilaquiles, hot cakes or waffles, menudo and pozole. Again, golf in the morning, followed by beach or pool, water skiing, scuba diving, and what have you. A lot of sun, which tires and readies one for that quiet nap after a large meal at noon. In the evening, refreshments in the bar, another big dinner, accompanied by wonderful music. Heaven! Nothing like trios singing romantic Mexican music. This time, Tina, the younger of the two Barboglio daughters, flew in from Dallas to join us and at some point in the evening we adjourned to the Disco section. When the music started, she upped and started for the dance floor, beckoning to any of the men at our table to dance with her. We urged Alberto to volunteer, being the youngest, and will never forget the poor guy trying to keep up with Tina to the rhythm of "Macho Man", which seemed to go on interminably. Finally they returned to the table, he, laughing and breathless, to be met by our loud clapping.

Next day, the four men were swimming together in the pool and stopped inside the water by the bar for a drink. An attractive young woman in shorts came up to the edge of the water and started a conversation, focusing on Alberto. At that moment, Manolo's wife, Maria Elena, and I were lying on couches by the pool, watching the goings on, when suddenly, Alberto's wife appeared from nowhere, and we heard all this shouting. Well, Mexican women can become as jealous as Mexican men, and

Sylvia wasn't about to have anyone flirt with her husband that afternoon. She gave the woman a complete dressing down, and told her to scram, then "stood by her man" until the invader had slunk away. We ladies were flabbergasted and amused.

Next year we decided on going to Cancun, which involved flying first to Mexico City for a day and a night. We had lunch there at one of our old haunts in the Zona Rosa, a German restaurant named "Bellinghausen" At night, we took in a show with Carlos Lico, simply because he was my favorite singer at the time. Our table was right by the stage, and I noticed that as he sang his heart out, he kept looking over at Sylvia who was sitting by me. I turned and found that she had falllen fast asleep with her mouth open, a true insult to his gorgeous voice.

Our rooms in Cancun were luxurious and more like individual suites. The beach is unique, in that its sand is white and fine, and extends far out into the peaceful waves where you can easily walk up to your shoulders. It is truly a paradise. One day we took a boat ride out to Isla Mujeres, (Women's Island) named that way because when the Spanish expedition landed in 1517, they found many female shaped idols representing the Mayan goddess of fertility, Ixchel. Where we docked, there were some huge turtles in a pond, and I immediately rode one, encouraged by the owners. Another day we took a tour out to the pyramid of Tulum, where Frank and I easily climbed to the top and looked out into the crystal waters. From there to Xel-ha, a lake where salt water mixes with sweet water, and where one can swim, while tiny fishes nibble at your legs and arms. Back in Cancun, we ended our evenings in one of the hotels' nightclubs, where all four couples danced until dawn.

SHORT EUROPEAN VACATION

In late October 1981, while shopping at The Popular, a department store in downtown El Paso, Texas, a folder was included in my purchases advertising a short "Theatre Trip" to London and Paris, 4 nights in each city, with theatre tickets for two nights in London, and tickets to the Moulin Rouge and Crazy Horse shows in Paris. The price was reasonable, so Frank and I decided we would invite Tony to go with us so he could see Europe for the first time. He flew from L. A. to New York, where we met at the airport, and went together to London. Every time we fly over London I get a lump in my throat, remembering that it is the city where my parents originated and where I spent the first seven years of my life. They were both such patriots. My mother loved everything British, starting with literature, which she taught me in turn to love. Right before the war, when we were to leave England, she stood in the kitchen lecturing my brothers about defending their country with their lives if necessary. (Thank God none of the five lost their lives in the various branches of defense.) Tony too was swept up in the marvellous sensation of seeing his grandparents' birthplace.

While there, we took tours to Oxford, Hampton Court, (I kept thinking of that Spaniard on our first trip pronouncing it "Anton Kur"), Stonehenge, Salisbury Cathedral, and that wonderful city which is Bath. One day we took a boat up the river Thames to Windsor Castle, and spent the day touring the castle, and then shopping and eating down town. Back in London we were lucky to find tickets to the theatre production of "Amadeus", one of the greatest of shows, but then theatres in London are so special. Old and creaky, the stages are a wonder of internal machinery which transform plain rooms instantly into mansions or gardens or whatever the scene calls for. And no one should visit London without standing for hours outside of Buckingham Palace to watch the Changing of the Guard. This alone is worth the whole trip in my estimation, and we saw that Tony was equally impressed with the pomp and circumstance. Naturally we could not leave the "old country" without a short visit to see my dear niece, Mary, and her husband, Mike, as well as their two handsome little boys near London. At this time they lived in a farm area in a quaint old house with a cow in their back yard. I especially wanted Tony to meet his cousin and her mother, who was once married to my brother Fred. We ended our short stay on this pleasant family note.

At this point I must add that as this trip took place in October, the World Series had started the day we took off from New York, and to Frank's dismay, the Yankees were playing the Dodgers that evening. Now, if I haven't mentioned it before, Frank is a diehard Yankee fan, and follows the games throughout the whole year, much more so the World Series. How could I have forgotten this in my excitement of making reservations for our trip? I will never forgive myself. The result was that as soon as we got to our hotel in London, Frank turned on the "telly" in our room, and found that the British viewer is totally unaware and unconcerned with the game of baseball, so we only heard football, cricket, and tennis results. In desperation, Frank, Tony, and I went out to look for a short wave radio to tune in to the games. It was very late by this time, and we ended up in Picadilly Circus almost at midnight, where we found a little shop that sold radios. It was closed, of course. Hoping that the owner lived upstairs, Frank found the bell and rang furiously until a man popped his head out of an upper window and said "Wot d'you wont?" When Frank told him what he wanted, he yelled back, "Are you mad?!" but he eventually came down and sold Frank the radio. That night Frank tried to tune in through the bathroom window, calculating the difference in time with New York, to no avail. The whole time we were vacationing, he had to rely on the headlines of the international Herald Tribune.

In Paris, besides the aforementioned shows and the usual trips to the Louvre and Notre Dame, we took a bus trip out to the Loire Valley to see the castles. The one that impressed us the most was Chenonceau, built over the River Cher. What a delight to walk on the fallen leaves, crunching our way through beautiful forests and breathing the early winter air where kings and queens once trod. I think Tony got a good impression of these two cities, even in such a short time. We flew back to New York and Mexico together, so Tony could spend Christmas at home with us.

In Mexico, the months of November and December are full of celebrations, starting with the first day of November, when the country celebrates All Saints' Day, followed by the second, which is All Souls' Day, or Day of the Dead, when the country remembers its dead. Some families place altars in their homes with a picture of their loved one, surrounded by favorite souvenirs from his lifetime, such as a favorite pipe, a pack of cigarettes, a hat he wore. Added to this, they place his favorite dishes, tamales, a bottle of tequila perhaps. Some altars are more elaborate than others, with a favorite dress laid out for a woman, and favorite music played all during the day. The whole altar is surrounded by marigold flowers which bloom at that time, and small candles are lit and placed on the altar. This festivity has been celebrated in the country for three thousand years by the indigenous people, an elaborate fiesta which the Spanish tried to eradicate when they conquered Mexico, but were unable to do. Believers in the afterlife surmise that the soul of the dead one will see and enjoy for that day the little niceties he loved during his lifetime. Little white skulls made of sugar are sold in the streets, with people's names painted on their foreheads, and these too are bought and added to the altars. People visit the cemeteries during these two days to take care of their loved ones' graves, and place bunches of marigolds to brighten them up. When my friend, Jo Withington, lived across the street from me, she often went to the market place to buy marigolds for herself and for me to place in vases in our homes because we liked them so much. If the vendor happened to ask her if they were for her "muertito", (little dead one), she'd answer no, they were for her. They must have thought she was mad to buy that type of flower for herself.

The 20th of November is the Day of the Revolution, which used to be celebrated throughout Mexico with an organized sports parade, followed by the Fire Department, and ending with Charros on horseback in their silver decorated outfits and wide brimmed hats, as well as Charro women in long skirts and rebozos, riding sidesaddle. The custom has gradually faded, and the Charros now ride instead at the end of the military parade which takes place on the 16th of September, Mexico's Independence Day.

December 12th is one of the most important festivities in all of Mexico, for it is the day that the country celebrates the apparition of the sacred Virgin of Guadalupe, one of the country's most revered symbols. The story is the following: in 1531 while tending his flock on the mount of Tepeyac, a humble indian suddenly saw an apparition of the Virgin with brillian sun rays in back of her. He was frightened, but the next day she appeared again to him, as she did on a third. This time she told him to cut some roses, which had miraculously appeared on the barren hill, and to take them to theArchbishop as proof of her appearance. The boy cut them, wrapped them in his cloak, and ran down to the church, where he opened his cloak so that the Archbishop could see the proof of his story. But lo and behold, the roses were no longer there. In their stead was the image of the Virgin, imprinted on the rough sack cloth. This image now rests on the altar of the Basilica of Guadalupe on the outskirts of Mexico City, and every twelfth of December thousands of faithful visit her church. In every city of Mexico there is a Guadalupe church with her effigy on display, where similar pilgrimages take place.

In December, the Posadas begin on the 16th and go on every night until the 24th of December. I mentioned these earlier, as it was at one of these parties where I met my future husband back in 1948. Later, when we were married and living in Campeche, I described how my neighbor, Beatriz, had taught me how to decorate a piñata to break during one of these parties.

In 1982 Frank and I went to Dallas, Texas, to attend the Barboglio's youngest daughter's wedding. We had previously attended their eldest daughter's wedding in Dallas a few years before. Several people from Torreon made the trip also, and we stayed at the sumptuously refurbished Adolphus Hotel. The wedding reception took place at the country club, and true to form, Tina had on an avant-garde wedding gown and head dress. She and her sister had gone into the fashion industry, producing a line of white cotton clothes with the name "Barboglio" on the label and selling them at Neiman Marcus and other stores with great success. We met many interesting people at the reception, as her husband is a well- known businessman in Dallas society circles.

ANOTHER ACCIDENT

In 1983 Frank was named Director of the IV Military Region in the Division of Health Services, which included the states of Coahuila, Nuevo Leon, Tamaulipas, and Zacatecas, which meant that the military hospitals in those states were under his command. This involved frequent trips to various cities, which always worried me because I knew how fast he drove. The ceremony took place in Saltillo, the capital of the state of Coahuila, which is about two and half hours by road from Torreón. On one of these trips, while driving with his military aid, the car hit an oil spill and skidded off the road, turning over twice. Frank hit the windshield and came out with a broken arm and collarbone while the soldier too ended up with a broken arm.. One of his military doctor friends drove out to the site to pick him up, and of course I was called to the hospital here where they were attending to him. Not knowing what to expect, and frightened that this time it might turn out to be more serious than the previous times, I arrived, found him with cuts on his face, but already in an arm-and-shoulder cast. It was miraculous that both of them weren't killed, and I was thankful that his lesions weren't worse, seeing the condition of the car which was completely "totaled", a beautiful Le Baron Chrysler. I wondered if his Saint Christopher medal in his car had saved him again!

I already mentioned that our mothers had both passed away in 1983, a sad month for both Frank and me. But the next year,

Frank retired from the army, automatically receiving the rank of General. Now he would continue with his private practice as usual at the Clinic, with no further duties at the Military Hospital. The very next year he was invited to Mexico City by the Secretary of Defense, General Arévalo, to receive a Distinguished Services Medal at a military ceremony. At that time, the General offered him a post in London for a year, as military doctor at the Mexican Embassy, with a salary that would be more than ample to live well in that city. Naturally, when he came home and gave me the news, we were both elated. What an opportunity! I could think of nothing else. We would rent our house here to a known family for the year we were to be away, but unfortunately, upon our return would probably be sent to another city in Mexico. So the offer had its good points and its bad. Our friends gave us a goodbye party and I started to plan my wardrobe. We would invite my sister Vic and her husband Dan to visit us while there, and of course, our son, Tony.......

End of dream. Military orders are often changed at the last minute, as ours were. Our trip was cancelled without any more ado and no recrimination on Frank's part. Like a good military man, he accepted the situation. I must admit that we were both very depressed with the change of plans, but looking at our happy life here in this area we thought of the old Mexican saying, "No hay mal que por bien no venga" which means "Nothing bad happens that isn't for a good reason."

LONG EUROPEAN VACATION

To assuage our disappointment, Frank decided we should give ourselves a three month holiday in Europe, so we took off for London, and rented a lovely little apartment in Shepherd's Market (a delightful central area). While there, we got to feel like real Londoners, walking everywhere, buying basic groceries and wine at the nearby little shops, and having tea in the afternoons at the various hotels, starting with the Ritz.

We took a tour to Ireland, stayed in Dublin, and visited the famous Trinity College. Walked miles, marvelling at the green countryside, in comparison to our own desertic surroundings. Another week we took the Flying Scotsman from London to Edinburgh, where we visited the medieval castle which dominates the city skyline, perched atop an ancient volcano right in the center of the "newer" city which in itself dates from 1850. Loved Princess street and all its surprising shops with lower prices than in London. Winding medieval streets beckoned to us, and we marveled at the Georgian and Victorian architecture throughout. After a couple of days we took a bus to St. Andrews, where we rented clubs and played the Princess course, but the sand traps were so deep, the gorse so thick, and the wind off the North Sea so icy and cutting, that I would have gladly given up had it not been for Frank urging me on.

We had invited Tony and his girlfriend, Debbie, to visit us and travel together on the continent. When they arrived, we took them the very first day for a ride on the double decker red tourist bus for a birds eye view of the city, but noticed they were falling asleep after the long flight. A few days later we took a train to visit my niece Mary and Mike and the family, who now lived in a lovely large house in Berkshire, about an hour away from London. Mike's charming parents were there. They had lived in India for years, where Mike had been born, and it was delightful to hear about their life in Bombay (now Mumbai) before they retired and came back to their own country. Nesta, my sister-in-law, lived next door, still looking well, and remembering my brother Fred with affection, although they had long been separated. The boys were grown, and there were four of them now. How lovely to still have family in England! However, I never would have changed my life in Mexico for one in England, had my mother decided to stay there during the war, nor do I know whether we would have survived the terrible bombings in London, as my sister was lucky enough to do.

After a few days in London, Tony, Debbie, Frank and I took a train to Portsmouth to board an overnight ship to St. Malo in France, where we wanted to visit the famous abbey at Mont St. Michel. We arrived in early morning, rented a car, this time a four door ample Peugot and drove up the causeway, where we parked, walking the rest of the way up into the quaint little town and umpteen steps to the church. Built in the middle ages of granite and limestone, it later became a Benedictine abbey, which it remains today. At a certain time of day I understand the tide comes in and disconnects the mount from the mainland, but we left in the early afternoon.

We drove on along the Brittany coast toward Normandie, where the great battles took place forty years before. Our son, Tony, is interested, almost obsessed, with World War II memorabilia, and knows each and every battle fought between 1939 and the end of the war in 1945, so it was a must, for all of us, to see the beaches, and recall the battle of D-Day. We stayed at a rustic little hotel at Vierville-sur-mer overlooking Omaha Beach. Early in the morning I rose to look out the window at the beach below, and the German bunkers, dug deep into the sand, where they had fired on our soldiers disembarking on that terrible day of battle. It brought tears to my eyes to think of the many lives lost forty years before. Then I spied a solitary figure in a black windbreaker walking slowly along the beach, bent against the cold wind, peering into the bunkers and stopping to look out at the angry ocean. Of course, it was Tony, finally reliving those hours which he had read so much about. After breakfast, we stopped at the American Cemetery and looked over the row upon row of white gravestones, stopping also at the little museums along the way which housed much of the memorabilia collected from the dead soldiers, both sides. There we saw cigarette cases, still with cigarettes in them, and usually a picture of a girl fitted into the opposite side; wallets, letters kept by the soldiers in their pockets, old uniforms, some with blood, poignant little articles that had meant enough to the soldiers to be carried into battle with them. There were films being shown too, old newsreels which we might have seen during the war, where boys stood smiling bravely at the camera, probably now long gone. We visited the British disembarkment area called Gold, and it was the same thing. We'd had enough by this time and continued along the Normandie coast to the next town where there were celebrations going on, being the Sixth of June, forty years after D-Day, with French war veterans wearing their medals, flags in the street and the Marseillaise being played. Tony felt he had to get out to mill around in the crowd, American and British flags on his jacket, and was immediately asked if perhaps his father had been in the final battle.

We drove on to Reims where we had lunch and saw the magnificent Cathedral. On to Verdun to spend the night. This name was significant in World War I, where the Germans and the French had fought the longest and bloodiest battle in 1916. When we drove through town it was already late, so we stopped at the first hotel we found, which turned out to be the worst hotel we have ever stayed at, with a dark bathroom at the end of the hall and creaky beds with lumpy mattresses. After a restless night, next morning we were offered strong coffee and hard croissants. We continued around the outskirts of Paris, (we wanted to leave it for the end of our trip), and on to Strasbourg where we crossed over into Germany. That night we spent in Munich at a beautiful Geisel Hotel where we had a sumptuous dinner in their restaurant, accompanied by piano and violins. On the way, we had passed Dachau and the death camps where Frank, Tony, and Debbie got off the car to inspect them. I could not stomach this, so refused. They came out a while later looking pale and silent.

We spent two wonderful days in Munich, Frank and I recalling our last visit there in 1973, with our friends, and then proceeded to Salzburg over those wonderful autobahnen which feel like silk, in and out of tunnels through the mountains, Tony enjoying each and every curve. Being a wonderful driver, he was fully able to keep up with the fast traffic in Germany. (When I had driven the little Seat car in Spain and France, we had gone so slowly everyone blew their horns at us as they whizzed by.)

I can't say enough about beautiful Salzburg, with the river running through the "Old Town", dominated by baroque towers and churches. It is the fourth largest city in Austria, birthplace of Wolfgang Amadeus Mozart no less. The movie, "The Sound of Music", starring Julie Andrews, was filmed there in 1965, twenty years before our trip, but the city still has bus tours that go to sites that appeared in the film, including the church where "Maria" got married. Debbie was the one who wanted to take this tour, so we went along, and she recalled scenes at each stop. One of the highlights of our stay was to visit Mozart's home, where they have his original sheets of music laid out under glass on desks. As Tony, Frank, and I had seen the play, "Amadeus", three years before, and knew about the jealousy of the other composer, Salieri, we were delighted to see Salieri's signature on one of the sheets of music. Outstanding, was a visit to the Mirabelle gardens filled with tulips of all colors, where we took many photos. Our hotel was the dignified Osterreichischer Hof, overlooking the river, and one evening while we were sitting in the bar before going out to dinner, I, always observant of people, noticed two young businessmen at an adjacent table. A few minutes later an attractive middle aged woman arrived, sat with them a moment, and then brought over two tall, stunning young women, introducing them to the businessmen. At this point, the older woman made her exit, leaving the four people conversing genially. I nudged Frank. An obvious tastefully planned escort service arrangement. All four left the bar after having one drink.

On to beautiful Vienna. I swear, after being in that city for four days, one realizes one needs at least a month to see the city well. Tony had been using a guide book in Munich and Salzburg which suggested deluxe and first class hotels, which up to now had turned out wonderful but very expensive. Now he had come up with another hotel of the same chain as in Salzburg, but we had no idea how to find it in this immense city. We asked several bystanders how to get there, and it was really comical, the way they attempted to be helpful in a language we clearly did not understand, gesticulating wildly and pointing, all to no avail. However, in each case we did understand the word "ring", which we grasped was an avenue which circled the edge of the city. With perseverance and a lot of luck, we finally drew up in front of our hotel. The first day we took a bus tour to get our bearings and see the points of interest we should come back to, but as we passed a lovely park, I heard the driver say that in the evenings there was live music and dancing. That evening we asked the concierge the name of the park, which I do wish I could remember, as I have told all my friends who are planning a visit to Vienna not to miss this delightful experience, and took a taxi to the park. Sure enough, there were tables on a large outdoor terrace in front of a restaurant with a dance floor, and at the far end, an orchestra playing Viennese waltzes, where many couples were already dancing. We ordered wine, and then to our surprise, a couple in formal attire, she in long dress and he in tails, commenced to circle the floor dancing with long strides, the way a waltz should be danced, until they had covered the entire floor. I presume this was to encourage the spectators to copy them, and as they exited, everyone clapped and started to dance themselves. There were all types of couples, some dressed up, some not, most of them overweight, a few of the ladies wearing flouncy summer dresses and net gloves halfway up the fingers. It was a real show. Although I wanted to join in, Frank said he had rubber-soled shoes, and refused to dance. Tony and Debbie weren't up to it either, as they probably didn't know how to waltz, and certainly not in the glorious manner of the entertainers. If we ever go back to Vienna I will be sure to instruct Frank to wear his dancing shoes!

We visited the Spanish Riding School, where there was no show going on that morning, so we merely sat in the balcony and watched the Lipizzaner stallions and riders perform and practice. Two musts were St. Stephen's Cathedral, where they had the plumed headdress of Mexico's Emperor Moctezuma, (I can't imagine why!), and Schönbrunn Palace, where we saw the famous pearls belonging to Maria Theresa of Austria, and where Princess Sissi, Elizabeth of Bavaria had lived. But there was so much more to see, and all this was only the tip of the iceberg, so to speak. On we drove to Innsbruck, settled in a broad valley between high snow-covered mountains, the second time for Frank and me. We took the funicular up to the top of the mountain, and there had a snack. Although we spent the night at the same hotel as years before, this time it did not enthuse us as much as the last time. Next day we drove on, passing Lichtenstein with its typical Bavarian type wooden houses with little flowering window boxes in front, and on to France, where we stopped in Dijon for a wonderful meal in a local restaurant, crowded with local residents. Just the right place to eat. Onward toward Paris, stopping for a tour of Fontainebleau, favorite hunting forest of French kings, and the magnificent Renaissance palace where Napoleon I abdicated in 1814. Finally, Paris. It had been a long drive, and this was where Tony and Debbie would leave us after a few days to fly back to Los Angeles. Frank and I would continue with our trip to southern Spain and then back to London for a breather before leaving for a trip to Scandinavia.

We toasted the end of our trip together at one of our favorite restaurants on the Champs Elysees, Fouquet's. It was sad to see the kids leave, for we had enjoyed being with them, and still felt invigorated from keeping up with their youth. Frank and I took a train that very night to Perpignan, where we had to spend the night and change trains next day for Barcelona.

Barcelona has to be my favorite Spanish city, as I probably said before. Frank had not been here, as I had with my lady friends in 1973, so I gladly saw all the sights over again, with the exception, because it was closed, of the City Hall. There lies that wonderful mural of Christopher Columbus, arriving before Isabella and

Fernando, King and Queen of Spain, with two natives and a tropical bird from America. It had impressed me on my first trip, and I had raved about it to Frank and was disappointed we could not admire it. We spent time at the Picasso Museum, where we discovered his early paintings before he became so modern. I was particularly taken by one of a little girl making her First Communion, her white veil partially covering her pretty face. We loved one of a doctor, sitting beside a patient, and were able to buy a reproduction for Frank's office. Of course we meandered down the delightful Las Ramblas walkway, and went one night to devour a platter of delicious Paella.

We rented a car and drove along the Mediterranean coast, La Costa Del Sol, passing sun-kissed resorts like Benidorm where we knew the jet set abided, and on through Tarragona and Valencia, a gorgeous old city. In Javea, we spent the night at one of the magnificent "Paradero" inns, sponsored all over Spain by the Spanish government, usually in old refurbished castles or monasteries. On to Granada and Sevilla. Enough has been said about these last two cities not to go into detail about their beauty, their architectural treasures, their churches, and their ambience. In the evenings we would amble down to the "old town" to stop at taverns for a glass of wine, where huge cured hams hung from hooks on the ceiling, and the counters displayed a variety of appetizers, the famous "tapas". Spaniards speak loudly, and always sound to me as if they are arguing, but we have learned that this is just their way. We returned inland, up the middle of Spain, past Alicante with its lovely palm-lined avenue, past beautiful countryside, white-washed houses, olive groves and orange trees. Every once in a while we would see a huge black bull made of tin, on a hillside, advertising Osborne brandy, until we reached Madrid. As we had visited this city thoroughly on our first trip, we flew back to our apartment in London, tired and happy.

After a few days relaxing, we took a cruise, stopping two days and nights in each city of Copenhagen, Oslo, Stockholm and Helsinki. Although it was summer, the weather was sunny but crisp in each city, and the difference with the rest of Europe was remarkable, in architecture, art, and people. The men looked like vikings, the women large, pink, healthy, and clean, their skin unmarred by tanning or makeup. I took Frank's photo between two Norwegian policewomen who dwarfed him. The streets and hotels and restaurants were pristine, the museums full of wonderful paintings by artists we had never heard of, (naturally we didn't miss "The Scream", in Oslo). Any visitor should not miss that marvellous Frogner Park, full of marble sculptures by the artist, Vigeland, where rosy, naked children frolicked in the beautiful fountains.

When we returned to London, we visited my niece and her husband again. We were fed royally, hardly finishing luncheon before Mary would bring out a tray of tea and crustless cucumber sandwiches. They invited us to the theatre in nearby Windsor one night, and the next day we took a train back to London and flew to Houston, Texas, and HOME SWEET HOME. Never has it looked so good to us. Our maid and the gardener had taken perfect care of everything, our back lawn and pool were bathed in sunshine, our eager welcoming animals were faithfully awaiting us, our personal effects in place, all this making us feel we should never have left home for so long. This is a feeling we have every time we come back from a trip, be it a long one, like this one, or even a short one. From my youth I remember the first line of a poem by Edward Guest: "It takes a heap of living in a house to call it home..." and as I write this at present time, I can say that we have lived in this same house for forty-eight years, a heap of living, and it is truly our home.

We settled down to our regular routines, Frank going to the office to consult from 9 A.M to 1 P. M. when he would come home for lunch, which here in Mexico is the main meal, have a short siesta, and returning to his office at 4 P.M. until 7:00 or 8:00 at night. We usually watched some program while having our light supper in front of the television. My usual routine was one of golf in the morning, twice a week, with Bobby and

Fran, lunch, siesta and time to read. Sometimes I had a social engagement in the afternoons, or I would get into the kitchen to make something special that the cook was not trained to make, such as a pie or a cake. Time was taken up with occasional letter-writing, to Tony or Vic, putting my album up to date, or going on constant errands. We had, and still have, a very relaxed life.

I had a birthday coming up in November of '86, so decided to have a party in the garden. The weather here must have changed since then, because I find that celebrating my birthday now in the garden in November is out of the question, for it is usually too cool. When I look back at photos of the party in our album, I'm surprised to notice the men in short-sleeved shirts, the ladies in silk dresses with no sweaters or wraps around their shoulders. I made the luncheon meal myself, as I always do for company, not trusting the maid to do it as I have found over the years that the average maid can cope very nicely with everyday menus, but when confronted with extra guests, flies into a flurry and makes a mess of things. Besides, in these cases, I usually decided to cook something out of the ordinary with ingredients she might not be familiar with, so what better than to do it myself, although with her helping hand to chop onions, slice mushrooms, dip chicken breasts into flour and brown them, or whatever the recipe calls for. The party was a success, and we all had a fine time, I more than everybody, for I received many useful gifts, but it grieves me now to see people in the photos who have since passed away. This always happens when we look up something in my albums, which I have kept faithfully ever since I was growing up. You can imagine that our hall closet is full of these relics, all duly dated, some of them falling apart, which help me to remember many incidents that I have related in this memoir.

In December we flew to Los Angeles to attend the premier of a movie Tony had worked on as Assistant Cameraman, "Streets of Gold", starring Klaus Maria Brandauer and Wesley Snipes, no small movie this, and of course we were excited to see his name in the credits. Tony and Debbie, Frank and I, went together. It seemed our son's career had finally taken off. Then we drove back in Tony's station wagon to spend the holidays at home. He had bought this large Ford station wagon in Mexico, a few years back, but had not gotten rid of his Maverick. In fact, today he still owns it, and it elicits compliments every time he drives it.

That Christmas was an unforgettable one, for although we went over to Debbie's parents' home for the customary Christmas Eve dinner, and the next day had her whole family over for Christmas day meal, it was obvious to all present that things were not going well between Debbie and Tony, which turned out to be a damper on the merry making. We had come to consider Debbie a future daughter-in-law, and could only hold our breaths until the bomb broke and we heard of their breaking up, which happened a few months later. Tony had asked us if it would end the friendship between Debbie's family and ourselves should they go their separate ways, and we said we hoped it would not, but that he had to make his own decision. So they broke up. We were very sad, but it was not up to us, and luckily, the friendship between the two families endured.

EASTERN CANADA

In May of that year we flew to Toronto, via El Paso and Chicago. We had long wanted to see Canada, besides our previous trip with Tony to Niagara Falls, and finally decided on a trip to the eastern part where we were fascinated with the cleanliness of the city amongst other things. One morning we visited the St. Lawrence market, and were impressed that one could probably eat off its floors, not at all like our Mercado Juarez in Torreón! From there we took a city tour to City Hall, Queen's Park, where there is a magnificent monument of Queen Victoria in front of Parliament, and St. James Cathedral. Took a chance and rang up John Summers, who is my English nephew Mike's brother, and he and Happy his wife came by the hotel in the evening. We invited them to dinner at the impressive revolving C&N Tower, overlooking the yet unfinished Olympic Stadium, (Frank could hardly wait to come back to see a ball game there) and although we did not previously know them, Mike and Mary in London had often mentioned them, and we knew they resided in Toronto. It proved to be a good idea, and we all enjoyed each other and the wonderful meal we shared. We were there for two more days, during which we shopped at the magnificent Eaton Center Mall, took in a movie, ate at various restaurants, and walked miles all over the city.

Next morning, we rented a nice little car, a Tempo Ford, and drove to the much recommended nearby Niagara-On-The-Lake, a beautiful little town which had flowering trees in the middle of the avenues, giving it a postcard air. Everything there was pretty and quaint, even the small hotel we checked into, with floral ruffled bedspreads. We commented to each other that it would be an ideal place to retire, but who were we kidding, we knew we would always remain in Mexico.

From Toronto we took a train to Montreal, about a four and a half hour trip, and checked in at a gorgeous Meridien Hotel. Our suite was so beautiful that I felt I was Liz Taylor, luxuriating with my room service while Frank took advantage and went to see a baseball game. I was happy for him, and enjoyed good rest, reading brochures about what to see the next day. After a city tour we walked around Vieux Montreal, the old city, stood in the Place d'Armes in front of the Basilica of Notre Dame where there were horse and carriages in front for the tourists, and continued down streets full of shops, beckoning to us with goodies galore, wonderful odors coming out from the many small restaurants along the way. We stopped at one that served thick slices of bread by an open grill, where one toasts the bread and spreads any of a variety of butters of different flavors on it. We chose garlic butter, and ordered broiled chicken which was roasting on another grill. Next day we explored underground Montreal, where a whole network of department stores, restaurants, movie houses and subways exist so that the inhabitants can shop freely during the long winters without getting out in the freezing weather.

Took a two hour bus ride to Ottawa, capital of Canada, where we were amazed at the beauty of the architecture, and where we spent time the second day at the Houses of Parliament, which resemble their counterparts in London. In fact we constantly commented on similarities with that city, especially when we found most commerce closed for Victoria Day, and an imposing statue of Queen Victoria in front of Parliament. Even the city tour in a red double-decker bus reminded us of the ones in London. Visited the National Gallery on Elgin Street, the War Museum, the Mint, and lunched at the Bayward Market at a sidewalk restaurant. A long walk over the bridge led us to Hull, in the province of Quebec, while Ottawa is in the province of Ontario.

The train ride next morning took us back through Montreal to Quebec, the city. I had taken a course in French at the Alliance Francaise in Torreón in previous years, but found I did not understand the language as spoken by Canadians. We stayed at the imposing Chateau Frontenac in front of a large plaza where we had dinner that night. A friend of ours back home had asked us to look up his nephew and French niece while in Quebec, even sending them a small gift. The young man was studying at the University, and proudly took us for a visit. We spent a pleasant day with them, although the wife's comment about Torreón annoyed me when she said they had once visited our city but that she could not stand it because of "beaucoup de poudre", a lot of dust. I was able to understand that part. Well, what did she expect from a desert town.

We took a tour which included the Basilica of Sainte Anne de Beaupre, a site about thirty miles from Quebec City. The church is a fine example of Gothic architecture, its huge pillars inside, hung with crutches, walkers, bicycle wheels, and photos of all the miracles granted. I was impressed at seeing two women with a child in front of St. Anne's statue, obviously asking for a miracle or giving thanks, who were reciting the Lord's Prayer in French, "Notre Pere, qui est dans le ciel...". It sounded so special I had to wait until they had finished. The church is parallel to the St. Lawrence River, and to get there we had to ride through a forest filled with maple trees fitted with spouts collecting the syrup. Naturally we bought some, and found it truly different from the commercial brands.

We flew home, stopping at Vic and Dan's overnight, to relate our new adventures. They always welcomed us and made us feel special. Dan would open up a bottle of whiskey and fix the best Scotch and sodas that we have ever tasted, or perhaps it was because of his great personality and running commentary as he made them. Vic would efficiently cook up a marvellous meal meanwhile. About this: I have never met a faster and more efficient woman than my sister, Vic.

Not for her the drudgery of a cook over a hot stove. It was almost like magic the way she would produce a roast or a chicken casserole with all the trimmings, and set it out tastefully to serve at the table. This is the way she was about everything. During the war, when she was married to her first husband in London, she worked as a secretary to a member of Parliament, and had to go into the War Offices underground regularly during the blitzes. Not many women would have been efficient enough to work for a member of Parliament or have the capacity to do so. We knew she and Dan would soon be moving to Denver to be closer to their son, Bill, and although we would miss having them nearer us, knew that this was the sensible thing to do, due to their advancing ages.

Again we arrived home safe and sound, happy to have had wonderful experiences in that great country which is Canada. Then Bill invited the three of us to spend Christmas in Denver with them, so we were happy to do so, seeing that Vic and Dan now lived there. We flew to El Paso and holed up in a hotel to wait for Tony, who would drive his big station wagon from Los Angeles, pick us up and then drive us to Denver. He took his time, and when he arrived, his vehicle was stacked with Lord knows what to bring home after Christmas. Frank sat in front with him, and I was stuffed in the back seat, sitting on top of something, with packages and bundles under my legs and on top of my lap. Since then, we have realized that Tony does not travel light. When he arrives these days by plane to see us he usually has five or six pieces of luggage, all packed tightly, with things he says he needs. We spent a wonderful Christmas with Chris and Bill and their family of three stalwart boys and two girls. Vic and Dan were present, so we made up a merry group that year.

We had missed Christmas at home, where we would have had the uncomfortable situation with Debbie and her family, now that Tony and she were no longer together. For New Year's Eve we were back in Torreón, and went to Bobby Moore's home for a big sit down dinner. And so, the holiday season passed.

Next summer we went to Hank and Sally's youngest son, Larry's wedding to a lovely girl named Ann, in Los Angeles. It was to be a big catered affair, Tony forming part of the wedding party. At the airport, we were received by Melanie, Tony's new girlfriend, as he was filming in Mississippi at the time and had asked Mel to receive us. She showed up at the airport in a cute khaki outfit of shirt and shorts and was so effusive that she won us over completely. Her wavy hair was fluffed out around her face and she looked absolutely darling. We liked her immediately. As Tony was to be out of town for another day, she had reserved a room for us at a nearby hotel, which worked out fine, as we found out later that she had already moved in with Tony and did not know how we were going to take it. She had flowers for us in the room with a welcome note, and that too pleased us greatly. What a thoughtful girl. Tony arrived just in time for the wedding, and the four of us attended together. The catered party was elegant and formal, and afterward, Sally had prepared another more informal party at home, where she served a wonderful repast with a huge chocolate cake for dessert. Sally was always very splendid with her meals, and I marvelled at her efficiency when entertaining at big family reunions. I could never have done them half as well, even with my trusty maid by my side.

WESTERN CANADA

Right after the wedding in L. A., we arranged at a travel agency to fly to Seattle for a few days and from there on to Victoria and Vancouver. Since our last trip to eastern Canada, we had been wanting to see western Canada, and this was our chance. Tony took us to the airport the day after the wedding, and we arrived in Seattle. Although we had a private tour which took us to all points of interest, we were not taken with the city and decided to leave the next day for Victoria. We took the ferry across Puget Sound, and despite the fact that it was summer, remained below because the air off the water was chilly. Ever since we stepped off the ferry we fell in love with Victoria Island, the incomparable picturesque city by the sea in beautiful British Columbia. Baskets of flowers hung from every lampost as we headed for the magnificent turn-of-the-century Empress Hotel. The lobby was huge and regal looking, the rooms large and comfortable, and English tea was served in the elegant dining room in the afternoons. But the next morning what we wanted to see were the famous Butchart Gardens, fifty acres of the most beautiful sculptured plantings in what used to be a limestone quarry. The perfection is incredible, and we lingered longer than what we thought we would, unable to tear ourselves away from such perfect beauty. In the afternoon we took a boat across the water to Vancouver, only to find that a cattle convention was taking place and there was not a room in the city. While talking to the lady in charge of hotel reservations at the wharf, I saw a folder peeping out from a case of brochures which advertised "The Rose Garden Guest House", and asked her to call them. We were really lucky, for they had a room. When we arrived we found a handsome couple waiting for us in a house with a surrounding garden full of roses. And when we saw our room we realized why the inn was called The Rose Garden. The owner had overdone herself with the decoration and there were rose patterned curtains, bedspreads, upholstery, and roses in a vase on the dressing table. I think she must have sprayed with rose scent, for the whole room smelled of roses too. As the house was in a residential district, far from town, she invited us to join her and her husband for supper. We accepted, and sat down to a chicken-and-dumpling dinner that I cannot easily forget because it was so delicious. Even my husband, who normally would shy away from dumplings, ate them with gusto. We appreciated her kindness, and when we thanked her profusely, she said she would like to take us on the morrow for a ride to two of the prettiest parks in Vancouver which we probably would not see thoroughly if we took a tour. She drove us first to Stanley Park and then to Queen Elizabeth Park, and I do not remember in which one it was that she led us to an immense Dogwood tree, which we had never seen before, laden with white flowers. What a beautiful sight and how unlikely we will ever see a similar one again. We rented a car next day and drove around town, walked around Chinatown, where we ate, and in the afternoon went to one of the great malls to do a bit of shopping. But being far from town was an inconvenience, so we decided we'd drive back to Seattle in the rented car and hand it over there. It was a lovely road trip, passing by Bellingham, which we thought looked very inviting for another time. When we got to Seattle we stayed at a different hotel from the first time, and perhaps because of this, it changed our outlook, and we thoroughly enjoyed the beautiful city. I especially remember the residential areas, one which I think was called Magnolia Bluff. High, banked lawns come to mind, with the houses at the top surrounded by profuse flower beds. Again I thought of our poor dry earth in the middle of a desert, which I had coaxed into an attractive garden of our own.

When we got home we had news from my nephew, Bill, that two of his kids, whom we had invited upon our visit in December, would be coming to see us in August. They would be arriving on the bus, after an overnight ride, poor little dears. Heather was about eleven and Tim fifteen. What to do with two children their age? Luckily we have a pool, where they spent a large part of their time, before our friends, Pete and Fran Barboglio, came to our rescue and invited us for a weekend at their cattle ranch, about two and a half hours away from Torreón. I'm sure this was the highlight of the vacation for the kids. Besides riding around with Pete in his pickup to check on the cattle, they got to ride horseback, as well as to ride on motorbikes that his son, Tito, had stashed away in the barn. Plus that, Pete made his famous barbecued steaks for us all, which Tim devoured.

After they left, I went to Mexico City alone for my niece Susan's wedding to a young man of Dutch descent. Frank did not accompany me because he had a military assignment. They made a nice couple, Susan so dark and pretty, and Jacob, so extremely fair. She is the little girl my brother Bob and Lyn adopted in Monterrey in 1960, who had blossomed into a lovely intelligent young woman. The ceremony and banquet were held in the gardens of the well known restaurant, Antigua Hacienda de Tlalpan, outside of Mexico City, and as the saying goes when a party is extra special, "echaron la casa por la ventana", meaning "they threw the house out the window". I dressed in a red silk dress, and danced every piece with my tall lanky brother, as Lyn does not dance. We must have made quite a pair, the six-foot-six man with his five-foot-two dance partner. I'm glad I attended the wedding, for Bob passed away a year later, and I will always have the memory of our dancing together that evening. He was the second one of my five brothers who had gone before me.

Another Christmas at home with Melanie and Tony, who drove from L. A., with Magnum, Tony's beloved Doberman. We enjoyed having them, for they were very much in love and Mel was smart and cute, and we got along fine. Another family wedding next year in L. A., and fast forward to 1990.

RUSSIA AND EASTERN EUROPE

We joined a tour in New York, first time we had ever been on a group tour, to visit Russia, Poland, Hungary and what in those days was still Czechoslovakia. But first we drove to El Paso, Texas to stay the night with our dear friends the Jacksons, who had lived in Torreón a few years back and with whom we had kept up a close friendship every time we went to El Paso. They had heard about my recent passion for western music, so they surprised us, inviting us for an evening at a western bar where there was a live band. Frank and I had always enjoyed watching western dancing, the way the men seem to glide forward, pushing their partners around the floor, and of course we tried it, but were disappointed with our progress in comparison to the couples around us, so mostly we sat tapping our feet and watching the dancers. But it was fun. Everything with the Jacksons is fun for that matter. Leo is six feet five inches, and Janet only five feet two, and when they dance together he bends over and seems to carry her around the floor, but they sure make a pretty couple. Plus, they are around ten or twelve years younger than we are, so they transmit their energy and their youth to us.

We flew to New York and spent two nights seeing stage shows, museums, and eating at fine restaurants. We met our group at JFK airport and noticed they were a very disparate bunch, ranging in ages from two young women, to two white haired ladies in their late seventies, several middle aged couples, and one very elegant bachelor wearing an obvious wig. The flight was long, and I took a sleeping pill this time, knowing that at the end of the flight we would still have a long train ride from Helsinki to Leningrad, and I didn't want to be falling asleep while travelling through Finnish and Russian countryside. It didn't work. I have never been able to sleep sitting down, be it on a plane or a bus for that matter. I stayed awake, and saw below us, when the clouds parted, Iceland, Newfoundland, Labrador, and the Faroe Islands. Of course, I later napped on and off on the train, only awakened by the Russian guards at the border who told me to remove my sunglasses so they could identify me, and later on by a buxom waitress serving tea in glasses with handles. When we arrived in Leningrad I was impressed that our huge hotel overlooked the greenish and somber looking Baltic Sea. The lobby was very pretentious, all in white marble, with statuettes and a fountain. Our rooms were spartan, but what called my attention was the width of the beds. They were like cots, with odd colored blankets tucked in firmly all around, and flat little pillows. The curtains were clearly made for other windows because they were too short, not wide enough, and made of some floral fabric that did not go with anything else in the room. But the room was clean, as was the antique bathroom, and as we had not expected much, it was very satisfactory. That night at dinner we got to meet some of our fellow travelers, and fell in with a sweet older couple from Minnesota. Together we saw most of the memorable sights of Leningrad, including the great Hermitage which I had longed to visit for several years. The opulent great marble stairs are ornamented with gold trim, and there are five buildings dedicated to Western art. We were able to see most of them, but I worried about the temperature of the galleries, as in some, the windows lay wide open to the sun, a soft breeze coming in. I wondered how this would affect the art eventually, such a magnificent collection, so many old masters that I had never seen, even in art books.

One afternoon we strolled down Nevsky Avenue and found a tea shop where we stopped for a refreshment. A middle-aged lady came to us, smiling, nodded when we asked for tea, and brought us two bowls of icecream and cookies. A combo of violin and chelo started to play, and we passed a relaxing happy hour there.

Next day, we saw it all, St. Peter and Paul fortress, the magnificent St. Isaac's Cathedral, third largest cathedral in the world, everyone oohing and ahing at every turn. Their architecture is so completely different, so ornate. In the evening some of us went to the theatre to see the Kirov ballet version of Don Quixote. Stupendous theatre with fabulous décor, but didn't care for the ballet music. The next morning early we were to fly to Kiev, but had to wait for the drawbridge to open at midnight, so sat with our woman guide in the hotel bar that night until time to take our bus to the airport. During this time we saw a few elegantly dressed young women walking around, and I asked our guide how it was that they were so well dressed, when there seemed to be nothing for sale in the stores. She smirked, and said that they were prostitutes, who bought their clothes in Paris, with the fabulous money they earned from their "work". Finally we were able to cross the Kirov Bridge at 2:20 A.M, when the drawbridge opened for twenty minutes, and went straight to the airport to take our flight to Kiev. We flew on an ancient Aeroflot plane, no seats assigned, all sitting where we could, overcrowded, no air conditioning, oversized wrapped bundles filling the narrow aisle, and my seat belt not functioning. Most of the rest of the passengers only had half a seat belt, and the back of our seats kept collapsing. No matter, I was resigned to the fact that we would not stand a chance if the plane went down or if it caught fire. Once we took off, a waitress, I hesitate to call her a stewardess as she was a big blousy woman in civilian clothes, started up the aisle balancing a tray, would you believe, with bowls of hot broth! Of course these had to be passed out from hand to hand as she couldn't make her way in between the rows of seats, and Frank and I immediately said we didn't care for any by wagging our heads and saying "Nyet". I was sure this was going to be our last flight and could see the headlines in the world newspapers the next day. Needless to say, we arrived in Kiev shaken but safe.

Kiev, pronounced "Keev" there, and the whole of the Ukraine, is Russia's "breadbasket". Our bus ride to the hotel in town was lovely, beautiful chestnut trees lining the highway, tulips and daffodils adorning the parks. Our hotel was a high rise, and like the last hotel, had floral curtains too short and narrow for the windows, and again, the beds were narrow with thin mattresses. We visited many churches, but the most beautiful small one was St. Andrews, up on a hill, painted a pastel blue, with gold and white trim. On each outing we went round and round a wonderful iron statue of a Cossak warrior atop a rearing horse, and when I finally asked our guide who it was, he told us it was Bogdan Khmelnitsky, who freed the Ukraine from the Poles. We took a calm, one-hour boat ride on the Dneiper River, sitting on deck with our elderly friends, noticing little beach cottages on the shores, and coast guard boats as we glided toward the grand Peace Arch and the statue to Mother Russia. Next day we went to the Lava Pechera Monastery, and several museums on the premises. Most outstanding were the miniatures which have to be seen through a microscope. I was fascinated by seeing a flea with gold shoes, a hair split in two with a little rose carved in the middle, a musician on half of a pear pit, with his little mandolin on the other half. Little things please little minds, the saying goes! But the whole time we were in Kiev, the memory of the nuclear plant disaster four years before in nearby Chernobyl was in the back of our minds, and we wondered just how safe it was to be there. We might never know. So far, so good.

Our flight to Moscow this time was on a sleek, newer Aeroflot. A General boarded with us, his chest covered in medals, and Frank, a new General himself, longed to exchange words with him. He was met in Moscow by a retinue of military men, and driven off in a long black automobile. We boarded a bus for an hour's ride from the airport into town, passing by birch trees, interesting little cottages with tiny fenced yards. Hotel was as grand as in Leningrad, although with the same narrow beds and odd curtains. I wondered if they had the same decorator for all their hotels. Had bread, cheese, soup, and a delicious stew, for a change, instead of those dreadful steaks fried in smelly oil. At most meals, Frank and I filled up with a lot of bread, excellent butter and cheese, and icecream, which we never touch at home. Next day the tour included St. Basil's, the exterior of Lenin's Tomb where we stayed for the impressive changing of the guard, and Gum Department Store which is really a series of small shops with nothing interesting in them. After lunch, a shopping tour, but very confusing money change. The price was written in Russian money, but when one bought an item, it was changed into dollars and then changed back into rubles, making it come out more expensive in dollars. Very odd system, so ended up by not buying anything.

Visited the Kremlin through Trinity Gate and many stairs. Saw the Armory, the Museum, and the Kremlin Church, with floor to ceiling icons, all painted on wood. Very impressive. That evening we went to the circus, different from any circus we've ever see in the States or in Mexico, and I've been to a lot of them with my son in Mexico. It included a high-wire act, a water ballet act, a tiger act with 14 beautiful sleek tigers, and a magic act. We were able to understand and appreciate it all. Magnificent. Next day a visit inside Lenin's tomb, where we all filed by his preserved body. The temperature is kept at 61 degrees, and to me he looked like something out of Madame Tussaud's in London. Outside we saw a bride depositing her bouquet on the front steps, which I understand is a custom. At some point we went into a food store, where they sold nothing, just nothing. Tins of cookies, tins of jams, cold extra-fat bologna, sausages, cucumbers and bread. Terrible. One has to form long lines for God knows what they might be offering that day at the end of the line. Perhaps an orange, perhaps a cabbage. I made a mental note never to complain any more about our local supermarkets when they didn't have some fruit or vegetable I wanted.

The next night was special: We went to the grand Bolshoi Theatre to see Swan Lake, only my favorite ballet in the whole world. I could hardly contain myself as we walked into the theatre, and when the music started I was so elated I thought I would burst out crying. We had previously seen this ballet in Los Angeles years before, but to see it at the Bolshoi Theatre was more than I could ever have hoped for. Our box was already occupied by several people, but as the ballet advanced, more and more men forced their way in and knelt in front of our seats, until about 20 people occupied our balcony, and we could barely see through them. That night I came out thoroughly disgusted with Russian men in general, thinking them uncouth, uneducated and absolute boors, for when the music finished, they started clapping uncontrollably and yelling Brava, Brava, Brava, loudly. They almost ruined my night at the Bolshoi, although not quite. After that I started noticing how they barged through doors ahead of ladies, almost treading on feet and letting doors slam in one's face, besides countless other little details which make up a western gentleman's behaviour. I have since had no reason to change my impression.

After the ballet, our guide took us to a sort of night club where they had live music and a raised dance floor. There were a few natives dancing, the men half tipsy, not knowing the right steps, waving their arms and making absolute fools of themselves. We ate sliced salmon and caviar and were served champagne and vodka and finally taken back to the hotel slightly after midnight. Next day we were happy to take our train to Warsaw.

It was an overnight train, and we had supper in the dining car, aided by a young Columbian student who heard us battling in Spanish and English trying to order. He had been in Russia for five years with a scholarship at the University of Moscow, which apparently is the place to learn about the refining of petroleum. We did not know this, and found him interesting. We went to bed at midnight and were awakened rudely by Russian border officials to see our passports. They even looked under our mattresses to see what we might be smuggling, followed by Polish officers who burst into our compartment without knocking, not a good introduction to Poland. However, once in Warsaw, it was sheer delight to walk down the sunny streets looking at fruits and vegetables at stalls everywhere, so unlike Russia. We bought tickets to a piano recital at a nearby castle for that evening, to hear one of Warsaw's best pianists play Chopin's music, the Polonaise, my favorite since I was a teenager, his études and Mazurkas. What better than to hear Chopin played than in Warsaw? A lot of "bests" on this trip. Next day we took a limousine with three other tourists to old Krakow, where I will never forget Remuh Cemetery where hundreds of old Jewish tombstones were returned and stood up close together after the Germans had used them as paving stones during the occupation.

We flew to Budapest, Pest really, as Buda is on the other side of the river. A young, excellent, woman guide was so enthusiastic in her description of the Revolution that she stole our hearts and had us on the verge of tears. Exhaust fumes and mad traffic almost did us in, but the castles were beautiful, as was a trip toMargit Island, a tiny island in the middle of the Danube river. Here, we remembered our good friend at home, Margaret Horkay, (Peggy, like me) whose Hungarian father had named her after the island. At night we partook of a marvellous Goulash dinner, accompanied by wild gypsy music in our ears. I made a mental note to ask Peggy how to cook Goulash when we returned.

On to Prague, now the Czech Republic, the most beautiful city in Eastern Europe, and a city of a hundred spires, they say, although there seemed to be four hundred of them. As one flies in, all the red-roofed buildings look colorful and attractive, and it only gets better when one walks through the city. Frank and I cut out on our own, used the subway system, and had lunch on a hilltop café, near the ancient Prague Castle. We walked over the unique Charles Bridge with its 30 statues of saints, and attended an opera by Stravinsky at the grand Opera House. Cared not for the opera, but at least we were able see the interior of the magnificent Opera House. Finished with a big final dinner party including folk dancing the last night, and prepared for our early flight next morning to Helsinki, where we would spend the night and supposedly fly home, ending the official tour. But on the morning we left, to our dismay, Polly, one of the oldest women in our group, found she had lost her passport, and was forced to remain behind. She looked very forlorn in the lobby when we all said goodbye, and I worried about her when we returned to Mexico, so much so that I wrote a letter to her London address telling her that Frank and I hoped she was safely home by now.

I received no response, and for some time often wondered what had finally happened to her. Then one day, about a year and half later I received a letter, saying she had just received mine which had gone to London, been forwarded to her daughter's home in California, and back to London. I breathed a sigh of relief.

When we finished our tour in Helsinki, Frank and I decided we could not go home before seeing England again, so we flew next morning to Heathrow, put our suitcases in lockers, and with hand luggage only, took a train from Paddington Station to Bristol, where we spent the night. Visited the old iron ship, HMS Great Britain, saw the hanging bridge, went into St. Mary Redcliff church, "the most beautiful Gothic church in all of England", according to Queen Elizabeth I, and had a long conversation with the keeper of the church, who would not let us go until he had shown us various poets' tombs, as well as the grave of the famous church cat. As we had no itinerary, we took a bus to Plymouth, and were absolutely enchanted with Devon's gorgeous green rolling hills, where sheep and cows lie in the sunny pastures. We found a precious Bed-and-Breakfast house near the bus stop, and walked around, finding many antique shops, and coming across a plaque listing the names of the Pilgrims who sailed from Plymouth to America in 1620. We sat on the edge of the quay in the sun to imbibe a tepid beer and feed the seagulls, and in the evening had supper at a quaint little pub. Next morning after a fine English breakfast of stewed prunes, eggs, bacon, kippered herrings, toast and coffee, all included in the price of the room, we stopped to talk with the innkeeper who was interested in the fact that I was English and had had five brothers in the war, seeing that he too had been in the armed forces. I noticed that once you get an Englishman talking, they can go on and on, despite the fact that at the beginning they might have been shy or reticent. Rather like opening the floodgates.

We took a bus to Cornwall, a place we had long wanted to visit ever since we read "The Shellseekers" by Rosamunde Pilcher. We got off at Truro, where we walked around, visited its church, and bought some packets of tea and spices, before hopping the next bus to Penzance. I also had in mind visiting St. Michael's Mount there, which as it turned out, became a comical episode. In Penzance we checked in at an old hotel recommended in a book long ago given to my mother by my son, Tony. The title was "An Epicurean Tour of Britain", published in 1963, the perfect present for a true epicure. Unfortunately, by the time she received this gift, she was really too old to enjoy it as intended, other than to read about some of the sites she had visited many years before. From our bay window we could look upon The Mount in the near distance, which next day we set out to visit, to compare with Mont St. Michel in France, visited five years before. We set out after a good English breakfast at the hotel, to walk the cobble stoned streets in town, where we looked into the tiny antique stores, jewelry stores, and quaint pubs, asking for instructions to get to the Mount. We were directed to take a bus along the oceanside to a stop where the bus driver would tell us to descend. When we got off, we were surprised there were no arrows or paths leading to a ticket office or a dock. Only a small tea house near the road, with a few stone steps to the beach below, where only rocks sat on the edge of a gray ocean. A lady in a raincoat and hat was standing there, and when we asked her where we could take a boat, she answered, "Oh, my son works on the Mount, and if I wave my hat, he'll come for me." Well, she obviously had already waved her hat, for there came her son, in a row boat through the choppy gray waves. When we saw that, we decided to stay on dry land. I stood on the rocks with the cold wind whipping my hair so that Frank could at least take my photo. He took so long to focus while waves lapped at my feet, that finally a high one came and wet me to my knees. At this point, roaring with laughter, we abandoned the beach and went into the tea house for something hot and a dry-out in the ladies' room. Most unsuccessful outing! We returned to the hotel for lunch and was told that on Saturdays the Mount is closed, but the mystery of how to get out there was not revealed to us.

(I have since learned, through the internet, that there are now boatrides and tours to the Mount.)

Back in London next morning, we changed trains and rode out to Reading station as Mike and Mary had intructed us to do. They met us, and we drove to their comfortable home to spend Sunday with them and the four boys, partaking of the delicious dinner they regularly served on Sundays: leg of lamb, potatoes, vegetables from their garden and trifle for dessert. The boys absolutely devoured everything, even a potato I had left on my plate. We were accompanied to the train next morning with Laurence, the third son, who had to travel to London for his classes at King's College.

In London we had no reservations, so told the cabbie to take us to a "nice hotel", which he did, extra-nice, where we were horrified at the amount of pounds sterling we had to pay. No matter, it was just for two nights. We were lucky to find scalpers' tickets to The Phantom Of The Opera. Frank complained that they were too expensive to see the same old story we'd seen before on television, but only a few minutes into the play, we were transported into the fabulous world of the Paris opera house at the turn of the century. When the broken chandelier illuminates and slowly begins to rise to the rafters, it is restored to its original grandeur, accompanied by the incomparable music of Andrew Lloyd Webber.

. Next day I suggested trying to find the house I had lived in with my mother and family, 37 Clifton Road, so we went to a tourist booth, where they explained which bus to take and where to get off. When we descended, we started up the hill and I immediately knew exactly where to turn to get to the old house. We stood in front, I, remembering the times we had gone in and out that big front door with a brass knocker. After a while, I got up the nerve to knock, but noticed there were now three bells to ring, so it was clearly no longer a one-family home. I simply went around the back gate and looked into the garden where I used to play with Trixie, our Cocker Spaniel, and where my brothers had made an igloo one year when it snowed heavily. Frank took my picture at the front door to send to Vic, who would really be astounded that I had remembered how to get there. A neighbor came out, and looked at us questioningly, so I explained that I used to live there fifty years before, and she was astounded and most pleased. It must have given her something to talk about when her hubby came home later!

We flew back to Helsinki next day and from there to New York, where our tour had started. On to Dallas and El Paso, where we spent the night with the Jacksons again. Missed having Vic and Dan living there, but they had moved to Denver, Colorado, to be nearer their son.

We flew home, and as always, flying over desertic Torreón and the hundreds of humble shacks near the airport, I turned to Frank, as I always did, and asked the same question: "Why are we living here when there are so many beautiful places in the world where we could live?" But of course, the answer was that we knew this was our home, where Frank had practiced his profession and where we had made a lovely comfortable life for ourselves. We could not see from the plane the many residential areas that had sprung up since we first arrived, so it was a facetious question, and I always regretted it when we finally drove up to our own house. When we looked out onto our beautiful garden, petted our ecstatic animals, said hello to our faithful maid and gardener who had taken such good care of everything in our absence, we wondered why we had ever left this paradise to venture into unknown territory, seeking more exciting experiences, even incurring risk, instead of remaining safe and sound at home.

In 1991 our friends, the two Spaniards with whom we always made beach trips, acquired a hotel in Mazatlán, so off we went again, the four couples, to spend a few days there to "estrenar", inaugurate, the hotel. This time we flew. We were each given large comfortable rooms, and it had a wonderful outdoor straw-roofed palapa by the pool, where we consumed many happy meals together. What a convivial group we were. I look back now with melancholy fondness, for two men of that group are now gone, and those wonderful little beach vacations ended with their loss.

In November of that year I celebrated my sixtieth birthday by inviting a group of my lady friends over to what is known here in Mexico as a "merienda", a variation of a tea party, where one serves a more substantial plate than sandwiches, such as tamales or green enchiladas, followed by a slice of cake and coffee. I received many gifts and good wishes, but more than that, I was happy to be in excellent health, enjoying life with my husband of thirty-eight years, and having my son doing well in his work as a free-lance cameraman in Los Angeles.

We had acquired two sleek black kittens that month, Tilly and Tommy, which I had seen at my seamstress's house on one of my forays to have clothes adjusted. Catalina lived on the second story of an old ruin of a house, and every time I climbed the outdoor metal staircase to visit her, I counted my blessings. Here was a poor woman in her late sixties, still sewing for a living in a miserable room that served as bedroom and kitchen, her sewing machine jammed in between the bed and the kitchen stove. She always received me with a smile on her face and an offer of a taste of something she might be cooking. She had long ago adopted a female cat, who had reproduced several times, so that the patio below was always full of cats and kittens. She fed them rice and beans, and whichever got there first were the lucky ones, while the others simply went without. Her last litter consisted of three striped kittens and two black, and they were all so adorable, as only kittens can be, that I decided to ask her for the two blackies. She acceded rapidly, and knowing she would not receive payment, next day I took over a huge bag of cat food, which I am sure they did not enjoy as much as their daily ration of rice and beans. No matter, I knew they would quickly get accustomed to it. Luckily for me, Frank is an animal lover like I am, so the two little kittens were welcomed into our home where they made our life even more agreeable. A year or so later, while buying plants at the plant nursery, my attention was called by two other little kittens, one calico and one black, playing amongs the flowers. I asked the owner about them, and he said he was going to "get rid of them", as they were a nuisance to his plants, so naturally, what could I do but bring them home too. Gradually, our menagerie grew. We had fed, over the years, a succession of cats who came to our doorstep, but little by little they had disappeared, and I hope my worst fears were not realized, knowing the fatal end alley cats often meet. These four were vaccinated and sterilized, and lived in our garden, but at night they were brushed and fed before being put away in two kennels we had built over the dog kennel. It worked out well for years. Three gradually died when they were about fifteen years old, and we still have Tommy, who is going on seventeen!

ZACATECAS

One year, when Tony and Mel came from L. A. to spend Christmas vacations here, we took a short trip to Zacatecas, a typical Mexican town we wanted the kids to see. As we rounded a bend, the beautiful aqueduct rose before our eyes as we drove into town, where we checked in at the Hotel Quinta Real. This hotel had recently been built on a bullring, a most original construction, and one which has brought many tourists to Zacatecas. The city has been named a World Heritage site, with narrow crooked streets and white flat-roofed houses, dating from 1546, when a rich silver vein was discovered, bringing many mining companies to the area. Its Cathedral is considered one of the most beautiful examples of churrigueresque architecture, with a notable façade richly sculptured in red stone, (cantera) and dating from the 1700s. After visiting the Pedro Coronel museum, named after a local artist, whose paintings are displayed within, we drove to the Convento de Guadalupe, a monastery about eight kilometers from downtown. Large religious oil paintings

275

hang throughout its corridors, despite the open air circulating through, making one wonder how they have survived the weather for so long. Perhaps the Zacatecas' mild climate has aided their conservation. Overlooking the city is a high rocky hill, crowned by a chapel, which one can approach by road or cable car, this last one giving the passengers a spectacular view of the whole city. It was here that the four of us stood that sunny morning, looking down upon the city, when I spied, in front of the chapel, what I thought was either a big rat or a tiny dog. I nudged Mel, asking, "What on earth is that?" She too was uncertain, but we gathered from the way it padded along that it was a dog. We went down the steps and sure enough, the poor little thing was all skin and bone with a long nose. I picked up the little figure, trembling from cold and from hunger, and went to a nearby stall to order two tacos without chile, which we fed to the puppy. It gulped them down and snuggled deep in my arms. I looked at Frank and Tony questioningly. They immediately responded that we could not possibly take it into our elegant hotel as it might soil the carpet and cry all night. But then Tony added, "If you want, when we're ready to leave tomorrow, we can drive up here, and if she's still around, we can take her home". Frank agreed, so that is what we did next morning. I worried all night that she would die of cold before our rescue, but when we arrived in front of the chapel, there she sat in the middle of the sunny plaza, waiting for us, or so it seemed. We fed her two more tacos, and then I bundled her up in my arms, and for the next three and half hours she slept on my lap while we drove to Torreon, trembling in her sleep all the way.

Needless to say, she grew into a lovely strong honey-colored dog, whom we named Daisy, who was to live with us for many years. Tony sent us a book on pet care from L. A. a month later, with the dedication, "For Daisy, who made our Christmas that much brighter"

Dan, Vic's husband, was diagnosed with cancer of the lung in 1991, for which radiation was prescribed. He was very brave about it and even kept playing golf during the first few treatments, but gradually grew weaker and weaker until he was hospitalized. I flew to Denver to spend his last weeks with Vic, first, while he was in the hospital, and eventually in a hospice, travelling to and forth with her every morning. I spent my time sitting in the hallways of the hospice, drinking coffee and reading, talking to many of the old people who were there awaiting their final hours. Vic would sit with Dan, recalling their life together, and then falling apart when she got home. Bill and Chris and their children often went to visit us at home, keeping me supplied with movies to watch in the evenings while I sat alone downstairs. Vic preferred to go to bed and try to sleep, but I could hear her tossing and turning all night. Not easy, losing one's husband, and I gave her the space she required. After it was over, I hated to leave her, but knew she would be well taken care of by Bill and Chris. But Frank and I would long grieve for jolly Dan, the ultimate golfer. We could not imagine Christmases and summer vacations without Vic and Dan together, brightening our days with their humor and good cheer.

When I returned home, Frank gave me additional bad news about our friend Bobby, who had spent those same weeks in the hospital in Torreón with complications after having her gall bladder removed. Also hard to lose a good friend. We had shared so many good times together, specially that unforgettable trip to Europe. So Frank and I were doubly depressed with our two great losses that year, realizing once again the fragility of life, and appreciating our days on earth with more intensity.

A VISIT FROM THE PRESIDENT

In August we had a big surprise: The Mayor of Gomez Palacio, who lived with his family across the street from us, approached Frank early one morning as he was leaving for his office, informing him that the President of Mexico, Carlos Salinas de Gortari would be arriving that afternoon in our city to inaugurate a new road, and had requested that the Mayor find a private residence for an overnight stay. We had heard that rather than stay at a hotel, this was one of his customary requests when he found it necessary to remain overnight outside of Mexico City. The Mayor asked Frank point blank whether we would be willing to receive the President that afternoon, a request which took my husband's breath away, and who responded he would have to ask me whether I would accept. When he did so, I was readying myself for a golf game with my friends and answered that it would be a huge inconvenience, and that frankly, I'd rather not, but when I saw my husband's disappointment, I changed my mind and acceded. I hurriedly went to the club to tell my friends the reason for my not playing that day, and I must admit they were more impressed than I with the honor of having the President in our home.

Carlos Salinas de Gortari was a very popular figure at the time, because of all the good works he had accomplished in the country. He had launched bold initiatives, such as the reversal of the lamented bank nationalization in 1982, as well as building a network of toll roads all over the country. I dashed home, and started getting things in order, putting new sheets on our king-sized bed, straightening up the bedroom and bathroom, and instructing the maid to dust everything carefully. I did not really know what else to do, but it wasn't long before three young men came to check the house to see what was needed.

They inspected the bedrooms, checked the sheets, fresh towels in the bathroom, and went into the kitchen to see if it was adequate. A few hours later, a huge truck arrived to disconnect our phones and our light and to connect their own lines. I began to regret our decision when they told us that the President would be arriving that evening, and that we had to be out of the house by then. One of the reasons they found our house adequate, is that our back garden gate leads on to another street, and the fact that we had two entrances gave him more security. The big problem was what to do with our pets. Carlos, our gardener, offered to take the dogs to his own home, but we left our cats outside with food to fend for themselves. Then our friends, the Barboglios, insisted we spend the night at their home while the President was in ours. The only one who was to be allowed to enter the gate was the gardener, so that he could turn on the pool filter in the morning and clean the porches. But the president's assistants had a problem with our T.V., as we have a Dish service with which we see U. S. programs, and they did not know how to get the Mexican stations. Frank was called urgently to instruct them what to punch, which he did, and just missed the president's arrival.

Next morning, we were invited to come back home and have breakfast with the President. When we arrived, our whole street had been blocked off with police cars, and all the neighbors were outside, ready to see what would transpire. We were ushered through, and into our house, where we waited patiently until he came out and formally was introduced. He was very gracious, and most appreciative of our hospitality. It was strange being served in our own home by a strange person, food that the President had ordered for breakfast, but we were charmed by his personality, despite the fact that he was a small unprepossessing man. Before he left we congratulated him sincerely for all the marvellous work he had done. When he was gone, the light company reconnected our electricity and phones, and we moved back, finding the kitchen in complete disarray where his cook had used every pot and pan in the cupboards and left them all dirty. I presume part of the President's retinue had had a grand feast the night before, as he himself had been invited to a formal dinner in town. So much for his visit. Within the year we were invited back to Los Pinos, the Mexican White House, for a formal dinner given in honor of the President of Germany and dignitaries. We sat with the President of the Deutch Bank, the Ambassador to Ecuador and a Mexican actor, along with their wives. Nice table, agreeable companions, excellent food, and I noticed in back of the President's table which was set up high against the wall, a marvellous mural of the Valley of Mexico, by one of Mexico's treasured landscape artists, José María Velasco. When we left, Frank left me standing on the terrace while he arranged for our car to be brought, and in the meantime I moved toward a group of people talking to our Poet Laureate, Octavio Paz, who was kind enough to nod at me appraisingly and raise his arm to include me in his group. Frank came for me too quickly though,and I regretted not being able to exchange a few words with the venerable old gentleman. It was an unforgettable evening.

We decided we'd spend Christmas that year in Ruidoso, New Mexico, at a ski lodge, so Tony and Mel and Mel's mother, Margaret, drove from Los Angeles to El Paso, Texas, where we met and drove together in Tony's big station wagon to Ruidoso. Mel's mother and I had long wanted to learn to ski, and although I was already sixty, and she a few years older, we decided we'd brave it and take classes and learn. Brave souls. She and I had not previously met, but when we did, liked each other immensely. Tony and Mel gave each of us gifts of a one- piece zippered ski suit, hers in black and mine in white. We were absolutely delighted. We took classes for the four days we were there, and I must say, I took to it like a fish to water. On the third day I was zooming down the beginners' hill, skis tucked under my arms like a professional. Margaret did well also, proving that if you set your mind to it you can learn at any age.

Next year Vic's health failed, and she had to sell her home and move to her son Bill's home. I immediately left for Denver to be with her, and spent two weeks in their guest room, sharing a bed with Vic. She was needing intravenous solutions almost every day, and was so weak she could not bathe without help. Chris behaved like a hostess, nurse, cook and bottle washer, during this time, and Vic was truly lucky to have such a wonderful daughter-in-law. Then Tony called me at their house to tell me that he and Melanie were going to get married on Friday, and could I come. Frank, at home in Mexico, had said he could not make it on such short notice, and I know it was because he was miffed at them both for not wanting to accept our open suggestion of a simple ceremony and luncheon in Los Angeles, and now suddenly doing things so abruptly. They had been going together for several years, and had had ample time to make plans for a nice wedding, but they preferred to do it on the spur of the moment. Vic was not doing well, so I told Tony that I could not leave her and fly from Denver to L. A. At the same time it broke my heart that Frank and I would not be at our only son's wedding. They married before a justice of the peace, and only Mel's sister and her husband flew there to be with them. Vic made a miraculous recovery, and I felt bad that I had not gone to witness their union. They chose not to go on their honeymoon in Europe until the following December when Frank and I promised we would take care of their house and dogs while they were away. When we went to L. A. that year to spend Christmas with them, we gave them a reception at a restaurant of their choice and invited all the Balderramas to join us. Too little, too late.

While playing golf with Bobby the year before she died, we found a little puppy abandoned behind a rock on the golf course. Perhaps its mother had just left her for a few moments while she went to find food, but she looked so forlorn that I picked her up, put her in my golf bag and took her home with me. As I said before, Frank was equally as fond of animals as I, so she was readily accepted, and Daisy seemed intrigued by this furry little puppy and went along with the adoption. Frank named her Punky, and she grew to look like a long-legged coyote. Whenever our cattleman friend, Pete Barboglio came over, he'd look at her and say, "If I came across her on my ranch, I'd surely put her away with all the other coyotes we've shot". But even if she looked like a rangy coyote, we loved her dearly. One year when I had a tea party and had invited a lady from Mexico City who was visiting her sister here in Torreón, she looked through our living room window and said, "What a beautiful garden, but why on earth do you have those ugly dogs!" Well, as you can well imagine, we felt like she had insulted our children!

HUATULCO, OAXACA

That Christmas, after having a big New Years' party at home, we decided to invite Tony and Melanie to join us on a trip to one of the newer beaches, Huatulco, on the Pacific coast in the state of Oaxaca. We four flew to Mexico City, changed planes and continued on to Huatulco. The area had not received rain that year, and as we flew over the jungle, so dense and dry and ominous, I thought with horror of going down and never being found. But then on every voyage we have ever taken, I always think something could happen to the plane and can even visualize the sudden drop from the sky and eventual crash into the ocean or the land below. I have always had a too vivid imagination, and my motto in life as been: Hope for the best, but be prepared for the worst. That is why I always check the emergency exits in planes and hotels. But as usual, we arrived safely in the warm humid atmosphere of Huatulco, being winter, when the weather is ideal, not as unbearably hot as in summer. What a paradise, still not totally invaded by tourists, but already with two lovely hotels to pick from. The second day, Frank and I, who had carried along a few of our golf clubs, went out to play on one of the lushest courses we have ever been, dotted with huge flowering Flamboyán trees, their red flowers brightening up the greenery of the surroundings. The breakfasts were unlimited, as is usual at all Mexican beach hotels. After that, we'd change and go to the pristine golden-sanded beach or to the enormous pool to spend the rest of the morning watching other residents or simply reading. Tony rented a water motor boat for a while, and zipped around over the waves. In the afternoon, after another huge meal at the hotel, we would rest in our rooms, before taking a taxi to one of the nearby towns, La Crucecita or Santa Cruz, where we found a variety of small stalls and shops and restaurants, to purchase native handicrafts and have a light snack.

In August of 1993 Frank and I celebrated our fortieth wedding anniversary and made it a welcome party for the recent newlyweds also. We had about fifty people at tables in our garden, a catered affair with a cancionero group playing guitars. There is nothing more romantic than the old Mexican songs. Each one expresses whatever the lover wants to say, which is why serenades are so popular when courting. That night they played all our old favorites, "Tú me enseñaste", (You showed me how), "Mía", (Mine), "Júrame", (Swear to me) and "Qué sabes tú? (What can you know?) as well as many others. Tony had invited his boyhood friends, and they made up a jovial table. Both couples received many useful gifts, and the evening went off well.

OREGON AND CALIFORNIA COASTS

That Christmas we were invited by Mel to meet the rest of her family in Salem, Oregon. We flew to L. A. and from there we joined Tony and Mel for the long ride to Oregon, stopping on the way for a visit to the Hearst Castle at San Simeon. It was truly a fun Christmas. First we went to her mother's home in Salem for Christmas eve, to meet her 96 year old mother, a delightful, pretty, very talkative old lady. All Mel's family was there, her two brothers and two sisters, a very congenial group. After Christmas, we spent a night, courtesy of the kids, at the distinguished old world Benson Hotel in Portland. Then we took off for Mount Hood, destination, another wonderful hotel, Timberline Lodge. If the reader is a skiier, he or she should visit this lodge one day. It is truly a marvel, 6,000 feet high on the massive south shoulder of the mountain, built during the Depression by the WPA (Workers Progress Asociation) by hand, from local stone in 1936. It is a masterpiece of Cascadian architecture.

Our rooms were warm and cozy, and the restaurant served

haute cuisine, so much so that I had to buy their beautifully illustrated cook book. Two beautiful Saint Bernards roamed the hotel, guardians of skiiers lost in the snow, presumably, although they looked pretty old to get out in that weather. Mel's mom decided she would not ski, so I set out alone the second day, behind Melanie and Tony. All went well, but the third day I got too big for my britches, and decided on a more difficult run. Tony had told me to be careful when jumping off the ski lift, as it was pretty high. I paid no attention, but when I saw how high the jump was, I hesitated too long, while the instructors below kept yelling "Jump! Jump!". When I finally decided, I landed flat on my stomach and ribs and was completely winded. They ran to pick me up and said they would send for the ski cart to take me back to the lodge, but I insisted I was alright, thus forcing one of the poor instructors to walk me all the way back to the hotel. Frank was sitting on the terrace overlooking the ski runs, having a nice hot toddy when we arrived, and I felt like a fool. I did commend the instructor for his dedication that evening though. No more skiing for me. We left next day anyway.

The drive back along Pacific Coast Highway, following the ocean was memorable. What a scenic ride, cutting through the Oregon Firs, stopping at lookouts to view the ocean below; driving further along the California coast with its huge, indescribable Redwoods. Mel and Tony had introduced us to a section of the Pacific coast that we might never have known but for Mel, who was a native Oregonian. They had chosen, with great care, Bed-and-Breakfasts along the road, that we might experience this typical experience. We stopped in Salishan Lodge, Newport, Yaquina Bay, and Mendocino, beautiful inns, wonderful food, roaring fires. Then, to my delight, we stopped to see my brother, Ted, in San Mateo, California. It had been many years since we had seen each other, and it was a reunion not easily forgotten, as he was still in good health at the time. He was a handsome, 75 year old man, with silver hair and clear blue eyes, and had not lost the dry wit from his youth.

Then, a big event in our lives: Our first grandchild was born in October of 1994. We flew to California, and straight to the hospital, where Mel lay, looking flushed and pretty, with a beautiful little baby boy in her arms. Oh, what a joy it was to hold him in our arms, a son of our son. I cannot describe the feelings we had that morning, and I know that other grandparents have that same feeling which can never be equaled, when seeing their first grandchild. Frank and I were elated, and couldn't see enough of him. I had taken some baby sweaters, kindly knitted by friends of mine in Mexico, but from the very beginning, Mel dressed little Anthony in cotton jogging suits, and we took him out proudly in his new pram along the edge of the ocean although it was a cool day. How different to when I had kept Tony all wrapped up like a taco for his first few days. I learned that Mel had very different ideas about how to raise a baby, and after a while I stopped making suggestions.

ENGLAND, WALES, STRATFORD, PARIS, BRUGES

In February of 1996 we got itchy feet again. No matter that we had been to Europe already five times, we felt that there was so much more to see that interested us. For instance, I had long wanted to visit Wales, where my Grandmother, Margaret Rowena Richards, was born, and where my Grandfather had first met her while visiting his aunt. They had eloped and married in London, leaving for America in 1890, and here I was over a hundred years later looking for traces of them. Our friends in El Paso, the Jacksons, still owned a travel agency, so they were happy to make up an itinerary for our forthcoming trip. We planned to include, besides London and Wales, Paris, Brussels and Bruge. This time we would take the "chunnel", underneath the channel, to Paris. Looking back, I think we have been extremely lucky that all our trips to Europe have been realized without mishaps, inconvenient delays or loss of luggage, and this one was to be the same. In a letter to Vic upon our return, dated April 12, 1996, (written on St. James Court Hotel stationery) which was returned to me after she died, I think I described our holiday better than I can do it at present time:

"Dearest Vic, The long-promised letter, although we have been in touch by phone. The highlights: In London we saw three plays, "Sunset Boulevard", good, but not a pinch on The Phantom; "Miss Saigon", which was excellent, but very sad; and a sleeper, "Jolson", which we enjoyed heartily, clapping ourselves silly with each song the actor belted out. He absolutely brought the house down. Of course, part of the fun is going to the bar at half-time to hear the British comments, and see what everyone is wearing! One afternoon we stopped for tea at the Ritz, despite our concierge telling us it was "absolutely impossible" to get in without reservations. All the ladies were dressed in their finery, although I wasn't, as this was completely spur-of-the-moment. Guess we were just lucky: shining silver service, snotty waiters, and a wonderful choice of teas and tiny delicious sandwiches. We visited out of the way art galleries, took a bus to Leeds castle, and another day to Brighton, where we toured the Brighton Pavilion, which Prince Regent, George IV, had asked John Nash to enlarge and remodel after an Indian Palace.

"Only spent one full day in Paris, where we were able to get tickets at the Grand Palais for an exhibitition of one of my favorite landscape artists, Corot. We admired the newly gilded domes, angels, gates and columns, all due to President Miterrand's renovation of Paris. We then entrained to Brussels. La Grand Place is really impressive, a beautiful square where sit the Town Hall and other buildings, all done in gilt paint. Took a streetcar out to see the fair grounds, without knowing how much to pay. A lady sitting across from us took pity and gave us an extra ticket she had in her purse. We were terribly grateful. Kind woman! Our hotel was pristine modern, as was the one in Bruges, where we had to walk through the fish market to get to the center of town. That city is really incredible. Every building is about four or five hundred years old, clean, beautifully kept up, the canals, churches, statues, cobbled or brick streets. I cannot believe we have been in Europe five times and never thought of visiting Bruges. There is a street that has small restaurants on either side, with waiters on the sidewalks hawking their wares, and the food one eats in any of them is unbelievable. I understand there is running competition between French and Belgian food, and frankly, I wouldn't know which to choose!

Back to Britain, again on the Eurostar under the ocean, and a bus to Wales, first Cardiff and then Swansea, both places where the Richards had lived. I don't know what I expected to find, but I was filled with nostalgia when looking down the streets Grandfather Hardy had walked with young Margaret Rowena. Stopped at the photography shop where they had had their photos taken, and which had only closed as late as 1970. Stopped at an art gallery which bore the address where the family used to live, and realized my hunt was futile unless I delved into the city archives. What for? Pointless. Besides it had started to pour, so we took another bus and went to Stratford-Upon-Avon, the most darling city. I have long treasured a water color of Anne Hathaway's cottage which our mother bought years ago, and now, as we stood before the little thatched house, I remembered Mom. We stayed two nights in Stratford, simply because we were in love with the 200 year old Shakespeare Hotel, and also because it had suddenly turned sunny. Had tea in the afternoons in the chintz-covered sitting room, wonderful dinners at night, (who says English food is bland?) and visited antique shops as well as the Teddy Bear museum, where I remembered my Teddies which I still have! I have long suspected Frank of being more of an Anglophile than I, and it is fun to watch him transform himself into a proper Englishman on these trips, with his tweed suits, English cap, and umbrella. Perhaps my mother inspired him years ago with those long talks they used to have about England.

"When we returned to London, we visited Mary and Mike, and they drove us out to Cambridge, where their son, Jonathan had just graduated. I almost froze while visiting each school, although only able to look in at the center grassy square surrounded by buildings. When Mary saw me trembling, she lent me her scarf to wrap around my neck and head and decided we should stop for hot tea in a tiny restaurant filled with noisy students. Britain during the month of February is definitely too cold for my liking. We flew out next day to Dallas-Monterrey-Torreon, happy to find a much warmer climate. Thus ended our equally marvellous sixth trip to Europe".

A year later, we took our first Caribbean cruise with our dear friends, Fran and Pete Barboglio. People we know had raved about cruises over the years, and we had finally selected the Holland American Cruise line, which has turned out to be the finest in our estimation and one which we have continued to choose. Starting with the gourmet cuisine, everything was done with finesse and taste. We flew out via El Paso, Houston and Fort Lauderdale, where we began our cruise after a wild ride on an airboat through the swamps, observing the poor old crocodiles which had my complete sympathy. Our first cruise stop was at the island of St. Maartens, followed by St. Thomas, and its streets of gold jewelry shops. I could hardly resist! Then our final stop was in Nassau, where I was interested in hearing the opinion of our local guide about the Duke and Dutchess of Windsor, who had spent years living there. I expected to see a statue, at least, of our beloved Duke, but no, their opinion was that they had been an idle couple, who spent all their time playing Bridge, and did nothing for the island or its inhabitants. Well! How disappointing.

I had visited Vic in Denver right before leaving on the cruise. She was in the late stages of cancer of the throat, but the first night she and I stayed awake until 3 A.M. talking and laughing, recalling funny incidents in our life. We'd start to fall asleep and then from one bed to another the conversation would resume. I will always have that one pleasant night in my mind when I think of the last time we were together. Next day she was down and moody, and nothing pleased her. When I left, I knew I would never see her again, as she was skin and bone, and the prognosis was bad, but her son, Bill, and his darling wife were giving her the best of care. We did get to talk again when Frank and I returned from our cruise, but she was not the same old Vic, and a few weeks later she passed away. At the time, I only half suspected how much I would miss her love and her sardonic wit for the rest of my life. I think of all the advice she gave me over the years, some not well-received, taken as criticism from an older sister. But she loved me dearly, and I adored and admired her all my life. With her passing, it was the end of the first six Browns. I find myself today trying to live up to her in many ways, and keep in close touch with Bill and Chris, who are such dear members of my fast dwindling family

PARIS, MADRID, AND LISBON

In 1998, Tony called and told us he had purchased tickets for the quarter, semi, and finals of the World Soccer Cup in Paris, and wanted us to accompany him so that he and his father could attend the games. Mel and Tony now had another baby girl, and Mel wanted to take the children to spend time in Oregon with her mother, so Frank and I rented an apartment for the three of us for ten days in Paris, instead of going to a hotel. It was owned by a French couple we had met in Torreón a couple of years before when they were working for the Renault assembly plant here. It turned out to be a wise investment, for although not cheap, it turned out more inexpensive than renting two rooms in a hotel for ten days. Tony was to fly from Los Angeles, and we would fly to Monterrey first, spend the night, and from there Dallas-Paris. (How inconvenient before we had our international flights of today). We arrived a day after Tony, who had checked in meanwhile at a nearby hotel, and went straight to the apartment. The French couple would supposedly receive us and then leave for their alternate home in the French Alps, but when we arrived, no one answered the doorbell at their apartment. Downstairs there was a small bar, where I eventually went in to ask if they knew where the owners were. All this, in my bad French, saying that we were from America, (was there any doubt?) and that we had rented the apartment and had our luggage in the courtyard. The sullen bartender finally took pity on us, and suggested we wait for a while sitting at the bar, as he had just seen Madame go out. About a half hour later Madame arrived in a flurry, as she had assumed we were to arrive at 10 P.M., not 10 A.M. Oh, well. We were pleasantly surprised by the apartment, with new curtains and bedspreads which she had made herself. Frank, especially,was amazed with her dilligence, and eyed me accusingly. Well, I USED to know how to sew. She and her husband had placed a piece of good cheese in the fridge along with a bottle of wine, as a welcome gift. A little basket of peaches and apples stood on the kitchen counter. We were so pleased that we asked them to go down the street with us to have lunch. They were a most pleasant couple, and they have since visited us twice in Mexico. Tony arrived about that time, and we settled down in the small apartment.

Frank, Tony and I would start out every morning with a light breakfast of fruit, coffee, bread and butter (there was a shop down the street which sold wonderful French loaves), and then walk all over Paris. We saw Museums galore, and one day when the two men had taken the rapid train to Lyon to see a game, I spent the entire afternoon at the Museé D'Orsay, a converted railway station which has the most marvellous art collection, afterwards walking two hours to get home by dusk. By the time I arrived, they were already there, worried I had gotten lost. (I am known for my lack of sense of direction.) I could never walk that distance today, even in my comfortable SAS shoes, I am quite sure.

Then Mary, my niece, and Mike her husband, called us and said they were flying from London to Paris to spend the day with us. When they arrived at the apartment, we went out to lunch at a special restaurant we had previously noticed, Le Notre, on the Champs Elysees, and from there to the Grand Palais to see a marvellous exhibition of Delacroix. Glad they enjoy art too! We had coffee with them, from where they left for the airport to fly back to London, and we told them how appreciative we were of their special trip to see us. They are so dear, and so thoughtful!

We had bought tickets via our friends in Paris to the Concert of the Three Tenors, so that night we went to the Champ de Mars, beneath the Eiffel Tower, found our seats, ordered champagne and prepared to listen to the magic voices of Pavarotti, Domingo, and Carreras. We were not disappointed. This for me was another dream come true, such as the Bolshoi Ballet in Moscow had been eight years before. How many "special nights" was I going to be able to enjoy in my lifetime, especially in the company of loved ones? I felt like pinching myself to be sure it was true. After the show we strolled down the Champs Elysées and stopped for a snack and drink at Fouquets, one of our favorite restaurants.

We tried to visit sites in Paris we had not been before, but decided to repeat, not only Versailles, for Tony's sake, but the incredible Rodin Museum, with its beautiful gardens and statues. It is always emotional to look upon this erotic sculptor's works, The Thinker, the Kiss, the Prisoners of Calais, and so many others. Recently, I had read about the Museé Cluny, or National Museum of Medieval Arts, where the famous tapestries of the Lady and the Unicorn hang. They had long intrigued me, along with their history, described by George Sand in her writings. Six beautiful red tapestries, each describing one of the six senses, (Hearing, Sight, Touch, Smell, Taste, and Love), hang in a red-illuminated room. Loving animals the way we do, it touched us to see the unicorn with his hoofs on the lady's lap, as well as in other poses. The hall has low light, to preserve the colors of the incredible tapestries.

One day we drove out to Monet's Garden, Giverny, and as we stood on the little bridge over the lily pond, I knew that little by little my dreams were being fulfilled. I long ago had bought a poster of this very scene, and now I was photographing it myself. Being June, the garden was in full bloom, and one could see many of the sections portrayed in Monet's paintings.

Early every morning Tony would take off for his morning run to Notre Dame Cathedral and back, a good way to start his day. Together, on the Ile de la Cité we again admired the wonder of the Sainte-Chapelle stained windows in the upper part of the chapel. Of course we could not leave without another visit to Napoleon's tomb in Les Invalides, where Tony took some marvellous photographs of the impressive casket from the upper balcony. As to the Coupe du Monde, they saw a total of five games, and France won the cup, much to the joy of the whole country. There was incredible celebrating on the Champs Elysées the day we flew to Madrid.

We had wanted Tony to see part of Spain, and to feel the flavor of the Spanish atmosphere, if only for a couple of days. Just to sit at a sidewalk café in the shade, having a glass of wine and watching the parade go by, was a treat. We visited the Palace, where King Alfonso and his wife Sofía live, the Prado, and the Museum of the Reina Sofía, where we saw Picasso's "Guernica", famous painting about the German bombing of the town by the same name during the Spanish Civil War. We had not heard of a newer museum, the Thyssen Bornemisza, but we were fascinated with the collection. Truly worth visiting to any art lover who visits Madrid. Before Tony left, we enjoyed a captivating Flamenco dancing show, where they took photos of us wearing attractive little red Spanish dancers' hats.

We bid Tony goodbye at the hotel to take overnight train to Lisbon. He was due to fly out of Madrid the next morning for L. A., back to his little family, and we already had our tickets for six days in Portugal. It was a sad end to almost two weeks of fun filled days, but we thanked the good Lord that we had been able to spend those perfect days together with our son. Our train ride was an experience. Our cabin was tiny but comfortable, with upper and lower bunks. Next morning at breakfast we learned about Portuguese coffee when we ordered it without milk, despite the insistence of the waiter. Talk about strong coffee! It really gave us a jolt. Our hotel faced the timeworn Avenida Liberdade where we were reminded of the popular song in Mexico at the time, "Lisboa Antigua", or Antique Lisbon. The sidewalks were paved with stones, uplifted in places by the ancient tree roots, and although the whole city was old, it was clean, and the buildings were beautiful. One had to admire its ancient beauty. The World Expo '98 Fair was going on, so we spent two days to visit the various pavilions, thrilled when we found the Mexican one, where they welcomed us with Tequila and Mariachi music. We hired a wonderful old driver who showed us the main points of interest in the city, the Castle of San Jorge, the tower of Belém, the Monument to Discovery, and the old Carriage Museum. Another day he rode us to various points outside Lisbon, of course the famed church of the Virgin of Fátima, Cascais by the ocean, the walled-in town of Obidos, Nazaré beach, and many castles where we joined guided tours to hear of their history. At nights Frank and I went to clubs where they sang Fado, accompanied by Portuguese guitars. Fado is truly the music of the country, a type of sad low wail, heart-breaking to hear, reaching into your very soul. At these clubs we nearly always ordered that delicious Portuguese green wine with grilled fresh cod, unknown in Mexico, for at Christmas time, only salted, dried cod is sold for making the famous Bacalao dish. We entrained back to Madrid, and found beautiful emails from both Tony and Melanie waiting for us at our hotel. With this, another perfect vacation came to an end.

OAXACA AND TAPACHULA

We had branched out and been seeing two congenial couples for some time, ever since our beach vacations had ended after the death of Sylvia's husband, one of the two Spaniards which we had enjoyed so much. The Fernandez and Cepedas were about our age, and our gatherings with them were more placid, usually for dinner at one of our houses. They and the Barboglios and ourselves decided it would be an interesting change to travel to Oaxaca, southeast of Mexico City, from where we could visit the famous pyramids of Montealbán and Mitla. Just being in Oaxaca would be a treat. We had already visited its beaches in Huatulco with Mel and Tony, and now we wanted to see the sites of the capital city. We stayed at the Camino Real Hotel which is a XVI century converted convent, still showing faded frescoes and having a lobby full of colonial paintings. Downtown, we visited the Cathedral, the XVII century Temple of Santo Domingo, one of the most remarkable and gorgeous churches in Mexico, with its gold altars; the museums, and bought some of the famed black pottery in the colorful marketplace. We took tours out to the pyramids, but aside from admiring them, found that we were not as nimble as before, and could not begin to climb them! At night we saw a wonderful show of the Guelaguetza folk dancing at the hotel. The costumes are colorful, pleated and flounced, and the girls' hair is braided with ribbons. Lunch at a restaurant in front of the plaza, where some of us ordered the renowned chicken in black mole.

About the time we were planning to return home, Juan Jose Fernandez called his brother in Tapachula, in the neighboring state of Chiapas, who insisted that we four couples fly to visit them for a few days. None of us knew them, except for Juan José and his wife, of course, so we strongly refused to stay at their home. But they insisted, until finally we acceded.. Their daughter was in Europe at the time, and their son studying in Mexico City, so they had their two rooms, plus two more at our disposal. That night we invited them out to dinner, and next morning when we arose and went to the dining room, Silvia, our hostess, had a full table set for the ten of us. Bowls of luscious fresh cut up fruit were already on the table, and fresh juice was being brought in by the maid. She and her husband owned a pineapple plantation as well as banana and mango trees, the fruit of which they exported to Mexico City supermarkets. We had a full, appetizing breakfast, served by Silvia and her maids, and then were invited for a ride around the city to see the sights. At one point she rode us right up to the border of Guatemala, to show us how close we were. Meanwhile, the men went to see their cattle ranch, and when they returned, two of which were ranchers, were envious of the lush greenery that the cattle were munching. One highlight for us was going for lunch under a large thatched "palapa" they had built for the purpose of barbecuing meat right on their plantation, overlooking the sea.. Hammocks were strung up, where we relaxed after lunch with a beautiful view. They were a charming, handsome couple, and Silvia was the perfect hostess, always up early, looking fresh and attractive in her cotton dresses, presenting gourmet luncheons every day. Never had we seen such generous hosts, and we were happy they had invited us to a city we probably never would have visited without an excuse.

SOUTH BEND, INDIANA
AND NEW YORK CITY

In November, we visited Tony and Mel in L.A., and then flew to
Chicago with Hank and Sally, where we rented a car to drive to
South Bend, Indiana for the Notre Dame-U.S.C. annual football
game. Both Frank and Hank have followed Notre Dame football
closely since they were children in L. A., influenced by their
Catholic school upbringing. It means a lot to them whether their
team wins or loses. The day of the big game, Sally and I went with
them to Notre Dame Campus to visit the Golden Dome, and see
the band's entrance into the stadium. Then we left them there to
go about our shopping. We had found a big antique mall earlier,
and believe it or not, spent hours there, going through all the
beautiful old collections, and buying up quite a few things. I still
treasure the dozen gilt-adorned Limoges cake plates, and a sugar
and creamer set from England among other pretties. It was hard
for us to tear ourselves away, in time to meet our husbands after
the game. (I believe N. D. won that year!) We had reservations
at the distinguished old Studebaker Mansion for dinner that
night, a real treat, peering at framed photographs and portraits of
many old family members who used to inhabit the mansion, and
enjoying the haute cuisine served. Next day we drove to nearby
Valparaiso, where our husbands' attractive youngest sister lived
with her husband on a beautiful farm in the middle of the woods.
We had lunch with them and spent a long afternoon reminiscing
about their parents and family, and the years when they were
all growing up. Family reunions are so wonderful, and I wish I
still had some of my original family members left. She and her
husband have since moved and built a magazine-pretty house
nearby, and her husband, Bill, has now retired at a very early
age. When we returned the rental car at the Chicago airport, we
suggested flying to New York for three days, where we proceeded
to paint the town red. Starting with breakfast at Rockefeller
Plaza, we watched the skaters, and followed with a visit to the

Twin Towers, where it was so cloudy on the top floor that we could see nothing! Looking back, we are fortunate to have seen this marvel before it came crashing down before our unbelieving eyes on 9/11 on T. V. We went to the theatre, ate at all the fine restaurants, including the newly re-inaugurated Russian Tea Room, visited the museums, and ended up the last night at the Carlyle Hotel Bar listening to the incomparable voice of Bobby Short. We enjoy being with Hank and Sally. They are a handsome couple, good sports, and amenable to all suggestions. Two years before, we had gone to New York after the Notre Dame game to meet with my nephew Bill, and Chris, his wife. We had enjoyed that trip too. At that time, Hank and Sally had flown home direct from Chicago..

In the year 2000 we had an unexpected phone call from my old friend, Mary, from high school. I had long ago lost touch with her, but she had tracked us down in the Torreon directory and wanted Frank and I to attend her and Herman's fiftieth wedding anniversary. I had been her "Madrina de Lazo" at their wedding, the one who places the silk rope around their shoulders, supposedly tying them together. We flew to Mexico City and were picked up at our hotel by Bobby, her eldest son, to attend the church ceremony where they would renew their vows. When they walked down the aisle, we could honestly see very little difference in them from when we had witnessed their marriage, conceivable proof of a happy union for half a century. After the Mass, we gathered at a pleasant country club for the festivities their seven children had planned. It was a gay occasion, where we danced and enjoyed a banquet while catching up on years gone by. We met their children, and I proudly showed them a small album I had made up with photos of Mary and myself in High School, on our bikes, acting crazy, as well as photos of Mary and Herman with Frank and I when we double-dated later on. We all had a good laugh. When we left, it was with a promise to get together again the next year to visit Veracruz, my first point of entry into Mexico.

In all fairness, living in Mexico is not all good. There are many things that one learns to overlook and live with. As you must have gathered by now, punctuality is not one of the Mexicans' good points. This applies to when you invite guests to dinner, have an appointment with a doctor, take a train, (sometimes even a plane), or order something to be made by some artisan or furniture maker. The title of "The Land of Mañana" is not loosely applied. Truly, people believe that one should not hurry oneself needlessly. Another aspect that has always distressed me is the lack of concern for animals. I often stop my car alongside donkey carts, and bawl the driver out for not feeding his burro enough. This does not endear me to him or to other drivers in back of us, but it infuriates me when I see them needlessly whipping a horse or another beast of burden. Stray dogs in the streets, hunting garbage, tear me up inside. Over the years I have brought home many stray cats and dogs, reason for which we have never owned a thoroughbred, but remain saddened by being unable to do anything about the rest. It is a losing battle here. Admittedly, in Mexico City there is a large animal protection group, but although I've been in touch with them and tried to start one here, people lose interest easily, and not enough money comes in for the necessities. Nothing make me feels worse than when I see an animal hit by an uncaring fast driver, and later see the poor animal run over many times until it forms part of the asphalt. The philosopher, Schopenhauer, rightly said that man has made the world a living hell for all animals, and this applies to the ones we hunt, or kill for food. I hope that one day in the future, man ,(including me) will finally learn how to survive completely on legumes and vegetables without having to kill innocent animals. Beggars in the streets are a common sight, and I always give to the very old ones or those who are incapacitated. I frequent two of the most needy old-age homes in this city and in Lerdo, a nearby town, with old clothes every month or so. There are so many needy persons. One of the reasons I have never wanted to go to India is because of the fear of seeing beggars and animals in worse plights than in Mexico. On the other hand, Mexico has so much beauty, the people on the whole are warm and caring, and it has given me and my family so much, that I would be ungrateful if I did not recognize and appreciate its gifts

.

SOUTH AMERICA

In the year 2000, Frank and I asked our good friend and travel agent, Romualdo, to make up a trip for us to visit four countries in South America. Romualdo himself has traveled worldwide, and is the kind of agent who not only includes the type of details you ask for, but throws in a few suggestions of his own, such as sidetrips and restaurants that he has enjoyed. One can rely on his good taste. The itinerary started out with four days in Rio de Janeiro, four days in Buenos Aires, three days in Bariloche, the crossing of the lakes between Argentina and Chile, and a flight to Santiago de Chile. From there we would visit Peru and Machu Pichu, which I personally had wanted to visit since grade school. We were to be met at each airport by our guide, who would take care of the bags and drive us to our hotel. Romualdo is a perfectionist, so he arranged the trip exactly the way we wanted it, choosing wonderful hotels and suggesting points of interest in each city.

In Rio, we were located right in front of the beach, which I thought Frank would enjoy because of the reknowned bathing beauties, but it turned out that it was still chilly weather in March, so there were no swimmers yet. Aside from being excited at being in this well-known city with its ornate sidewalks, we visited all the designated points. We rode the cable car up the Corcovado mountain to admire the Christ Redeemer at the top. We found it so tall when we looked up at it from its base that we decided it was best appreciated from afar. We checked out Sugar Loaf Mountain, the Copacabana and Ipanema beaches, a typical nightclub with wild dancers and transvestites who tried to get Frank to have a photo taken with them, (he flatly refused), visits to the ultra-modern Cathedral, the Church of San Benito, and an expensive visit to a jewelry factory, H Stern, where we bought some exquisite aquamarines for me. We ordered codfish in restaurants, longing for the exquisite broiled cod which we had eaten in Lisbon, but they served it differently here, and not half as good.

From Rio we took a flight to Iguazu, on the border with Brazil, Argentina, and Paraguay, where we were taken to a wonderful wood-smelling hotel named Hotel Las Cataratas, named for the nearby magnificent falls. I can't say enough about the falls. What really impressed me was the fact that they were in the middle of the jungle, unlike Niagara Falls in urban surroundings, making one feel you were discovering them for the first time. Back at the hotel, we found wild raccoons playing on the lawn, and I sat there, feeding them in the evening sun. We sat on the pleasant indoor terrace that night, listening to the water crashing on the rocks below while we sipped our drinks. Next day we were taken to the Boca del Diablo, Devil's Mouth, where 275 falls sprout simultaneously from various cliffs. I can't believe now that I left Frank on the shore, where he did not want to board a rickety boat, and went by myself with an old driver to the very mouth of the main fall, where a movie had been filmed several years before. Clearly I was much braver then.We were also taken to visit a famous bird and reptile park before we took our plane to Buenos Aires the next day.

We had specially requested reservations at the Hotel Alvear, an elegant, old, recently refurbished hotel, and were not disappointed, especially when we heard that Sean Connery had just had lunch in the glassed-roofed dining room the day before. We lost no time in making reservations for that evening at the "Viejo Almacén", the Old Warehouse, where we were fascinated by the various couples on the stage perform the Tango, that most sensuous of dances. We had seen it done many times before in movies, but nothing compares to seeing real Argentinian dancers embrace each other tightly and move rhythimically together, their legs and feet crossing each other as they bend and sway to the music of the violins and the "bandoleón", a type of accordion. I was transported. We ordered, to go with our wine, the famous "empanadas", a small piece of pastry folded over a meat filling, but found them rather dry, in comparison to the wonderful Cornish pasties.

Next morning we were taken on a city tour by the pleasing young man who had met us at the airport. Argentinians are known to be vain creatures, and he told us a joke on them, saying that when the sun comes out, they all look up and smile, thinking that God is taking their photograph. The truth is that they are a good-looking race, having a mixture of Spanish, German and Italian blood in their genes. They speak with an attractive cadence, and although we were prepared to think them conceited, found them very agreeable and friendly. Our guide insisted we visit a suede factory where we could buy jackets cheaply. I believe now that he must have received a commission on sales, as the three that we bought we saw later in Bariloche for much lower prices. Naturally we asked to be recommended to a good restaurant specializing in meat, that being the main staple of that country. But after asking the waiter for suggestions, and ordering, we were taken aback at the amount of meat on each plate, surely enough to feed four people. At restaurants in the future we learned to order one plate for the two of us, and even then we had leftovers.

We visited the well known churches, drove down Alvear Avenue, Palermo gardens, and the Barrio La Boca, a quaint fishing district, one of the most colorful in Buenos Aires where the houses are painted in various bright colors. When later we visited the Museum, we found many paintings with this quarter as the subject. Of course we walked around the Plaza de Mayo, the political heart of the city, and forum for protesters who have demonstrated since 1976. On one end is the Casa Rosada, Pink House, Argentina's presidential palace, a long low neoclassical building.

Again, at night, a Tango show at the Casablanca club. I would never tire of watching these couples dance. It is the most fascinating of all steps. Next evening we went to the Café Tortoni, a popular old coffee house where Tango is performed on a small stage, and where political and cultural leaders rub elbows with visitors. When the master of ceremonies looked into the audience and asked if anyone would care to dance with him, I was more than ready to try, but an old lady beat me to it, and my opportunity was lost forever!

One morning we visited the Recoleta cemetery to look for Eva Perón's tomb. We remembered how impressed we had been with the formidable statues on the tombs in Milan. The entrance is imposing, with marble colums, and we found many elaborate marble mausoleums belonging to influential and important Argentinians. Madame Perón's tomb is a simple one, but there were fresh flowers lying on top.

We found taxi drivers talkative and amiable, and after coming out one night from dinner at an attractive restaurant by the river, Frank paid the driver with a 100 Austral bill, equivalent to one hundred dollars, and he returned back a fifty Austral bill plus change. Next day when we wanted to pay our films with that bill, they rejected it, telling us that they were obsolete as of the beginning of the year. Apparently, taxi drivers got rid of the ones they had not changed at the bank by giving them as change to their clients. So much for the charming taxi drivers!

We took a short flight to Bariloche situated in the foothills of the Andes, surrounded by lakes and mountains, part of Patagonia. It has the appearance of a little Swiss village, with many of its buildings made of wood or stone, and is known mainly as a spa and ski resort, but in the summer it is full of tourists for its beaches and lakes. After WWII it became known as a haven for former Nazi war criminals, according to the Simon Wiesenthal Center. What we noticed was that the whole downtown smelled of chocolate, one of its main exports. Our hotel, the Llao Llao, was about twenty minutes from town, built on a hill with its own golf course. The second day I left Frank playing golf and went to town to shop for leathergoods. We were to meet at the hotel bus stop, which had a small bus which took one up to the hotel. When I got there at noon, as we had arranged, I found Frank sitting morosely at a little table with his right arm in a cast. He told me he had slipped on a wet grassy hill, and the golf cart had run over his wrist. He had made his way back to the hotel, where they gave him first aid and accompanied him to a small clinic, where they X-rayed and bound his wrist and arm up to the elbow. The funny part was that in order to pay the bill he had to get into his money belt which he wore under his undershirt. He could not manage the pants and belt with his left hand, so had to ask the nurse to unzip his pants and the belt, and take out the money. A little embarassing!

That afternoon we still took a ride up to a beautiful lookout point where one can look down through the hills to the ocean. They had two huge, beautiful Saint Barnard dogs up there, supposedly used during the winter months to rescue stranded skiiers. We took many pictures with them.

Next day we were ridden to the wharf where we were to take our boat for the crossing of the lakes to Chile. The water was calm and emerald green, perhaps due to the reflection of the verdant mountains surrounding it. It was a placid trip, and after making two stops, we finally arrived at Puerto Frías, where we were transferred to a small bus to take us to our overnight stay in Peullá. However, when we arrived there and looked at our rustic rooms, beds were unmade, the carpets dirty, and frankly the place did not look very inviting. We asked if we could continue our trip on the boat to Puerto Varas, where we were supposed to dock next day. They agreed, reluctantly, and we arrived at the next town that evening and were ridden to a clean little motel. Next morning we were taken in a van to Puerto Montt, where we took our short flight to Santiago in Chile. There we were met and taken to a beautiful Hyatt Regency Hotel. Next day, an attractive young woman came for us to take us on a city tour.

She was not only pretty, but well versed in tourist information. She kept up a running commentary from the front seat to such an extent that we could not really appreciate all the buildings she was describing. By the time she let us off for lunch, we decided we would rather see the rest on our own.

We were very impressed with Santiago. It is a beautiful modern city with parks and plazas, and we visited the official Government Palace, known as the Palacio de la Moneda, where Frank had his picture taken with two handsome guards. From there we walked up the hill that had the landmark statue of the Virgin Mary. We toured the magnificent Cathedral downtown, where we admired a beautiful marble statue of a Pietá, amongst others. At the Museum I was fascinated with several paintings by artists I had never heard of, so I bought several of the reproductions in postcards, and wish now I had acquired more. Naturally we wanted to visit Pablo Neruda's home, which we found is furnished like a ship, and there I bought a small book of his love poems, so passionate, so deeply moving. Our little guide called and wanted to drive us to Valparaiso on Sunday, but I knew that she would give us a running commentary all the way, making us miss the scenery, so we preferred a tourist car with another couple, and enjoyed the ride and the scenery. At one of the stops we found some llamas, which I wanted to pet, but was warned that they spit. I refrained. We passed one of the main wineries on the way, Concha y Toro, which is one of our favorites here at home, and arrived in Valparaiso. I don't know why I was so taken with this town, but perhaps it was when I learned that it had been a boom-town during the period when ships traveling between the Atlantic and the Pacific used to have to dock here. This changed with the building of the Panama Canal, and the golden age of Valparaiso was over. It was a staggering blow to its economy, and only in the past few years has it made its way up in importance again. But the cobblestoned alleyways, the funicular railways and the stairway footpaths to ascend the overlooking precipitous cliffs, fascinated me. The hilltop houses were only painted in front; the backs, overhanging the cliffs, were left rustic and unfinished. It was the kind of town I felt I would like to stay in for a period of time, painting, if I painted, or writing, as I do. We would have liked to visit Pablo Neruda's favorite house, now a museum, a few minutes away from the center of town, overlooking the water, but we had to be on our way and visit the neighboring town of Viña Del Mar, only a short drive away

Viña Del Mar, usually referred to by Chileans as just "Viña" is one of the country's most fashionable beach resorts. The attractive houses and hotels, the manicured lawns, the Casino, the golden beaches are all something of a contrast to the ramshackle streets of Valparaiso, which I felt had so much more personality. Still, each in its way has something to offer. Isabel Alllende has written an interesting, passionate account of a famous woman who followed her lover through the conquest and settling of Santiago and other cities in Chile. Unfortunately, I read it after we had returned from our South American trip or I would have appreciated the country even more.

We had been watching CNN European version of the news every night in our hotel rooms throughout the journey, and now were dismayed to hear of a revolution in the streets of Lima, Peru, which was to be our next stop. We had paid in advance for our flight there, hotels in Lima and Cuzco, as well as the trip to Machu Pichu. But after seeing the soldiers and the gunfire in the Plaza, where our hotel had been reserved, we decided sorrowfully to cancel that part of the trip. The travel agency made arrangements for our flight back to Mexico City instead, and we were reimbursed later by AIG for that part of the vacation. Sadly, as the years go by, I really doubt we will ever be able to return, so must satisfy ourselves with videos of the place I most wanted to see ever since I was in grade school.

In 2002, fifty years after Frank had graduated as a medical doctor with the rank of Major from the Escuela Médico Militar, and now a Retired Brigadier General, we attended his class reunion in Mexico City. We stayed at the military hotel which is next to the school grounds, and met with eleven of the fifteen doctors who had graduated with him in 1952. One had entered the priesthood shortly after graduation and was stationed in Costa Rica, three of them had recently died, the others either lived in Mexico City or had arrived from various parts of the republic, making a total of eleven. Several of them were staying at the same hotel, and the first morning we met for breakfast. How pleasant it was, for me especially, to see the wives, who at one time had been their sweethearts at the same time Frank and I were dating. Frank had been in contact with some of his companions over the years when he went to Mexico City for promotions, and also at the twenty-fifth class reunion when, as a Lt. Colonel, he had attended alone. It was the month his father had passed away, reason for which he only went to the Mass, and did not stay for the celebration. The first morning, after breakfast, and a solemn Mass, the eleven doctors were taken to visit the new military School of Odontology, the new Gynecology and Obstetrics Clinic, and the Military Hospital where they had all specialized in the past.

Meanwhile I branched out on my own and called my childhood friend, Roberto Humphrey, to meet me at the Franz Mayer Museum downtown. It is in front of the Alameda park, a XVIII century building which had once been a hospital, and holds the principal collection of decorative arts in Mexico. I had long wanted to visit it. We strolled through every hall, looking at the marvellous display of hand-tooled antique silver; textiles, centering on rebozos, sarapes and rugs; devotional figures from Mexico and Guatemala, polychromed and gilded; and mainly, authentic Talavera pottery, a type of majolica glazed earthenware, originally introduced to Mexico in the XVII century, and now appropriated by workshops in Puebla. There are many artesans who copy these patterns, but the authentic one is only manufactured in Puebla, and has its seal on the bottom of each piece. On the second floor is the library containing thousands of rare old books which we only fleetingly glanced at. We went out to the cloister surrounding a court with a fountain in the middle and found on one side some tables and chairs and a small section that served cool drinks. It was always interesting to be with Roberto. He had so much to tell me about what he had been painting lately, what he had sold, and who he had sold them to, many of whom were well known personages. On weekends, he and a friend always drove outside Mexico City to visit small towns which still have the flavour of old Mexico. We walked from the museum toward the Palace of Fine Arts, Bellas Artes, where we had lunch in the restaurant on one side of the lobby, not before admiring the huge murals by Rufino Tamayo and Diego Rivera adorning the palace walls. By the time we arrived back at the military hotel, the men were just returning.

That night in the school auditorium a ceremony was held where the doctors were each awarded a plaque thanking them for fifty years service to the military. Next morning after breakfast we gathered in the courtyard of the school, where a stage has been set up for the doctors, the Director of the school, the Surgeon General, and the Secretary of Defense. We ladies sat in chairs in the courtyard, and the President of Mexico, Vicente Fox, made a speech and then shook hands with each and every doctor. When he left the stage, he came down and shook hands with the ladies, at which time I was able to take his picture. He is a tall and handsome man, and now graces our album where we have photographs of the ceremony.

That night was the final gathering, a dance at the Military Casino, which brought back memories of when Frank was a student and we used to attend the yearly dress ball there. Even though many years had passed, I must say that both the doctors and their wives all looked very well, and we found that we still had many fond memories in common.

OUR TRIP TO THE
HEARTLAND OF MEXICO

We had a visit from Frank's two brothers, Armando and his wife, Zulema, who lived in Chihuahua, and Hank and Sally, from Los Angeles, with their daughter Vicky and her two teenaged children. Vicky and her family live in Iran, her husband being a handsome Iranian who sends her to visit her family in the U. S. every other year. She and her two children were visiting her parents when they decided to come to Mexico. We had plans to guide them on a tour through the heartland of Mexico, where so much history was made during the nineteenth century.

After having them for a couple of days in our home, we left, in two cars, for Zacatecas, the nearest city of our tour, where we visited many of the places we had already seen with Melanie and Tony a few years back. Frank's family was especially fascinated with the old Convent, and its multiple oil paintings, done by priests during the past century. We took the cable car over to the Cerro de la Bufa, (where we had found Daisy), the hill from which Pancho Villa and his army had taken over the city of Zacatecas in the 1914 Revolution. Of course we stayed at the famous hotel made from a bullring, and walked the stone streets of the city in the evenings. From there, we drove to San Luis Potosí, the capital of the state of the same name. The city was in the midst of a fair, jam-packed with people, stands selling all sorts of curiosities in the main Plaza. We were able to elbow our way into the magnificent XVIII century Cathedral facing the imposing Municipal Palace. Several streets are closed to traffic in the area, giving one the freedom to meander around at ease. It was so nice sharing our days with Frank's brothers and family, especially for Frank, who had not had the opportunity of being with both his brothers at the same time for many years. The three of them would walk ahead of us, talking animatedly, while we three ladies and the kids dragged behind, leisurely poking our noses into each and every stall. After asking, we found our way up to a great restaurant which served typical Mexican dishes, exactly what the family wanted to taste, accompanied by live piano music. Our tour agent had luckily reserved a motel for us at the entrance to town, so we later savored a peaceful rest on the veranda while the kids were able to frolic in the garden and pool.

On our way to San Miguel de Allende, we stopped at Dolores Hidalgo, the most revered town in the heartland of Mexico because here it was that the priest and "Father of the Nation", Don Miguel Hidalgo y Costilla, had first cried out for Independence on that famous night of the 15th of September, 1810. We visited his tiny home, full of memorabilia, where a dear old man gave us a tour of each room and showed us the bell tower where the priest had rung the bell while calling for the uprising against the Spaniards. He went on about his capture, and almost cried when he related about Hidalgo's head being cut off and displayed inside a cage at the Alhóndiga de Granaditas (a huge grainery) in Guanajuato. Gruesome!

We drove onwards to San Miguel de Allende, keeping an alert eye out for the hotel where we had reservations, leading from the highway. Of course, one of the kids spied it first, and as we drove through the stone archway and down a rock-paved road, flowering bougainvillea vines brushed the car. At the end was the old Hacienda El Atascadero which has been adapted to a hotel. Our rooms were Colonial styled, tastefully decorated and comfortable, with Indian woven bedspreads. The bathrooms had been modernized. We sat on the stone terrace and had beers that evening, followed by a quiet dining experience in the dining room, overlooking the gardens with their huge overgrown trees. Next morning we planned to go into town to visit the unique Gothic styled church and other historic sites.

We had completely lost count of days and dates, and for two mornings in a row, both Sally and I had forgotten to wish our husbands Happy Birthday when we arrived at the breakfast table. Hank and Frank are one year and one day apart, dates that were forgotten until we were reminded by them. Everyone chuckled, while our remorse was obvious.

San Miguel has conserved its architecture, its culture, and its original stone or cobbled streets. There are magnificent colonial edifices, combining baroque and neoclassical elements, such as in the parochial church, a unique pink stone structure. The city is considered a national monument, and hosts yearly world-famous events such as chamber music festivals, theatre and jazz festivals, theatre, and symphonic orchestras among other important programs. A large percentage of the inhabitants are foreign, American, French, German and other nationalities, who own or rent homes, occupying themselves mainly in the arts, such as writing, painting and sculpting. There are many art galleries, offering local and international works, a bohemian paradise, offering an average temperature yearlong of 61° to 72° F. We were told we could walk around freely at night, as there is strict police vigilance because of so many resident foreigners.

From San Miguel de Allende we drove about 92 kilometers to Guanajuato, the capital of the state, and one of the most historical and colonial cities in Mexico, owing its fame and fortune to the rich veins of silver and gold discovered by the Spanish many years ago. To enter the city, however, one must drive through dark, old, subterranean stone tunnels, very picturesque, but rather frightening. Luckily, a young boy offered to get into our front car and guide us to the main plaza, where our hotel was located. Once there, we were supposed to back into the garage underneath the hotel, and again, a young fellow volunteered to get into the SUV and back it in for us, quite a feat, with about an inch on either side of the vehicle. I would never recommend this hotel to anyone, other than perhaps to go into the lobby and look at the décor. We had asked our travel agent for a downtown hotel, and apparently this was the best one, two hundred years old and supposedly very grand. Perhaps it was grand in its day, but sadly, no longer. We made our way through dark passages, on foot, and up into the lobby, where we were astounded with an

Arabian Nights type of decoration: Huge paintings and tapestries hung on either side of the walls, red velvet upholstered furniture, thick old chinese or turkish rugs, all dimly illuminated by huge chandeliers. It was like discovering a ill-lit, forgotten tomb. After literally gawking at the old paintings, we checked in and climbed the creaking carpeted stairs to our rooms. In contrast to the over-decorated lobby, these were extremely spartan, each with a double bed, mattress sunken in the middle, one straight backed chair, a table with a tiny T. V. on it, and an ancient looking bathroom which turned out to be clean and functioning. (Later we were to find that the sheets and towels were like cardboard, and the T. V. only showed one local station.) When we came down from our rooms, we held a whispered conference, and decided we would change our reservations from the three nights we had originally reserved, to only one night. It was late, and we were too tired to hunt around for another hotel. The adjacent dining room looked attractive, with long dark wooden tables, high-backed Colonial styled chairs, heavy drapes and chandeliers, resembling something out of Don Quixote, so we decided we would have our dinner there. And this is where we almost changed our minds about the hotel, for the supper was exquisite. The chicken in mole sauce was rich and brown and mouthwateringly tasty. The kids asked for tacos, and they too were golden and crunchy, filled with a succulent barbecued meat. After the meal, and feeling better about our surroundings, we walked around the crowded Plaza, although rain was threatening, and sat for a while on the iron benches under the huge trees, realizing that this was truly a lovely example of life in the Mexican province.

A man in a large van came for us next morning to tour the city. He was a young architect, part-time tourist guide to earn extra money, so naturally he focused on the architectural style of the buildings. We visited the famous, beautiful nineteenth century Doric Roman Juarez Theatre, which my mother and I had visited on our trip together years before, admiring the French styled lobby, and theatre decorated in the Moorish style. The kids wanted to visit the Mummy Museum, where 119 mummified bodies are preserved in perfect condition due to the high mineral content of the soil they were buried in. One woman had been buried while pregnant, and one could see the perfectly formed baby inside her. One doctor had been buried in his tailcoat and top hat, (now crushed flat!), still stylishly dapper, despite his missing teeth. There is something dreadful, yet fascinating, about looking upon these people who had once lived, and loved, in this historic city. On a lighter note we visited the artist, Diego Rivera's birthplace, where there is a very minor collection of his works. So much to see, but we had to drive on to Aguascalientes. We stopped briefly in León, where my mother and I had once spent the night, and admired the progress of the lovely city due to the conscientious Governor of the state of Guanajuato, Vicente Fox, who was soon to become President of Mexico.

When we got to Aguascalientes, (which translates into Hot Waters, due to the abundance of hot springs in the area), Sally, Zulema and I wanted to shop for linens, so the men left us for a couple of hours with the kids, during which we saw, and bought, a selection of tableclothes, table mats, napkins, blouses, and all sorts of products from the textile factories in the city. I can hardly tell the difference to this day between some place mats I purchased in Brussels, Belgium, and the ones I bought in Aguascalientes. The city is very festive in April and May with its annual Fair of San Marcos, when bullfighting, cock-fighting, expositions, theatres and music invade the whole city, but as we were there in August, it was calm and much more suited to our mood. We left Aguascalientes around mid-day and made it back to Torreón in time for a late supper, enjoyed at a nearby restaurant. What an agreeable short and sweet vacation we had, having the added pleasure of Vicky from Iran, with her two charming teen-aged children. This was the last reunion of the three brothers, Armando 74, Frank 72, and Hank 71, until a few years later in Chihuahua besides Armando's deathbed. When we look back, we wouldn't have changed it for the world. Another reminder of how fleeting life is, and how family means so much throughout.

VERACRUZ, FULL CIRCLE

A year later, as promised, we flew to Mexico City, where Mary and Herman picked us up and drove, first to their favorite resort in the state of Veracruz, a rustic little hotel on the beach. They had become attached to the family who owned it, and made a yearly trip to spend time there. The rooms were austere, cool tile floors and a double bed with nothing but a sheet, for no one needed more. My only complaint was the 25 Watt bulb on the wall lamp over the bed, making it impossible to read at night, considered a "must" by Frank and me. The only air conditioning was from the tepid breeze sweeping through the windows in the evenings. The first night, when we went to bed, Mary told me, "Meet you on the beach at 6 A. M., okay?" and I realized with a sinking heart that her inner clock was adjusted to a different time zone than mine. However, I made an effort, went down beside the gray ocean around the specified time, and found that she had already been there and gone back to the hotel, where she was having breakfast with Herman. More surprises awaited us. They had decided to show us some of the surroundings before driving eventually to the city of Veracruz. The first outing was to Antigua, to see the house Cortez had lived in over four hundred and fifty years before. Whether he had really lived there or not was anybody's guess, but a tiny barefoot boy of about six came out of nowhere while we were standing in front, and proceeded to give us a verbal tour of the history of Cortez's arrival in Mexico and occupancy of the house. A large tin placard hung on the wall backing up the child's story, informing the visitors that this is where the great man had lived briefly in the XVI century, and that it was constructed from river stones, adobe bricks, and coral reef. Only a few walls still stood, mostly uprooted by thick vines and roots from the trees, so that one could hardly step inside. But the child amazed us with his speech given from memory, and he gladly accepted our money before he scampered off into the woods.

Herman knew of all the right places to drive, having vacationed there with the family for many years in a row, so one day he drove us to a pleasant little restaurant at the very edge of a river, where we ordered Mexican food, typical of the region. Another day, one of the highlights of the trip, we drove to the pre-Columbian archaeological ruins, Tajín, which was one of the largest cities in Mesoamerica during the Classic era. There we wandered among the pyramids, admiring the most famous one, the Pyramid of the Niches, which has seven stories and 365 niches. The sun burned down, limiting our desire to see each and every one of the many pyramids. At the entrance, the Totonaco dancers, known as the Voladores, (flyers), were starting to climb the hundred foot pole from where they would gradually descend, hanging by their feet while whirling around the pole, a most dangerous feat. At the top, a solitary man played a mournful tune on his flute. When they finally landed on the ground, they passed the hat and everyone contributed, only amounting to a few measly pesos for having risked their lives.

Finally, we drove to the city of Veracruz. I had wanted to return for many years, to see if my impressions would be more favorable now that I was a grown woman, accustomed to the way of life in Mexico. We drove down wide avenues with beautiful palms in the middle, into the center of town, where sat the Cathedral in front of the Plaza I remembered from childhood. There, on one side, we found the Hotel Imperial, where my parents and I had stayed in 1939 when my mother and I came off the ship from England. The lobby, now a little run down, was cool and shady, and toward the back I caught a glimpse of the same little gold elevator cage I had ridden in so many times during that unforgettable week in my life. Frank took my photograph in front of it, my eyes brimming with tears, while remembering my still young parents of those days. I felt my life had come full circle.

We checked in at a more modern nearby hotel, and that night, being Saturday, we went to the Plaza, where the uniformed Naval Band played for the people to dance in the square. We sat at a small table and the men ordered beers, while Mary and I went to the edge of the dance floor to watch the dancers of all ages, who took their dancing seriously, executing the steps of the "danzón" with care and rhythm. It wasn't long before two men came over and asked us to dance, and although we informed them that we were with our husbands, they insisted on just one dance, so we finally accepted, as by this time the music was making our feet go by themselves. After one piece, we thanked the gentlemen and made our way back to the table, where our husbands had not even noticed our absence. Later we coaxed them onto the floor and danced a few pieces, but it was obvious that only the local citizens had the necessary rhythm in their bones.

Next day we visited the beautiful downtown Naval Museum, a well documented building, filled with memorabilia from the 1914 U. S. occupation of the city which lasted for seven months. President Wilson had sent Marines to attack the Naval Military Academy to prevent the unloading of a German ship carrying a cargo of munitions. The cadets defended their port, and there were many lives lost on both sides, a sad event in the history of U.S.-Mexican relations. We visited the old Spanish Fort of San Juan de Ulúa, across the Malecón, (embankment) which had been the repository for the treasures to be shipped out to Spain four hundred years ago. Built of coral reef and rock, it was originally a fort against buccaneers and pirates, then a customs warehouse, a torture jail during the time of the Catholic Inquisition, a military warehouse, and a prison. The cells were dank and dark and one wonders how anyone could have survived in them in that hot humid weather. The old man who lives on the island told us a tale of Juana la Loca, who supposedly was kept in one of the cells until, with white chalk, she drew a picture of a sailboat on her wall, telling everyone she was going to escape on it. One day her jailer found that she was gone, and ancient lore has it that she really sailed away on her boat. There was a section near the fort that displayed old jewelry found on the ocean floor, from one of the Spanish boats which sunk before it could make its way back to Spain. The old castle was not open to the public, being in ruins, but it had served at one time as a presidential lodging.

One cannot go to Veracruz without stopping for coffee at the famous coffee house and restaurant, La Parroquia. Coffee in the state of Veracruz is known throughout the country as the best, and this restaurant has an huge brass coffee maker which has served clients for many years. One must also visit Boca del Rio, which used to be a separate town but which has now become part of the city of Veracruz. There we had Huauchinango a la Veracruzana, red snapper fish served in the local style, accompanied by music from the marimbas. There are so many places to go, and so many historic places to see in that state, that it should be one of the "musts" for all tourists. Plus this, Mary and Herman are both dear people to have as friends, ready and willing to go anyplace at any time. This trip, as well as the one we took to Oaxaca and Chiapas, and the one we took to the heartland with Frank's family, was one of the most pleasant and instructive vacations we had had in a long time, and all in the same country where we live. Again, as when we returned from our Mexican trips, we decided we should travel more throughout the country, rather than going across the pond to Europe.

THE SUMMING UP

Our life together has been one long adventure, starting out in Campeche which was like a four month honeymoon. We had very little money in the beginning, depending completely on Frank's army wage while he perfected his craft as a gynecologist at the Military Hospital, where he gradually developed into the outstanding beloved doctor of his many patients over the years. We have been very lucky to have a wonderful son who has been successful in his career, now married to a lovely girl, and three beautiful grandchildren. Besides this, incredibly, we have been blessed with outstanding good health. At this writing, Frank is 83 years old, and I am 77, both still mentally and physically active (for our ages!) and full of hope for the future. Frank retired a few months ago, hoping to have more time to read and play golf, as well as to indulge his favorite sports of baseball and football on T. V.

Last year I was going to the gym three or four times a week but decided to buy a treadmill and do exercise here at home instead. This way, Frank also exercises, and we have, in addition, a stationary bike and a step exerciser, so the playroom has become our gym out by the pool.

I have been a voluntary worker in a magnificent foundation which opened a few years ago in Torreón, the Arocena Museum. It is stocked with a religious art collection belonging to one of the oldest families in this city, and abides in the refurbished building of the old Casino, where many years ago the whole of Torreón society used to gather for weddings or New Year celebrations. Every time I go up its marble steps, I remember the past, when we used to skip effortlessly up this same stairway, dressed in long evening dresses, our men in tuxes or dark suits. It is now one of the finest museums in the north of the republic. I enjoy my work, along with four other ladies, translating descriptions of the various art collections which are shown temporarily in its halls.

The development in the Laguna area has been incredible since we arrived in Torreón in 1956. We have many more beautiful residential areas, three more golf courses, two large modern malls with large department stores and cineplexes, new boulevards, bridges, overpasses, modern supermarkets in both Torreón and Gomez. Residents have a choice of cable T. V.and one called SKY. At first we had a large dish on our roof and bought stations from the U. S., but now we have a choice of Dish or Direct T. V. from the U. S. There are two large theatres where a local symphony orchestra plays once a month, and where ballets and plays are shown almost constantly.

Our social outings are less than when we were younger, because many of our friends are no longer with us. We go out to breakfast or lunch occasionally with other couples, or sometimes I have ladies over for tea parties on our terrace, where Frank and I usually have our midday meal, overlooking our garden. My oldest friend, Fran, now ninety, but with more joie de vivre than most of us, still gives breakfasts and luncheons. Summers, Tony and his little family come to spend three weeks with us, enjoying the pool and the garden, at which times we are the happiest. Frank celebrated his eightieth birthday recently with a catered luncheon on the porch and Tony flew in to attend the luncheon and give a beautiful speech about his father.

I am lucky to have a wonderful little maid who not only cooks, cleans, and irons beautifully, but who sets the table outside tastefully. I have come to believe that she is "playing house" with my possessions, for depending on what she makes for lunch, she uses tablemats and dishes to go with the menu. When she makes enchiladas or tacos, she will set out my Mexican plates, and so on. She is truly a jewel.

Although we still travel, I have not described many of our trips, realizing that my story of "Growing Up In Mexico" has included perhaps too many vacations taken outside of the country. For this reason, I have omitted referring to our various interesting cruises, one to Alaska to celebrate fifty years of marriage, after Tony and Melanie gave us a beautiful family party in Los Angeles; one up the eastern coast of the U. S., from New York to Canada and back, and one outstanding Mediterranean cruise. I've omitted our last trip to Europe, focused on northern Spain, which we chose to do entirely by train, finding it harder than we expected. I realize that we have been very fortunate to be able to afford all these trips, perhaps because we only had one child to support, in contrast to other couples here who had five or six children to put through school.

Mainly we have been fortunate to have spent our lives with each other in this wonderful country which is Mexico, to whom we owe so much. We are grateful to all the many people who have been our friends over the years, some of whom we continue to see. The ones who have passed away, have left us with us with joyful memories. I can only end this memoir by saying, with love in my heart, VIVA MEXICO!